TEMPLARS

Edward Burman
read Philosophy at the University of Leeds.
He now lives and works in Italy and has
written a study, in Italian, of the
fifteenth-century sculptor
Silvestro Aquilano. He is also the author of
*The Inquisition: The Hammer
of Heresy* (1984).

By the same author

THE INQUISITION
The Hammer of Heresy

The TEMPLARS
KNIGHTS OF GOD

EDWARD BURMAN

Published in the UK by
Thorsons Publishing Group
Denington Estate, Wellingborough,
Northamptonshire NN8 2RQ
and in the USA by
Thorsons Publishers Inc.
Park Street, Rochester, Vermont 05767

First published May 1986
Second Impression December 1986

British Library
Cataloguing in Publication Data
Burman, Edward
The Templars
1. Medieval History
I. Title
641.6'4653 TX 813.Ag
ISBN 0-85030-556-X
ISBN 0-85030-396-6 Pbk

Crucible is an imprint of
The Aquarian Press,
part of the Thorsons Publishing Group

Printed and bound in the United States

Distributed to the book trade in the United States by
Harper & Row Publishers, Inc.

Distributed to the book trade in Canada by
Book Center, Inc., Montreal, Quebec.

CONTENTS

LIST OF ILLUSTRATIONS

between pages 64 and 65

PREFACE

THE Order of the Poor Knights of the Temple of Solomon, then as now referred to more commonly as the Knights Templars or The Temple, was one of the great medieval military orders, whose brother knights were from 1119 to about 1300 the image of the crusading knight. Literature, popular history and folklore between them created an enduring vision of this perfect knight, dressed in a white mantle bearing a red cross. Then in 1307 the Templars in France were arrested and tried on charges of heresy and magical practices, to be followed soon afterwards by their brother knights throughout Europe. The Order was suppressed in 1312, and its last Grand Master was burned at the stake in 1314. A shroud of mystery, ambiguity, and inherent contradictions has ever since engendered legends and romanticized versions of their story, and has fascinated both historians and occultists.

The vast literature on the Templars has recently been synthesized for the English reader in two excellent studies of important and interesting aspects of Templar history: Malcolm Barber, in *The Trial of the Templars* (1978), has provided a meticulous analysis of the trial proceedings to which any general survey such as this can only be indebted, whilst Peter Partner, in *The Murdered Magicians* (1982), has written an absorbing study of the development of the myth of the Templars *after* the suppression of the Order and its integration in the 'Templarism' of Freemasonry. Similarly, for that aspect of the story, this book is indebted.

Yet, in an important sense, both these books begin where the actual history of the Templars finishes—at the moment of the trial—although both furnish a brief history of the Order from its inception. The aim of this survey is to provide a detailed account of Templar activities in the two centuries of their active involvement in western history.

Emphasis is placed on the early years, using where possible contemporary chronicles in conjunction with reliable general histories of the crusades. An attempt has been made to portray what the Templars actually did, and thus to illustrate to what extent their natural function was already curtailed *before* the trials took place. When their role in the military and financial history of the crusades is properly appreciated, the decline and suppression of the Templars no longer appear as a sudden, inexplicable catastrophe.

Clarification of the role of the Templars is important since the phrase 'the Templars' is often used loosely with little regard for the fact of their historical status. Writers assert that the Templars 'were this' or 'did that' or possessed such-and-such a castle with no attempt to qualify their statements. To assert that they 'held' a certain castle can be both true and misleading, since it may have been held for a very brief period; similarly, it may be true that the Templars were an important military force between, say, 1147 and 1187, but it is certainly not true of the first thirty years and the last two decades of their history. In the same way, to affirm that there were four thousand Templars in France is to obscure the fact that perhaps a tenth of this number were knights while the remaining 'Templars' were serving brothers, cooks, stewards, grooms, and agricultural labourers. Furthermore, the difference between Templar history—and their possessions in the East—in the twelfth and thirteenth centuries is so immense that few generalizations hold good for both.

While the focus of this book is obviously on the *Templars* in the Holy Land, it must be stressed that the activities, power, and wealth of the Hospitallers were always at least equal to those of their rival order. The Hospital, after the mid-twelfth century, performed the same functions as the Temple and possessed an even larger number of castles in the East. But while the trial of the Templars, with its lurid and sensationalist overtones, has kept the Templars in the foreground of historical interest, the Hospital has been relatively neglected. Both Orders, and their respective Masters, were often present where perhaps only one is mentioned; it must therefore be assumed that generic statements concerning the military orders, and many references to the Templars, conceal the equally important presence of the Hospitallers.

Although this does not purport to be a scholarly study of Templar history, an attempt has been made to use original texts and chronicles as much as possible. Extensive quotations from contemporary writers have been used, especially in the first two chapters, where they provide an authentic idea of Templar strength in the Holy Land. Secondary works, such as those on the crusades, have been used to provide salient facts while avoiding as much as possible second-hand opinions. All the translations, including those from Gabrieli's collections of Arab sources, are mine.

1

GENESIS

THE Knights Templars came into existence towards the end of the second decade of the twelfth century, in response to the exigencies of pilgrims in the recently constituted Latin Kingdom of Jerusalem. Their foundation was eventually to lead to the forging of a new ideology which, in the words of Joshua Prawer, 'fused two current ideals of mediaeval society, knighthood and monasticism, into a code for a community of warrior monks'.[1] But their original function—the protection of pilgrims on the dangerous road from the port of Jaffa up to Jerusalem—was both less ambitious and much more urgent.

When Baldwin I became the titular King of Jerusalem on 18 July 1100, after the death of his brother Godfrey of Bouillon, he inherited an unstable and precarious kingdom. The city of Jerusalem had been recaptured after more than four centuries of Moslem rule, but many of the victorious crusaders had returned to their estates in Western Europe during the winter following the campaign.* The Latin Kingdom existed, but there was as yet no stable government, no system of taxation, and no reliable defence network either along the coast or around the newly conquered cities. Communications were intermittent and always difficult: Jerusalem was effectively cut off from the northern crusader counties of Antioch and Edessa by minor Moslem emirates, and the failed attempt to create an overland route from Europe to Jerusalem in 1101 rendered the kingdom even more isolated than before. When Baldwin I arrived, in the face of the concerted opposition of the Patriarch Daimbert and the Prince of Antioch, it was 'to inherit an empty treasury and a scattered dominion, made up of the central mountain-ridge of Palestine, the plain of Esdraelon and a few outlying fortresses set in

* i.e. the winter 1099-1100.

a hostile countryside, and a tiny band of lawless, arrogant knights and untrustworthy native mercenaries'.[2]

The great Moslem fortress of Ascalon was too strong for Baldwin to attack, and, as we shall see, raiding bands from that city constantly menaced travellers on the road from Jaffa to Jerusalem. In 1110 an army of Egyptians managed to reach the walls of Jerusalem; three years later raiders from Ascalon achieved the same feat. In 1115 they almost succeeded in taking the vital port of Jaffa, pillaging the Christian settlement during the attempt, and in the years leading up to the end of Baldwin's reign in 1118 his kingdom was continuously harassed in this manner. The only factor that saved the Christian kingdom was the inability of Moslem forces to unite under a single leader.[3] This situation of endemic insecurity provides the context in which the idea for the foundation of the Knights Templars may be understood.

The crusading states, with their imposing array of castles, fortresses, and sea-ports, were slow in developing the physiognomy we have come to recognize and were by no means secure in the early twelfth century. Present-day maps tend to falsify the situation in this period, since castles and other properties were acquired gradually—and often erratically— in the absence of an overall strategy between secular rulers, the Church, and the military orders. Later castles make the early crusader states appear stronger than they were, while castles often passed temporarily into the hands of crusaders and then back into Moslem hands. For instance, the castle of Banyas was only in Christian hands from 1129 to 1132, and then again from 1140 to 1164; the Templar castle of Chastellet at Jacob's Ford was founded in 1178 and destroyed by Saladin two years later; the important northern frontier castle of Baghras passed in and out of Templar hands almost once a generation from the 1130s to the end of the thirteenth century.[4] The presence of these castles on a map of the Holy Land can thus be misleading: the Kingdom was never static, and often much weaker than it might now appear to have been.

Even such castles as did exist were of limited efficacy, since Moslem armies could move between them at will—and often did so. A small garrison could do nothing against a large force passing even within bow shot; on the other hand, the enemy force might have other objectives and no desire to engage in a long and perhaps strategically useless siege. The military historian R. C. Smail has explained this fact as follows:

Routes and areas were held or commanded by medieval garrisons only in the sense that those garrisons dominated them in time of peace and could suppress civil disturbance or minor enemy raids. But when warfare was fought on a scale likely to endanger the Latin occupation, no fortress or group of fortresses could restrain the passage of an invading force.[5]

Precariousness, temporality and easily disruptible communications were essential parts of a shifting and often fragmented entity in which warfare was an important feature of everyday life. There were no lasting times of peace.

Dangers for Pilgrims

Jerusalem itself was virtually isolated, while the incipient economy of the Latin Kingdom was based upon the sea-ports—where Italian merchant colonies of Genoa, Pisa, and Venice were already established during Baldwin I's reign. Roads from Jerusalem to Antioch and Edessa, and after 1109 to the new crusader state of Tripoli, were controlled by the emirates that occupied the land between them; the roads to the coast were menaced by brigands, and occasional better-organized harassing armies. Yet the attraction of Jerusalem as a destination for devout pilgrims was strong enough to overcome fear of these difficulties. As early as 1105 Chastel Arnoul was built to protect the route to the coast, although it was destroyed the following year.[6]

Passages from first-person accounts of the dangers will illustrate the difficulties better than any summary: for instance, Saewulf, a Norse pilgrim, wrote a vivid account of that final stage of his long journey. After a disastrous storm at Jaffa which caused the death of a thousand fellow pilgrims and the loss of thirty ships, he describes the overland journey up to the Holy City in 1102:

We went up from Joppa to the city of Jerusalem, a journey of two days, along a mountainous road, rocky, and very dangerous. For the Saracens, always laying snares for the Christians, lie hidden in the hollow places of the mountains, and the caves of the rocks, watching day and night, and always on the look out for those whom they can attack on account of the fewness of their party, or those who have lagged behind their party through weariness. At one moment they are seen all around everywhere, and all at once they disappear entirely. Anyone who makes that journey may see this. Oh, what a number of human bodies, both in the road and by the side of it, lie all torn by wild beasts . . . On that road not only the poor and the weak, but even the rich and

the strong, are in danger. Many are cut down by the Saracens, but more
by heat and thirst; many through scarcity of drink, but many more perish
from drinking too much. [7]

Saewulf's description of the Saracens suddenly appearing and then
disappearing again is extraordinarily forceful and true to life. But his
stress on the number of deaths from heat and thirst, and the fact that
even the rich are vulnerable, is interesting in view of the later history
of the Templars and the function they came to exercise throughout
Europe.

In 1106–7 Daniel, Abbot or Prior of a Russian monastery, recorded
the same journey. His first stop was made at the church of St George,
a third of the distance from Jaffa to Jerusalem, at Lydda, where St
George had been martyred and where there was a good water supply.
He continues:

There are plenty of springs at this place, near to which pilgrims come to
rest for the night in great fear, for the place is deserted, and not far from
the town of Ascalon, whence the Saracens issue and massacre the pilgrims
on their way; there is thus much to be feared from this place to the point
at which one enters the mountains.

They count it quite 20 versts* from St George to Jerusalem. The way
is across rocky mountains, and is a very frightful and troublesome one. [8]

These experiences are further corroborated by Abbot Ekkehard of Aura,
who speaks of the 'innumerable and unheard-of torments' of the same
route, with daily martyrdoms and many dangers which bring 'grief
and anxiety' to the pilgrims. [9] Such descriptions emphasize the difficulty
of travel within the Latin Kingdom of Jerusalem in its first ten years.

But in about 1110 there was an important shift in crusader policy
and mentality, a shift which helped to pave the way for the new ideology
of the warrior-monk. Until that date cities had been destroyed as soon
as they were captured, for instance Jerusalem (1099), Acre (1104), and
Beirut (1110); but thenceforth they were spared and some of the original
population stayed on to live under the new rulers, for instance at Sidon,
Tyre, and Banyas. The process of colonization had begun, but was
at first concentrated along the coast where trade could sustain a new
economy. Jerusalem was at this time a city three-quarters empty, to

_____
* 1 verst = 3,500 feet.

be visited only for brief periods on pilgrimage. Living conditions were difficult, with thieves pursuing their profession unharried in the uninhabited areas of the city.[10]

The next decade saw a concerted effort by Baldwin I to repopulate his capital, the emotional centre of the Kingdom. William, the Archbishop of Tyre, half a century later, explains the situation as follows:

> At this time the king realized with great concern that the Holy City, beloved of God, was almost destitute of inhabitants. There were not enough people to carry on the necessary undertakings of the realm. Indeed there were scarcely enough to protect the entrances to the city and to defend the walls and towers against sudden hostile attacks.[11]

Baldwin's aim was to find men willing to settle in Jerusalem, and then to create work for them. This process began in mid-decade with repopulation by Syrian Christians from Transjordan, who were given houses and sometimes land as well. At the same time, in order to protect the city against marauding bands of Moslems, a new part of the northern wall of the city was built.[12]

Next, Baldwin attempted to encourage immigrants by providing economic incentives: he exempted all foodstuffs entering his capital from the taxes which had previously been collected at the David Gate, nowadays the Jaffa Gate. Corn, beans, and barley were thus exempted, and a tax of 8 per cent imposed on these goods if they were exported from Jerusalem without being sold.[13] Thus cheap housing, food, and land were part of an intelligent strategy designed to increase the population of the city and thereby to strengthen it. Yet Jerusalem remained an anomaly within its own kingdom, possessing no Italian merchant colony, no sea-port, and only one market. Pilgrimage was the city's principal *raison-d'être*, and Prawer is right in saying that its existence was 'preserved artificially for sentimental reasons'.[14] To change this situation, the policy of repopulation was of paramount importance, together with the establishment of safe overland routes and security within both city and kingdom. It is easy to understand why Baldwin II—who succeeded his cousin in 1118—welcomed the initiative of a group of knights who offered to provide protection on the dangerous road from Jaffa to Jerusalem. If that fundamental lifeline could be rendered safe, Jerusalem would stand a better chance of surviving and prospering.

Laying the Foundations

It is often asserted that the Knights Templars were *founded* in 1118 or 1119, but such a bald statement of the facts is confusing. This assertion is based upon two celebrated accounts of the Order's early history, both written by men who were neither eye-witnesses nor even contemporaries. The earliest account is that written by William of Tyre, about fifty years after the event; the other version often cited is that of Jacques de Vitry, Bishop of Acre from 1217 to 1227, written a full century later. Apart from the obvious problems of historical objectivity, both accounts were written by men with tainted motives: William was a vehement critic of the Templars, as we shall see; Jacques de Vitry was informed of the origins by the then Master of the Order, who had *his* motives for providing the version usually accepted within the Order.

Archbishop William of Tyre describes the origin of the Knights Templar as follows:

In this same year [1118] certain pious and God-fearing nobles of knightly rank, devoted to the Lord, professed the wish to live perpetually in poverty, chastity and obedience. In the hands of the patriarch they vowed themselves to the service of God as regular canons. Foremost and most distinguished among these men were the venerable Hugh de Payens and Godfrey de St Omer. Since they had neither a church nor a fixed place of abode, the king granted them a temporary dwelling place in his own palace, on the north side of the Temple of the Lord. Under certain definite conditions, the canons of the Temple of the Lord also gave them a square belonging to the canons near the same palace where the new order might exercise the duties of its religion. [15]

This brief account concurs with that of Jacques de Vitry, who was close to the Templars at Acre and probably derived details of the Order's history from Pedro de Montaigu, the Grand Master:

Only nine men at first undertook this holy project. They did service for nine years, wearing secular habits, such as the faithful gave them out of charity; but the King and his Knights, having compassion on the aforesaid noblemen, who had given up all for Christ's sake, and together with the Lord Patriarch, supported them out of their own means, and afterwards bestowed upon them gifts and grants for the benefit of their own souls. [16]

The most striking difference is the appearance of the number *nine,* which William of Tyre also uses later. Both authors assert that there were nine knights who served for nine years before the Council of Troyes provided them with a Rule. Since that Council took place in 1128, the date of a putative foundation would appear to be 1119. This date is in fact accepted by most recent historians of the Templars,* and is further substantiated by a contemporary chronicle: Albert of Aix relates that at Easter 1119 a group of pilgrims on the road from Jerusalem to Jordan was massacred at 'a lonely place' by ferocious Saracens from Ascalon and Tyre. Unarmed, and severely weakened by virtue of being at the end of their Lenten fast, these pilgrims were unable to defend themselves. Three hundred died by the infidel sword and sixty were taken prisoner, together with the spoils of their dead companions. The immense shock of such a massacre on the eve of Easter may be imagined, and Albert describes how both the King and the Patriarch of Jerusalem were 'deeply afflicted with sorrow' (magni afflicti sunt doloribus).[17] Malcolm Barber suggests, plausibly, that this event may have been the catalyst which led to the attempt to found an order for the specific purpose of protecting pilgrim routes. In fact, neither William of Tyre nor Jacques de Vitry states whose idea the new order had been.

But there exists a further, almost contemporary and quite different version of the 'foundation' of the Templars, written from a different perspective without the possibility of manipulation by the Knights themselves. It was written by Michael the Syrian, Patriarch of the Syriac Church at Antioch, who has been described as 'a careful and conscientious historian' by a leading modern historian of the Crusades.[18] In a section of his chronicle entitled 'Histoire des Phrer frances', he writes:

At the beginning of the reign of Baldwin II, a Frank came from Rome to pray at Jerusalem. He had made a vow never to return to his own country, but to take holy orders, after having assisted the King in war for three years, he and the thirty knights who accompanied him, and to terminate their lives in Jerusalem. When the King and his nobles saw that they were renowned in battle, and had been of great use to the city during their three years of service, he advised this man to serve in the militia, together with those attached to him, instead of taking holy orders, to work towards saving his soul, and

---

* For instance, Barber, The Origins of the Order of the Temple, p. 224; Bulst-Thiele, Sacrae Domus Militiae Templi, pp. 20-21.

to protect those places against thieves.

Now, this man, whose name was Hou [g] de Payn, accepted this advice; the thirty knights who accompanied him joined him. The King gave them the House of Solomon for their residence, and some villages for their maintenance. The Patriarch also gave them some villages of the Church.

In many ways this account makes more sense. Baldwin observed an accomplished knight who had vowed to remain in Jerusalem, and after the disaster of Easter 1119 perceived how this man and his fellow knights could usefully perform the function of protecting the pilgrim routes. Hence the concept of the warrior-monk.

From the allocation of quarters in the House of Solomon derived the Templars' full title of 'The Military Order of the Knights of the Temple of Solomon'. Both Baldwin and the Patriarch would clearly have been favourable to such a group of knights, and willing to provide hospitality and support. The King could feel more secure with them lodged in a wing of his own palace, and it seems possible to dismiss the attempts by some writers[19] to create a mystery about this fact and suggest there was some secret collusion—or newly-discovered knowledge—behind the decision. The later part of William of Tyre's account of the foundation corroborates the above hypothesis:

The King and his nobles, as well as the patriarch and prelates of the churches, also provided from their own holdings certain benefices, the income of which was to provide these knights with food and clothing. Some of these gifts were for a limited time, others in perpetuity. The main duty of this order— that which was enjoined upon them by the patriarch and the other bishops for the remission of their sins—was 'that, as far as their strength permitted, they should keep the roads and highways safe from the menace of robbers and highwaymen, with especial regard to the protection of pilgrims'.[20]

This primary function was to remain the mainstay of the Templars' existence: even such apparently disparate activities as banking and agriculture were originally conceived in terms of providing a service for pilgrims.

What emerges clearly from these near contemporary chronicles is that a group of knights, between nine and thirty, united under the leadership of Hugues de Payen with the idea of affording protection to pilgrims. It seems likely that this occurred in the year 1119, if not at the suggestion of the King and Patriarch of Jerusalem, then at least with their support. Du Cange gave the names of the presumed original knights as follows: Hugues de Payen, Godefroid de Saint-Omer, André de Montbard, Gundomar, Godefroy, Roral, Geoffrey Bisol, Payen de Montdésir, Archambaud de Saint-Aignan. Traditional historiography follows his lead in asserting that these men conceived and enacted a plan to found a new military order.

Yet it is possible that the idea for the order came much earlier and from a more distant source: the clue lies in the close relationship between Hugues de Payen and his secular overlord Hugh, Count of Champagne—one of the greatest landowners and most powerful secular lords of twelfth-century France. Hugues, from the village of Payens eight miles north of Troyes in the old county of Champagne, was more than the minor figure he is often made out to be. He was a powerful knight who, Barber suggests, took the cross after the death of his wife and had perhaps even gone on crusade with Hugh of Champagne in 1104. [21]. He was later closely associated with the Count, was present in Champagne in 1113, and perhaps returned to the Holy Land in 1116, [22] an intriguing hypothesis which reminds us of Michael the Syrian's statement that Hugues de Payen was in the Holy Land for three years before founding the new order.

Hugh of Champagne had himself returned to the East in 1113, and Bulst-Thiele has suggested that the foundation of the order was *decided* at that time: this suggestion derives from the testimony of a letter from Bishop Ivo of Chartres, in which he exhorts the Count not to enrol in a *militia Christi* or *militia evangelica* because he was still married. Ivo had heard that Hugh of Champagne had already vowed to enter such a *militia,* and Bulst-Thiele concludes that it was 'probably the order of the Temple still without a name'. [23] In fact, Hugh formally joined the Knights Templars in 1125—while there were still supposed to be only nine knights—and since he was also the man who provided the land for the foundation of the Abbey of Clairvaux for St Bernard, the Templars' patron, he is clearly a key figure in both foundations. But his role remains unclear: both Hugues de Payen and André de Montbard—St Bernard's uncle—were his vassals, but his active presence in the early years of Templar history is elusive. However, it seems reasonable to suppose that the *idea* of an order like the Templars dated back to the time of the First Crusade,* that the *decision* to found such an order was made in 1113–15, but that the *foundation* actually took place after Easter 1119.†

But it would be unrealistic to speak of 'foundation' of the order known to later periods in 1119. At least twenty years were required before the Knights Templar emerged as a fully-fledged military order with a hierarchical structure, Rule, and discipline for which they became famous. Not until 1147 were they granted the right to wear a red cross on their mantles. The Order had great difficulty in expanding during those early years, and more than once in the first two decades was in serious danger of breaking up. It was in the 1130s, with the support of St Bernard and money and gifts flowing in from all Christendom, that the Order began to take on something of the form by which we recognize it. And even then it was a further decade before the West began to hear of its exploits, during the crusade led by Louis VII of France in 1147–8. Only then, one might argue, is it really possible to speak of the Templars in a meaningful way.

The First Knights: Years of Crisis

With no specific ethos, no official role and little power or finance, the first knights—whether nine or thirty—presumably occupied themselves with their obscure self-appointed task. Nothing is heard of them in contemporary chronicles: Fulcher of Chartres, chaplain to Baldwin II and chronicler of his reign up to 1127, does not mention them. But faint echoes of their activity do exist, and one feels them slowly emerging from the obscurity of their humble role.

The Cartulary of the Order opens with a letter from Baldwin II to St Bernard commending two knights of the Temple to him, and asking him to obtain papal approval for the Order. It begins: 'The

---

* It is important to note that a similar association of knights had been formed many years earlier: 'Already before the First Crusade a group of nobles in south-western France had formed an association for the purpose of protecting the monastery of La Sauve near Bordeaux and the pilgrims who visited it'. (Forey, *The Templars in the Corona of Aragón*, p. 4).

† An interesting parallel which may have provoked the decision was the foundation charter of the Knights of St John, *Pie postulatio voluntatis*, also of 1113.

Templar brothers, whom God has raised up for the defence of our province and to whom he has accorded special protection, desire to obtain apostolic approval and also a Rule to govern their lives.'[24] Evidently this was written before Baldwin's death on 15 October 1126, and emphasizes the Order's uncertain status in those years—although at least one historian has doubted the letter's authenticity.[25] Apart from this document, the earliest evidence of the Templars' existence would appear to be the fact that in 1120–1 Count Fulk V of Anjou lodged at the Temple in Jerusalem and may even have become a lay brother. After this visit he provided the new Order with an annual subsidy of 30 Angevin livres.[26]

Then in mid-decade the evidence begins to accumulate: in 1124 a document in the Cartulary mentions Templar rights near Marseille,[27] while in the following year Hugues de Payen is cited on a grant of privileges made by the Patriarch of Jerusalem to the Venetians as *magister Templi*.[28] It was also in 1125 that Hugh of Champagne was said to have joined the Templars. From 1126 to 1136 Albion, editor of the Templar Cartulary, gives 104 documents which show the increasing activity and wealth of the Order. Already the grant citing the Master mentioned above suggests a certain importance either of Hugues personally or of the Order by 1125, but it also seems that all was not well: at precisely that moment internal pressures and external criticisms nearly put a premature end to the fledgling fraternity.

In 1126 Hugues de Payen left Jerusalem for the West. The object of his mission was to recruit new knights and establish the Templars with greater authority. Up to this point they had obtained no striking success, and had been largely ignored by their contemporaries. It would seem that Hugues' journey was provoked by fear that his Order was on the point of failure, since a letter intended to 'bolster their courage' was written from Europe to his brother knights in Jerusalem. Jean Leclerq has established on the grounds of style and content that the author of this letter was certainly Hugues de Payen himself.[29]

It was clearly written to reassure knights more assailed by doubt than usual in the absence of their Master and his companion on the journey André de Montbard. The letter may be divided into seven sections as follows:

1. Hugues asserts that the knights' original vocation has been weakened by the devil, and then seeks to reassure them by means of spiritual quotations.

2. He states that the military nature of the order is a major objection raised against them, and replies to this objection by insisting that since the basic intention is religious the purpose of the order is primarily religious and only then military.

3. The devil tempts the brothers with pride and ambition, and the idea of achieving higher rank. Hugues insists that they must resist such desires with humility. With patience and humility they will best serve God.

4. Referring to the same temptations, he reminds the knights that neither rank nor dress confer Christian grandeur.

5. To the possible objection that military duties might be an obstacle to the peace of mind essential for contemplation, he argues that even contemplatives must perform some labour and cannot live without devoting time to activities other than contemplation.

6. He emphasizes the necessity of duty and perseverance, since these qualities will enable the knights to resist the temptations of the devil which threaten their vocation.

7. The multiform nature of the devil's suggestions is stressed, especially the notion that the Templar brothers are mere servants. Hugues insists on the idea of an association of free brother knights, and how service in such an association can lead to salvation.[30]

These brief sections, written in unscholarly Latin with frequent references to the Scriptures, vividly illustrate the doubts, temptations, and criticisms which the early knights suffered. The fundamental impulse behind this near failure can be traced to the novelty of the concept of a warrior monk. The originality of the ideology which was slowly evolving within the Order was such as to cause even greater tensions: the fusion of warrior and monk was a truly extraordinary but essential achievement. Indeed, Daniel-Rops hàs argued that before the First Crusade it might 'have been feared that western Europe would divide into two groups: on one side the military clique, on the other a more cultured caste of clergy and bourgeoisie'.[31] Thus the originality of the Templars lay in a new kind of synthesis of these two social categories of knight and monk, and the contradictions underlying the emerging ideology existed within the minds of individual Templar brothers.

The contradictions had already been made manifest during the First Crusade, since the motives leading powerful men to go on such an expedition were clearly manifold. They included religious zeal, the desire for mercantile advantage, simple land hunger, and the historical rivalry between the Eastern and Western Empires. On arrival, and after victory, men reacted in unexpected ways, modifying their ideals to suit circumstances and bringing to the surface the doubt and contradictions which afflicted the first Templars. Rosalind Hill cites an interesting example of these conflicts, and their consequences:

Godfrey de Bouillon, who is depicted in most of the twelfth-century texts as a man of devout faith and heroic simplicity, broke a solemn oath to the Emperor Alexius, while Bohemond, whom many people detested and who alienated even the author of the *Gesta* by his determination to grasp Antioch at any price, was among those who spent the whole night of Christmas Eve in prayer at Bethlehem with Fulcher of Chartres.[32]

Similar contradictions appear to have threatened the Templar Order before its ideological synthesis was finally achieved by St Bernard.* Hugues de Payen's letter provides a fascinating insight into the growing pains of his Order as he travelled to Europe to seek the aid of Bernard himself. But beyond this, the letter also allows a glimpse into the personality of the Order's first Master, as a devout, strong, and persistent knight possessing in full the qualities which he enumerates as essential for members of the Knights Templars. From this letter it is possible to imagine the arguments and justifications that Hugues presented to the Council of Troyes as he sought support for the Order.

* R. W. Southern has noted the contradiction in the Cistercian ideal, fostered by St Bernard, between complete self-abnegation, poverty, simplicity, retirement, purity, and refinement of spiritual life on the one hand, and on the other the Order's reputation as aggressive, arrogant, with military discipline, outstanding managerial qualities, and a tendency towards cupidity (*Western Society and the Church*, p. 252).

2

THE TEMPLAR
IDEOLOGY I: 1128-36

THE Templars are thus remarkable for having forged a distinct and
lasting ideology which 'fused two current ideals of mediaeval society,
knighthood and monasticism, into a code for a community of warrior
monks',[1] and which was the basis of the inherent mystery that
encouraged later attempts to construct myths about the Order. But
this fusion was not immediate. In fact Marion Melville has convincingly
argued that the ideology was based upon two successive influences:
first, the ascetic and mystical spirit of north and north-eastern France;
and, second, the chivalrous spirit of Provence—a concept of courtesy
and elegance in which everything, from clothes to horses, was insistently
'belle'.[2]

The first influence derived from the mastership of Hugues de Payen
and the direct patronage of Bernard of Clairvaux (i.e. from 1119 to
1136); the second derived from the equally successful but quite different
mastership of Robert de Craon, or Robert the Burgundian (from 1136
to 1149). Under these early Masters of the Temple, each of whom
ruled for an unusually long period, the ideology and lasting identity
of the Order were definitively established. As we shall see in this chapter,
the Latin *Rule* of 1128 reflects the austerity of Hugues and Bernard,
while the French expanded version of a decade later contains paragraphs
which read like sections from a treatise on chivalry. The successful
synthesis of these contradictory elements forged the original character
of the Knights Templars and made the Order the model for all future
military orders. Even the Order of St John later modified its character
as the result of the Templars' success.

Bernard of Clairvaux and the 1128 Council of Troyes
The Council of Troyes opened in January 1128 with the primary purpose

of considering the claims of the Knights Templars, represented by Hugues de Payen and André de Montbard. It was in part perhaps the fruit of the letter from Baldwin II quoted above, and in part the result of pressure exercised by Hugues during his eighteen-month stay in Europe. But it had come about mainly on the initiative of Bernard of Clairvaux, and from that moment he began to figure prominently in the history of the Order.

William of Tyre recounts the events leading up to the Council as follows:

Nine years after the founding of this order the knights were still in secular garb. They wore such garments as the people, for the salvation of their souls, bestowed upon them. During this ninth year, a council was held at Troyes in France. There were present the archbishops of Rheims and Sens, with their suffragans; the bishop of Albano, the pope's legate; the abbots of Citeaux, Clairvaux, Potigny; and many others. At this council, by order of Pope Honorious and of Stephen, patriarch of Jerusalem, a rule was drawn up for this order and a habit of white assigned them. [3]

But the presiding spirit of the Council was Bernard, here concealed by the modest epithet 'Abbot of Clairvaux'. He it was whose influence had brought it about, and who embodied the complex aims and inherent contradictions of the Knights Templar in his own person. Until his conversion at the age of twenty he had been destined for a knightly career, and the spiritual conflicts of his own life informed the spirit of the new Order. His mother, Aleth, sister of André de Montbard, was descended from the counts of Tonnarre, so he had inherited some ducal blood from the Dukes of Burgundy. The Order of the Temple was imbued with the ideals and convictions of the knightly class of Burgundy. Furthermore, the Council took place only eight miles from the birthplace of Hugues de Payen, eighty miles from Bernard's birthplace at Fontaine, and fifty miles from Montbard. The Abbey of Clairvaux stood thirty-five miles to the east of Troyes on land that had been granted by Count Hugh of Champagne—in whose territory all the above places lay.

Discussions about the Templars took place in this feudal context, in the presence of a papal legate but not of the Pope himself. At that moment Bernard's influence within the Church was reaching its zenith. Under his leadership the once failing Cistercian Order had grown from

7 abbeys in 1118—a year before the foundation of the Templars—and was to reach 328 abbeys by 1152. This increase brought him immense power that is difficult to understand today. He challenged the philosophical speculations and rationalism of Peter Abelard, criticized what he considered the aesthetic excesses of Abbot Suger of St Denis in Paris,* was powerful enough to rebuke publicly bishops, archbishops, and kings (Louis VI and Louis VII of France) without fear of reprisal, and was called upon to arbitrate in contested episcopal elections. In his treatise *De Consideratione* he specified the duties of the Pope, and generally acted as 'the conscience of the higher clergy'.⁴ What Bernard attacked was doomed to failure; what he approved flourished. Thus his support for the Knights Templar was practically a guarantee of the Order's success.

The Cistercian Order, recently founded as an élite and austere order, was on the verge of failure when Bernard renounced his knightly career in the spring of 1112 and entered the monastery at Citeaux. He arrived with thirty fellow knights, and the Order began to flourish immediately. In 1115, when the Count of Troyes offered to found a new house, Bernard was chosen to be the superior of the Abbey, which took the name Clairvaux. Within a few years the once failing organization had become what R. W. Southern has described as 'one of the masterpieces of medieval planning':

In a world ruled by a complicated network of authorities often at variance with each other, the Cistercian plan represented a single strong chain of authority from top to bottom. There was a single supreme legislative body in the triennial General Chapter of all Cistercian Abbots; a simple system of affiliation and visitation which embraced every house in the order; a uniformity of practice; a wide freedom from every local authority whether secular or ecclesiastical. The Cistercians achieved at one stroke the kind of organisation that every ruler would wish to have: a system complete in itself, wholly autonomous, equipped with a thorough organisation for internal supervision, isolated from external interference, untroubled by those sources of dispute about services and rights which choked the law courts of Europe. The Cistercian system was the first effective international organisation in Europe, more effective even than the papal organisation because it had narrower aims and a smaller field of operation.⁵

---

* Founder of the style that was to become the Gothic. See the letters in Erwin Panofsky, *Meaning in the Visual Arts* (Harmondsworth: Penguin, 1970), pp. 141-55.

This structure, inspired by St Bernard, was largely imitated when he applied himself to the expansion of a parallel military organization. That he should do so is no surprise: the military nature of Cistercian discipline has already been referred to in the previous chapter. Bernard was a knight by birth, was to preach the second Crusade under the auspices of Pope Eugenius III, and Abbot Suger once thought of entrusting Bernard himself with an army. Many people believe that Galahad, the ideal knight or taskless gallant, was Bernard himself.[6]

Be that as it may, the twelfth century was the age of St Bernard, and it was he—nephew to one of the original knights, and later spiritual inspirator of the putative founder, Hugh of Champagne—who was now called upon to decide the future of the Knights Templars: the Council was established at his bidding, in Champagne, and carried out under his personal supervision. It answered in full the demands of Hugues de Payen in providing papal approval for the new Order, provided a new impulse which rapidly brought about a change in recruitment patterns, and increased the number of knights in proportion to the enormous success of the Cistercians. But, most important of all, it provided the first *Rule* for the Order of the Knights Templars, certainly inspired by St Bernard and perhaps even dictated by him.

This fact of the *Rule*, of becoming an approved Order, was of vital importance in the medieval world. Joshua Prawer has explained it as follows:

In mediaeval usage *ordo* meant far more than an organization or corporate body, since it included the idea of a social and public function. Men who belonged to an *ordo* not merely followed their personal destiny, but filled a place in Christian polity. The warriors as a class were now an *ordo* with an *officium*.[7]

This *officium*, or office, was central to the ethos of the Templars. It is made explicit in the second paragraph of the *Rule*, known as the Latin or Primitive *Rule*, which was annexed to the minutes of the proceedings of the Council of Troyes.

The Latin Rule

The *Rule* consisted of 72 articles or paragraphs, which became 76 in the later French translation. The idea of a 'new knighthood', later made explicit by St Bernard, is already present in paragraph 2, the real prologue to the *Rule*, where emphasis is placed on the *office* of knighthood and the fact that knighthood had up to that moment deviated from this primary office:

It despised the love of justice, which pertained to its office and did not do what it should. Instead of defending the poor, widows, orphans and the Church, competed to rape, and kill. [8]

This original view of the purpose and aims of knighthood was represented as a restoration of lost values so that the Templars 'resuscitated' the Order of Chivalry to its original purity. Prawer comments: 'An ideal of "pure" chivalry was then thought to have once existed, though corrupted by time, and the Templars were bent on restoring its pristine purity.' [9]

What is most interesting here is that the Templars were looking back to some imagined form of lost perfection, an ideal order of chivalry which had perhaps never existed. We shall examine later the literary manifestations of this nostalgic vision.* For the moment it is sufficient to observe that this myth was highly developed by writers in the same historical and even *geographical* mental frame as the Templars themselves: notably, of course, Chrétien de Troyes, author of courtly romances such as *Lancelot* and *Perceval* which express similar nostalgic ideas of chivalry. It is in this context that the identification of St Bernard with Galahad may be understood. The Templars themselves already looked back to an imagined ideal knighthood as later sects and secret societies dreamed back to the Templars.

This concept is emphasized in the beautifully austere language of the prologue to the *Rule*:

Devant toutes choses quiquioques seit chevalier de Christ, eslisant tant sainte conversation, toi entor la profession, covient ajoustier pure diligence e ferme perseverance, qui est si digne et si sainte, et si haute est coneue a estre, que se ele est gardée purement et pardurablement, tu desserviras a tenir compaignie entre les martirs qui donerent por Jhesu Christ lor arms. [19]†

---

* Raymond Williams has stressed the perennial concept of past 'golden ages' in his book *The Country and the City* (Chatto and Windus, 1973); see especially Chapter 4; 'Golden Ages', pp. 35-45.

† Above all things whoever is a knight of Christ choosing only holy conversation, you who have taken the vow should add pure diligence and firm perseverance, which are worthy and holy and recognized as elevated virtues, so that if you observe it in all its purity and eternity you will be worthy of keeping company with the martyrs who give their souls for Jesus Christ.

It is clear that the diligence and perseverance echo the plaintive language of Hugues de Payen writing to the brothers left behind in Jerusalem. But the language is new, more powerful, and dignified.* This second paragraph sets the scene for the remainder of the *Rule*, much of which consists of short paragraphs of no more than a couple of lines, by explaining the meaning of the new concept of Christ's knighthood.

The remaining paragraphs of the Latin *Rule* are devoted to the practical matters of everyday life, with obvious derivation from the rules and mental attitudes of the Cistercian Order. Yet, as Leclerq observes, it is dangerous to generalize from the provisions of this *Rule* since it merely tells us 'how they *ought to* live, and not what they actually did'.[11] When the *Rule* was composed the Templars still counted a small number of knights, but experience and increased numbers necessitated constant additions until the original 72 paragraphs became 686 in the final version.

The *Rule* specifies that the Templar habit should be white, or black or brown (§17), and that the robes should be 'without any superfluity, and without any ostentation' (§18). It stresses that they should live in common and take their meals in silence (§21),† and that they were allowed to eat meat three times a week—except when the holidays of Christmas, Our Lady, or the Twelve Apostles fell within the week (§26). This social act of community in the refectory was clearly as important for the Templars as it was in monastic life, and one of the earliest penances specified is that of taking meals alone (§45-6). Each knight was to have three horses 'and no more' (§51), and hunting was expressly forbidden (§51).

Already at this early stage the presence of secular brothers, who would be called upon to perform the everyday duties of the order, and married brothers taken on temporarily, was provided for (§65-6 and §69); similarly, provision was clearly made for looking after elderly, pensioned Templars and sick members of the Order (§60-1).‡ But amongst these simple and almost monastic rules, which possess little originality and may or may not have been strictly followed at that

---

* The novelty is enhanced by the unusual stylistic combination of southern and northern twelfth-century French.

† § 31 is even more explicit on the importance of silence.

‡ Cf. the hospital at Denny in Cambridgeshire (p. 95).

early period, two factors stand out: first, the immense power of the Master, and second, the unusually strong vehemence of the paragraphs against women, which were later used in attempts to prove the existence of homosexuality amongst the Templars.

The misogynistic tendencies appear in the last paragraphs of the Latin *Rule*. Paragraph 70 states categorically that 'The company of women is a dangerous thing, and the devil has turned many men from the path to paradise by providing female company.' The next paragraph stresses that it is dangerous to look on women too much, and contains the notorious assertion that 'And for this none of you must presume to kiss wife, widow, maid, mother, sister, aunt, or any other women . . .'* (§71). This extreme denunciation may appear excessive to modern eyes, but simply reinforces the concept of 'Christ's knighthood' and distinguishes the idea of knighthood conceived by Hugues de Payen and sustained by St Bernard as different from that then appearing in Provence amongst the first troubadours. It is a provision which may well have been ignored during the second period of the formation of the Templar ideology under Robert of Craon.

The power of the Master was already paramount, and was made explicit in two paragraphs of this *Rule*. In one of these, entitled *De Licencia Magistri*, 'On the Powers of the Master', which in the later French translation was modified to the less austere and more straightforward *Dou maistre*, it is stated that the Master may 'provide the horse and arms of a brother to whomsoever he wishes' (§35). Thus free powers of recruitment are given to the Master of the Temple: in this case specifically for Hugues de Payen. But another paragraph at the end of the *Rule* goes even further and places unlimited power in the hands of the Master: it states categorically and unequivocably that all the preceding rules contained in the paragraphs of the Latin *Rule* are to be followed—or not—*at the discretion of the Master* (§73).

The provisions of the *Rule*, in establishing an elementary structure and order, thus answered fully the fears and desires that Hugues de Payen had brought to Europe from Jerusalem. It was still far from the complexity and thoroughness of the final form of the *Rule*, but it may be said to represent a personal triumph for Hugues de Payen

---

* 'Et por ce nul de vos presume baisier de feme, ne veve, ni pucele, ne mere, ni seror, ne ante, ne nule autre feme . . .'

and to have paved the way for the definitive organization of the Order. Although the force of St Bernard's personality is present in the *Rule*, it is also likely that some of the more practical provisions bear the signature of Hugues de Payen; perhaps there had already existed some rudimentary rule or code of conduct, upon which the Latin *Rule* of 1128 was based. Be that as it may, the first part of the ideology of the Templars was forged by the combined intelligence and action of these two extraordinary men, each of whom possessed to a high degree the qualities of diligence and perseverance which the *Rule* stressed.

Recruitment and Expansion

The Knights Templars underwent a rapid expansion throughout Europe immediately after the Council of Troyes. The first and most obvious success was in France itself, especially in Burgundy. The recruitment drive continued there for several years, with a large number of knights joining the order in 1133.[12] But the most important action was a matter of bureaucracy: Hugues named Payen de Montdidier as Master of the Temple in France, thus making the first step towards the creation of an international organization which became in a relatively short time the equal of that of the Cistercians.[13]

Hugues visited England and Scotland soon afterwards, and apparently received donations of land and money in both countries.[14] It was almost certainly at this date, late 1128 or early 1129, that the original London Temple was established in Holborn, outside Holborn Bars, with a garden, orchard, boundary ditch, cemetery, and the first round church. This Temple possessed houses and land on both sides of the northern part of Chancery Lane, and remained the administrative centre of Templar power in England until the Order moved to the New Temple—between Fleet Street and the Thames—in 1161. Although details are not specified, the Anglo Saxon Chronicle for 1128 states that Hugues 'was received by all good men, and all gave him treasure, and in Scotland also'.[15] But the English Templars really began to prosper with the accession to the throne of King Stephen in 1135. Here again feudal connections were of great importance: Stephen himself was the son of Stephen of Blois, who had gone to Jerusalem with the First Crusade, and Adela, daughter of William the Conqueror; his Queen, Matilda, was heiress to the crusading house of Boulogne, which had provided two rulers for the Latin Kingdom of Jerusalem. Godfrey de

St Omer had been a vassal of the Count of Boulogne.

Therefore it is no surprise to learn that the first recorded grant of land to the English Templars occurred in 1137 when Matilda, Queen of England and niece to Baldwin I of Jerusalem, endowed the Order with the Essex manor of Cressing.[16] This land, later the site of an important preceptory, is typical of the early Templar properties: it included an estate at Uphall, and the manor and half-hundred of Witham, and stood on the main road from London to Colchester. It was gradually extended by small gifts of between 1–5 acres until, by the end of the twelfth century, it included land in the villas of Terling, Fainsted, Great Leighe, Naylinghurst, across the River Brain from Temple Cressing, towards Braintree, at Bradwell, Galdingham, Mundon, and Layer de la Hay, with houses at Sudbury and Maldon and the manor of Finchingfield. The whole property comprised about 160 tenants by the end of the century and Lees concludes that 'the central position of Temple Cressing preceptory, within comparatively easy reach of London, the fertility and diversity of the soil, the excellence of the pasturage, and the convenient roadways and waterways, gave it a value out of proportion to its size'.[17] Although the consolidation of this estate took many decades, it is important as being the first Templar land outside London and represents an example of both the method of donation and method of expansion in those years. The earliest example of the name of an English Master recorded is that of the Oto described as 'milites Templi' who witnessed the 1153 *Carta Conventionum*, the agreement to the succession between King Stephen and Henry Duke of Normandy.[18] As in the case of Hugues de Payen witnessing the document of 1124 cited above, this would appear to attest to the importance of the Master in the legal and military hierarchy even before that date.

The Templars also appeared in Spain within two years of the Council of Troyes: the first definite mention of their presence in north-eastern Spain dates from 1131, while Forey argues that 'The Temple . . . appears to have been receiving privileges from Alfonso I by 1130'.[19] Rapid expansion on the Iberian peninsular was facilitated by favours shown to the Templars by the rulers of Catalonia and Aragona in return for help with the *reconquista*, or reconquest, of Spanish territory from the Moors during the 1130s.[20] It seems probable, paradoxically, that the first military action fought by the new Order was in fact in Spain.

Alfonso I granted the Templars exemption of the tax on one fifth of all booty taken from the Moors, and on his death left a controversial will which gave one third of his kingdom to the Templars. Although this inheritance was later successfully contested, it illustrates the vital role played by the Templars in the *reconquista*. In return for this military support they were given land in Aragon, Catalonia, Valencia, Mallorca, and eventually in Andalucía.

In Italy the expansion was less rapid, and the Order never became so powerful in that country of fragmented and independent states and duchies as in the rest of Western Europe. The Templar presence was closely related to the role of Italian cities and ports in trade with the Latin Kingdom: for example, it seems likely that they were already present in Lucca, home of the silk trade, in the 1130s. Although the first documented presence there dates from 1158 it is certain that the Order was already well established by that time.[21] But the earliest and most significant presence in Italy was at the ports of the Adriatic coast from which the crusaders and merchants set sail for the East— Barletta, Bari, Brindisi, Siponto, and Messina.[22]

In the Holy Land, progress was slower and the Templars did not begin to possess any significant number of castles until much later. An inventory of property in the lordship of Tyre as late as 1243 shows remarkably little property belonging to the Templars: while 21 villages and 51 half villages are accredited to Venice, and 4 villages to Pisa, only two-thirds of a single village is accredited to the Templars.[23] Altogether the religious orders and clergy possessed 12 per cent of the lordship in 1243. As Prawer observes: 'The remarkable feature of the lordship is the insignificant number of possessions belonging to the clergy and the Military Orders . . . the generally held view about the encroachment or the preponderance of ecclesiastical possessions, as compared with lay possessions, cannot be accepted for the whole of the Kingdom.'[24] Yet, as we shall see, the peculiar nature of the Kingdom was its predominantly urban and cash economy: it was money rather than possession of land that sustained power in the new colony. However, the Templars did come into the possession of at least some castles early in their career: the important frontier zone of Amanus, a March that lay between Asia Minor (Cilicia) and Syria, may have come into Templar possession as early as 1131. It included the castles of Baghras, Roche Roussel, and Darbsak, and might have been given to the Templars when Fulk of Jerusalem travelled north to Antioch in 1131. At the very latest it was given to the Templars by Raymond of Poitiers when he led a campaign against the Armenians of Cilicia in 1136-7. It was probably the first important gift to the Templars in the Latin East.[25]

In all, there exist about 600 charters granted to the Order under Hugues de Payen and Robert de Craon, with half of that number being in Provence and Languedoc, a third in north-east France and Flanders, and the remainder in England, Spain, Portugal, and elsewhere in France. They include the rights to land, and other rights such as markets and fairs, revenues, houses, prebends, tithes, rents, annuities, villeins, serfs with family, moorish slaves, and Spanish Jews.[26] This rapid expansion testifies to the new importance attributed to the Knights Templar after the Council of Troyes, and the injection of new life which came to the Order with the vital support of St Bernard. Without Hugues' determination and St Bernard's influence, the Order may well have failed; but by the late 1130s it was well on the way to its later wealth and power. It is, however, interesting to note that the greater part of this wealth lay in Western Europe, and thus contradicted to a certain extent the avowed purpose of the Order as it was established in 1119. Already the scope and character of the Knights Templar had changed considerably.

In Praise of the New Knighthood

The last significant contribution of St Bernard, and in a sense of Hugues de Payen, was the treatise *Liber ad Milites Templi De Laude Novae Militiae*. This treatise, probably written in 1135, seems to have been prepared in response to requests made by Hugues, whose tone may be imagined after reading the letter quoted in Chapter I. It is in fact addressed to 'Hugh, Soldier of Christ and Master of the Militia of Christ' and constitutes a subtle and closely argued justification of the concept of a warrior monk.* It consists of some thirty pages, divided into four chapters: 'In Praise of the New Knighthood', 'On the Profane Militia',

---

* As recently as the mid-nineteenth century translations of the *De Laude* were made for soldiers of the papal army (cf. *Delle Laudi di una nuova milizia, libro di S. Bernardo reso italiano, tedesco, francese ed inglese*, Roma: Tipi della Civiltà Cattolica, 1860).

'Of the Soldiers of Christ', and 'On the way in which the Soldiers of Christ should conduct themselves'.

That this treatise is a reply to Hugues is made clear from the opening words:

Once, twice, three times, if I am not mistaken dearest Hugh, you have asked me to write some words of encouragement to you and your fellow knights, so that, as a result of my status, while I cannot use the lance against the tyranny of our enemies, I can at least take up my pen . . .[27]

These are clearly the words of a knight by birth, and the language throughout the treatise enforces the conception of Bernard as a knight militant for the Church. The only reason he cannot fight is because of his physical weakness and sickness. Bernard glorifies the killing of non-Christians, finding a sufficient justification in the fact that the fighting and the killing are performed for Christ:

. . . the knights of Christ fight the battles of their lord in safety, not fearing to have sinned in killing the enemy, nor fearing for their own deaths, since neither dealing out death nor dying, when for Christ's sake, contains anything criminal but rather merits glorious reward. In this way, fighting for Christ is Christ attained. Truly he who freely takes the death of his enemy as an act of vengeance, will more easily find consolation in his status as a soldier of Christ. The soldier of Christ kills safely, and dies the more safely. Not without cause does he bear the sword. He is the instrument of God for the punishment of evildoers and for the defence of the just. In fact, when he kills evildoers it is not homicide but malicide, and he is considered Christ's legal executioner . . .[28]

This successful decriminalization of the act of killing in the name of Christ is a superb piece of propaganda, which accurately reflects St Bernard's education, thought, and actual concerns. It defends the actions of the Templars with a far more authoritative and convincing voice than that of the Master of the Order, and in bestowing St Bernard's blessing legitimized the idea of the warrior monk. After the *De Laude*, the new concept was never again seriously criticized.

Martyrdom had been promised to combatants in the Holy Land since Urban II's declaration of the First Crusade at Clermont in 1095, when he said: 'Now we promise to you wars which carry with them the reward of glorious martyrdom, wars which assure the title to temporal and eternal glory.'[29] The idea already existed, and had indeed been adopted by the earliest Templars. Martyrdom was already promised

in paragraph 2 of the Latin *Rule*, while the distinction between killing
an infidel and wounding a Christian is made explicit in the later
paragraphs of the *Rule*: one of the most serious crimes a Templar can
commit, equal to simony, heresy, and revealing the secrets of a Templar
chapter, and to be punished by expulsion from the house, is to kill
a Christian (§226); only slightly less severe, resulting in loss of the
Templar habit, is the punishment for wounding a Christian (§235).
Thus the murder of a Christian is forbidden, while the killing of infidels
is not only sanctified but can lead to martyrdom in the name of Christ.

The novelty of this concept is stressed both in *De Laude* and in
the Latin *Rule*: paragraph 9 of the *Rule* states that 'This new type
of religion came into being . . . so that knighthood should be admitted
to religion and thus religion armed by knighthood should progress
and kill the enemy without guilt', while St Bernard asserts that 'a
new kind of militia is reported to have arisen in the world . . . '.[30]
This element of originality was thus legitimized by the treatise that
St Bernard wrote for one of his favourite sons, and that went far beyond
its immediate scope in justifying with the immense authority of its
author a concept which was to have far-reaching consequences: 'The
preservation of the liberated Holy Sepulchre and the defence of
Christendom against the Infidel were indeed a mighty factor in recruiting
the European nobility, but their spiritual and social message to a warrior
class in search of identity and ideals proved even more potent.'[31]

When Hugues de Payen died in 1136, the Order he had founded
had become of international importance and had virtually alone created
this new concept of knighthood. In a sense a survey of the history
of the Templars might be based upon a single question: given this
privileged start, and the papal privileges soon to be granted, did the
Knights Templar justify by their subsequent actions the formation of
a tailor-made ideology and the support of St Bernard?

3

THE TEMPLAR
IDEOLOGY II: 1136–46

HUGUES was succeeded by Robert de Craon, or Robertus, Burgundio, who came from a powerful family in the town of Craon in Anjou. He was an excellent administrator and a diplomat of 'great finesse'.[1] Above all, he belonged to the more sophisticated nobility of Languedoc and was imbued with the qualities of courtly life and elegance that prevailed in that part of France during the twelfth century. His character was different from that of his predecessor, but he was equally devoted to the Templar Order and had perhaps been a brother Knight from the beginning. As the Order began to expand rapidly in the 1130s his gifts as an administrator were perhaps those most needed. It was under his mastership that the Templars achieved their hierarchical structure and international organization, and obtained from Pope Innocent II the autonomy which enabled them to act independently of the ecclesiastical and secular rulers in whose jurisdiction they operated.

Innocent II had from the beginning of his pontificate in 1130 been assailed by the alternative papacy of the antipope Anacletus II. In his constant struggle for supremacy he had been sustained by St Bernard and was from the beginning favourable to the Order which was flourishing under Bernard's sponsorship. Already in 1135, at the Council of Pisa, the Pope had granted the Templars a mark from his own treasury, two ounces of gold from the Chancellor of the Roman Church, and a silver mark from all prelates of the Church to be paid annually.[2] When Innocent II was eventually able to enter Rome as uncontested Pope he met Robert of Craon for a series of discussions. Perhaps as the result of Bernard's visit to Rome the previous year, Pope Innocent II issued the epoch-making bull *Omne Datum Optimum* of March 1139. Robert's mastership changed the character of the Knights Templars profoundly. The Order had been the brainchild of men who were members of the first generation of Franks in Latin Syria, with their special qualities and experience but limited imagination. Now it was to be modified, both in scope and in everyday practice, into a knightly Order reflecting the values of the Provençal nobility.

Omne Datum Optimum

The declared object of this bull was to create a new category of chaplain-brothers for the Templars to serve them in their now widespread houses, but its actual effect was more dramatic: it freed the Templars of all ecclesiastical authority save that of the Pope and made the Master and Chapter fully responsible for the Order. Its title, 'Every Best Gift', and its introduction, 'Bishop Innocent, to our dear son Robert, Master of the knights of the Temple . . .',[3] announce the astonishing tone of the bull.

This translation of the most important part of the bull will give a good idea of its tone and content:

Every best gift and every perfect gift is from above, coming down from the Father of lights, with whom there is no change nor shadow of alteration. And so, beloved sons in the Lord, we praise almighty God because of you and for you, since your Order and venerable institution is famous throughout the whole world. For *by nature* you were *children of wrath,* given up to the pleasure of the world, but now through the inspiration of grace you have become receptive to the message of the gospel and, having left behind wordly pomps and your own possessions and also *the broad way that leadeth* to death, you have humbly chosen the hard road that *leadeth to life*; and to prove it you have most conscientiously sworn on your breasts the sign of the living cross, because you are especially reckoned to be members of the Knighthood of God. In addition to this, like true Israelites and warriors most versed in holy battle, on fire with the flame of true charity, you carry out in your deeds the word of the gospel, in which it is said: *Greater love than this no man hath, that a man may lay down his life for his friends.* And, following the command of the chief shepherd, you are not at all afraid to lay down your lives for your brothers and to defend them from the pagans' invasions and, as you are known by name to be the Knights of the Temple, you have been established by the Lord as defenders of the Church and assailants of the enemies of Christ. But although with endeavour and praiseworthy devotion you are toiling with all your hearts and all your minds in so sacred an undertaking, nevertheless we exhort all the members of your Order in the Lord and we enjoin both you and those serving you for the remission of sins, by the authority of God and Blessed Peter the Prince, to protect the Catholic Church and, by fighting the enemies of the cross, to rid that part of the Church which is under the tyranny of the pagans from their filth.[4]

This generous and affectionate bull clearly gave the Templars a much wider field of action, and a scope far different from that established by Hugues de Payen twenty years earlier. It has justly been described by a recent historian of the Templars as 'the Magna Carta of the Knights Templar'.[5]

The Templars were now free to devote themselves to defending the Catholic Church against all enemies of the Cross. The Pope goes on to assert that the House of the Templars would thenceforth be under the tutelage and protection of the Holy See, and that they would be allowed to keep booty taken from the Saracens. The new role of chaplain-brothers was instituted with a one-year novitiate, although it does not appear to have been observed for many years. The chaplains were to be free of all diocesan control. Perhaps most controversial of all, from the point of view of enemies of the Templars, then and later, was the granting of the right to construct their own churches. This privilege was granted with the extraordinary—though coherent after the strictures of St Bernard—motivation that it would be 'indecent and dangerous for the professed friars to mix with the rabble of sinners and those who keep company with women'.

The French Rule

It was probably at Robert de Craon's instigation that the original paragraphs of the Latin *Rule* were translated into French; since the new *Rule* includes paragraphs devoted to the chaplain-brothers, it is likely that the translation was made after *Omne Datum Optimum*, probably in 1139-40.[6] Yet it is important to understand that the new *Rule* was never really finished: up to the end of the thirteenth century new paragraphs were added—often historical examples furnished by the Templars' own battles and defeats—and this process of adapting to meet new contingencies would have continued had the Order not been dissolved.

The key part of the *Rule* was, however, completed between the revisions and additions of Robert de Craon in 1139-40 and the fall of Jerusalem in 1187, when paragraphs determining hierarchical functions in the Kingdom became obsolete and would not have been included had the *Rule* been thoroughly revised after that date. The version of the *Rule* which has survived in several manuscripts was edited in 1886 by Henri de Curzon in the Old French text, with paragraphs 1-76 also given in Latin. It is composed of five parts:

§1–76   *Part I:* translation in 72 paragraphs of the Latin *Rule*, together with introductory paragraphs.

§77–278   *Part II:* a section comprising the hierarchical statutes of the Order. The titles, privileges, and duties of dignitaries and brothers are specified, together with the duties of conventual life.

§279–543 *Part III:* a) the daily life of the brothers, matters of discipline in the convent, on the march, and in war (§279–385). b) the holding of ordinary assemblies, public confession, the testimony or accusations that they must bring, and the penal code of the Order (§386–543).

§544–656 *Part IV:* new clarifications concerning the penal code, as if the short, 1-3 line sections of the original penal code were insufficient. This section, probably written in the thirteenth century, includes examples from Templar history.

§657–86   *Part V:* minutes of proceedings of the ceremony for receiving new brothers into the Order.

De Curzon believed that there were at least four major revisions of the *Rule*, with many additions. In some cases, modifications were made to earlier parts of the *Rule*, but the structure as presented here may be accepted as the one that governed everyday life for the greater part of Templar history.

Two changes, possibly instigated by Robert de Craon, made to the Latin *Rule* in the first version of the French *Rule* are of considerable interest. The first concerns the provision in the Latin *Rule* of a probationary period of one year for newly-enrolled knights; in the corresponding paragraph of the French *Rule* this requirement disappears, suggesting a loosening of discipline and requirements for the purposes of recruitment in the later 1130s (cf. §11). The most extraordinary change, given our knowledge of later accusations, is made in the second paragraph: a phrase in the original version ('. . . moreover where non-excommunicated knights are gathered you must go'*) becomes the exact opposite in the French *Rule*: '. . . we command you to go where excommunicated knights are gathered'. This controversial change has engendered many attempts at explanation, but may be taken simply as indicating the power of the Templars and the degree of independence from ecclesiastical control that the Order had already achieved. Before looking at the general nature of the *Rule* it might also be stressed that no·mention is made of pilgrims by St Bernard in the *De Laude,* or Innocent II in *Omne Datum Optimum,* or by the two versions of the Templar *Rule*—as if that original function had been overlooked.

The French *Rule* opens with a list of the Templar hierarchy, the privileges and duties of each rank being specified. For instance, the Master 'must have four horses, and one chaplain-brother and one clerk with three horses, and one sergeant brother with two horses, and one gentleman valet to carry his shield and lance, with one horse . . .' (§77). His duties and equipment are listed with immense detail and care.

According to this *Rule*, the hierarchy of the Knights Templar is as follows, with privileges, duties, arms, rights, and equipment detailed in the paragraphs given:

Master	§77–80
Seneschal	§99–100
Marshal	§101–3
Commander of the Kingdom of Jerusalem	§110
Commander of the City of Jerusalem	§120–4
Commander of Tripoli and Antioch	§125–6
Drapier	§130–1
Commanders of Houses	§132–6
Commanders of Knights	§137
Knight Brothers and Sergeants of the Convent	§138–41
Turcoplier	§169–72
Under-Marshal (a sergeant)	§173–6
Standard Bearer (a sergeant)	§177–9
Sergeant-brothers commanders of houses	§180
Rural brothers ('frères casaliers')	§181
Sick attendant brothers ('frères infirmiers')	§190–7

*'ubi autem milites non excommunicatos congregare auderint'.

In addition to these ranks, the Templars had vast numbers of servant brothers ('frères de métier') who performed the essential everyday tasks of such a large Order—grooms, cooks, servants, and labour for other menial tasks. Furthermore, some of these offices, for example that of the Drapier, responsible for the locally recruited troops trained in the manner of the Byzantine light cavalry, were unique to the Holy Land. On the whole, however, the ranks—and especially the higher ranks—conformed to the feudal structure of medieval Europe. The key distinction was always between knight and sergeant, even in those cases in which sergeants, as the result of the lack of knights in a small house or as a result of personal qualities, occupied posts apparently equal to their 'brother knights'. This distinction was marked by the brown or black mantles worn by sergeants, while only the relatively small number of knights wore the celebrated white mantle. Although the *Rule* states that they would eat 'in common', in practice the Templars ate at separate tables according to rank, but in the same hall (cf. §286–7).

There were also looser ranks of temporary and associated knights and sergeants. The associates ('affiliés') included married brothers ('frères mariés', and 'confrères'), while some members joined the Order for a previously stipulated period, such as the duration of a single crusade; these were called brothers *ad terminum* ('frères a terminé'). A further, and more complex, category consisted of those who paid a yearly fee *pro fraternitate* as lay or associate members in order to secure the spiritual benefits, prayers, and intercessions with which the Templars were privileged (cf. §673). And as the Order expanded throughout Europe anomalies of title and rank multiplied, so that there appears to have been no universal application of terms such as preceptor and commander. A confusion concerning the use of titles was increased in the thirteenth century, when the Templars maintained a fleet for the transport of pilgrims and goods from France and Italy to the Holy Land; other roles and therefore ranks were developed, such as Commander of the Ship or Commander of the Fleet, parallel to Hospitaller usage.[7]

At the core of this huge structure, the Knights Templars who wore the white mantle, later with the red cross, and who created the legend were from the beginning a small minority. They constituted a military élite served by an army of esquires and servants, and the whole Order—hierarchy, finances, agriculture, organization, recruitment—was geared to a single purpose: the maintenance of this body of well-equipped and well-prepared knights ready at any moment to go into action. This required vast resources, and the estimated numbers of knights in proportion to other brethren will illustrate this fact: in fact, in the Holy Land during the twelfth century the number of knights present was remarkably small. The feudal levy was of 670 knights and several thousand foot soldiers, while the total force of knights in the Latin Kingdom reached 1,200. Of these, perhaps 300 were Templars.[8] With such a number it is likely that the biggest Templar garrisons consisted of perhaps 50–60 knights, with as many as 400–500 other members.[9] In 1178, when the Moslem leader Saladin destroyed the garrison at Le Chastellet, there were 80 knights and 750 sergeants.[10] Some castles and garrisons were often deprived totally of knights in order to defend other sites, and many were garrisoned with a force of sergeants. The greatest defeat in the history of the Templars, at Hattin in 1187, saw the death of 100 knights according to the verse chronicler Ambroise.[11] These figures give a good idea of the size of the forces involved in many military actions in the Holy Land.

In Western Europe, numbers were even lower: Matthew Paris emphasizes the importance of the individual houses when he asserts that 'every manor can furnish, without grievance, one soldier, well-armed and fully equipped, for the succour of the Holy Land, even with all things which appertain to the full equipment of a soldier'.[12] Later events are more precise in establishing the proportions between knights and other brethren, which we have no reason to believe different from those of the twelfth century. At the revolt in Cyprus in 1192, Templar forces present included 14 knights, 29 other mounted men, and 74 foot soldiers.[13] Similarly at the trial in Paris of 138 Templars who were interrogated by the Inquisitor-General, only 14 were knights; of 546 Templars who came forward to defend the Order in 1310, 18 were knights.[14] Perhaps the estimate of a ratio of 1:10 made by Henry Lea is accurate: he estimates the total force of the Order shortly before its downfall as 15,000, of whom 1,500 were knights.*[15] He observes that when the Templars were taken at Beaucaire in 1307 there were 5 knights, 1 priest, and 54 serving brothers.[16] There is no good reason to doubt that this was a normal establishment, and that Lea's overall estimate is acceptable.

---

* Other estimates at the time of the trial vary from 5,000 to 20,000.

The *Rule* was mainly concerned with this small military élite. One of the most detailed paragraphs is in fact §138, in which the clothing and equipment of the knight are carefully listed (as we shall see in Chapter 4). They were to wear the white mantle at all times, except when sick in hospital; it was to be worn properly, and they could neither drink nor eat without it (§279). At least in the early years the knights maintained the rigorous life ordained for them in line with that of the Cistercians. They were to say 26 paternosters at the moment of waking, and a further 60 before eating (§683). Meals were to be taken in silence, with neither wine nor water at table (§31 and §183); they were only to eat what everybody ate together (§289). Furthermore, to stress their religious vocation, they were to observe two Lents each year, one before Easter and another before Christmas, with forty days of fasting in each period (§76 and §351). This rule could be modified in the event of war, or at the discretion of the Master in case of necessity.

The *Rule* provides simple penalties for infractions of this discipline, most of them not going beyond a few lines. There were two main categories of offence, distinguished by penalties for them: things for which a Templar 'lost the house' ('pert la maison'), and things for which he 'lost his habit' ('pert son abit'). The main offences for which the loss of the house was the punishment were simony, revealing his chapter, killing a Christian, larceny, and heresy (§224–31), while those that incurred loss of the Templar habit included refusal to obey the rules of the house, fighting against other Templar brothers, wounding a Christian, and giving the alms of the house to lay people (§233, 234, 235, 249). As we have seen, later additions to this rudimentary penal code suggest that these brief sections—laconic and almost abstract, as if no one would ever commit such crimes—turned out in the light of practice and expansion of the Order to be insufficient. They were repeated in greater detail in paragraphs 544–656.

The *Rule* concludes with the formula for the reception of a Templar brother. Before the new brother is allowed into the General Chapter, the Master or presiding Preceptor opens the proceedings:

Fine brother knights [*Biaus seignors freres*], you see that the majority has agreed that this man should be made a brother. If there be someone amongst you who know something which prevents him from becoming a brother according to the Rule, then say it, since it is better to say it before he has come before us. (§657)

If there are no objections, the candidate is then brought before the chapter. The leader of the chapter makes it clear to him that the life of the Templars is hard:

> You see us with fine horses and fine harness and eat well and drink well and possess fine clothes, and it therefore appears to you that you will be much at your comfort. But you do not know of the harsh commandments which obtain here within: because it is a hard thing that you, who are master of yourself, should become the serf of another . . . if you wish to be on the land this side of the sea, you will be sent to the other side; if you wish to be at Acre, you will be sent to Tripoli . . . (§661)

The next fourteen paragraphs consist of an interrogation of the candidate, to discover whether he is ready to suffer for God, to ensure that he is not a member of another order, to check that he is neither married nor engaged, that he has no debts, and that he has no feud or outstanding legal proceedings. This patient investigation must have dissuaded any but the most convinced of candidates.

The final grand question, that still resounds magnificently after seven centuries, leaves no room for doubt that the prospective knight is leaving behind him the trappings of his life up to that moment: 'Do you wish to be, for all the days of your life, servant and slave of the house?' To which the candidate replies: 'Yes, if God wills, sire'.* After this oath the newly-received brother is required to swear loyalty to the Master and to serve the Order. He is given the above-cited rules, and told clearly what to do to avoid losing either habit or house; practical rules of how and when to sleep, eat, and behave are given him, together with the number of paternosters and other prayers that he must say. The final resounding paragraph of the *Rule* runs as follows:

> Now that we have told you the things that you should do and of what you must beware, and those that cause loss of the house, and those that cause loss of the habit, and of other rules; and if we have not told you everything that we should tell you, then you may ask it.—And God permit you to speak well and do well. (§686)

The tone of the reception and the severity with which the Master interrogates and reminds the candidate of the difficulty of Templar

---

* 'Volés vos estre, tous les jors de vostre vie mès, sers et esclaf de la maison?' 'Oïll, se Dieu plaist, Sire.'

life leave no doubts about the difficulty of the vocation and the seriousness of purpose. The similarity of the reception of Gérard de Caux at the end of the thirteenth century suggests that these characteristics remained constant in the reception process throughout the history of the Knights Templars.*

Further Papal Approval

With the French *Rule* and the immense moral support provided by *Omne Datum Optimum*, the Templars were now truly an international order, already important in several spheres but as yet without any great military success.

Omne Datum Optimum was repeated frequently in the next century† but succeeding popes did not hesitate to add new bulls to Innocent II's initiative. Celestine II, his legitimate successor, died within a year of his election to the Holy See on 26 September 1143, yet found time to issue the important bull *Milites Templi* on 9 January 1144. This bull established two precedents: it awarded indulgences to benefactors of the Order of the Temple and gave them permission to hold a collection in their own churches once a year.[17] Celestine's successor, Lucius II, also held the Holy See for less than a year, after which brief period the Templars were further favoured by the election of Bernardo Pignatelli of Pisa as Eugenius III, on 15 February 1145.

Eugenius III, whose reign lasted for eight years, was a friend and disciple of St Bernard and had been a monk in the monastery of Clairvaux. Bernard wrote to him: 'What matter that you have been raised to the Chair of Peter? Walk on the wings of the wind, if you will; you cannot escape from mine affection. Love will recognize a son crowned even with the tiara.'[18] Bernard immediately began the composition of the five letters which constitute his *De Consideratione*, advising Eugenius how to act as pope and thereby composing what Daniel-Rops describes as the 'Charter of the Papacy'.[19] It is not surprising that this pope should almost immediately issue a bull favouring the Templars, also a child of St Bernard's inspiration. On 7 April 1145,

---

* Cf. Michelet, *Le Procès*, I, pp. 379–86. Barber, *Trial*, gives an English translation, pp. 253–7.

† Eight times between 1198 and 1205, during the pontificate of Innocent III.

seven weeks after his election, the bull *Militia Dei* was promulgated,[20] while in July of the same year he renewed *Milites Templi*.[21]

Militia Dei gave the Templar Order the right to build its own chapels independent of diocesan authority and to bury its dead in the cemeteries of these chapels. This reinforcing of the privilege already granted in *Omne Datum Optimum*, giving them the right to build their own churches, suggests that they may have had some difficulty in implementing it. The matter of the cemeteries was soon to become controversial.

The constant support of Eugenius III was to have a further important consequence. It seems that the Pope was invited to attend the General Chapter held in Paris in 1147—a sign of the close relationship and mutual respect between the papacy and the Templars at that time— and it was then that Eugenius granted the Templars the right to wear the red cross on the breast of their mantle.[22] Thus, by 1147, the Knights Templars were firmly established as an important military order both in the Holy Land and in Western Europe: they had a *Rule*, a distinctive and recognized form of dress, a well-defined hierarchical structure, and possessed wealth and land throughout Christendom. It was also in 1147 that their military fame began to spread as the result of an important action during the Crusade of Louis VII of France, which departed from France for the Holy Land in that year, with the blessing of St Bernard and Eugenius III.

⚜

4

KNIGHTS MILITANT
1147–87

THE military situation in which the Knights Templars began to operate was one of tortuous complexity. Frankish dominion of the East was itself divided into four Crusader States: the Kingdom of Jerusalem, the principality of Antioch, the County of Tripoli, and the County of Edessa. The *Kingdom of Jerusalem* was bounded to the west by the sea from as-Darum to the Nahr-al-Kalb, just north of Beirut; its eastern frontier ran from the Gulf of Aqaba, on the Red Sea, northwards to the East of the Dead Sea and the River Jordan and into the Lebanese mountains. The *Principality of Antioch* was much older, with its own Patriarch. Until recent times it had been part of the Byzantine Empire, and had never therefore been 'lost' to the Moslems as the other three states. Antioch controlled the overland route into the states from Europe, and the sea coast from the castle of al-Marqab in the south. Its northern boundary went north of Misis to Marash, then skirted Aleppo to the north and ran east of the Orantes River to Kafartab, whence its southern frontier stretched to the sea north of Shaizar and the territory held by the Assassins. The *County of Tripoli* stretched from the shore near Nahr-al-Kalb to a point north of Tartus, and then from Ba'rin the frontier ran south-west of the Orantes River and the city of Hom. It then ran from Jubail to the sea. Finally, the short-lived *County of Edessa* was situated north-east of Antioch and extended across the River Euphrates. Its northern frontier ran from Marash, in present-day Turkey, to Besni and Samsat; there it turned south towards modern Syria and passed between Edessa itself and Harran.

These four states were themselves often in conflict over policy and were further weakened by the presence of independent Moslem emirates and the strongholds of the Assassins within the area they sought to control. This paradox is explained by the fact that the 'occupation of the whole breadth of Syria was an ideal . . . perhaps never perceived and certainly never pursued by the Syrian Franks'.[1] Smail has shown how routes that passed within Frankish territory were regularly used by Moslem armies and that communications between Aleppo and Damascus with Mesopotamia were never broken by the crusaders.[2] Frontier cities such as Edessa and Antioch were contended by the surrounding non-Christian and Christian powers, which shifted, merged, allied or attacked as their temporary exigencies required. Religion was often subservient to immediate political and military needs: the Sebastocrator Isaac, brother to Emperor John of Constantinople, fled from the court in 1130 and spent the following nine years plotting with various Moslem and Armenian princes.[3] The same Emperor's nephew, also called John, became a Moslem and married the daughter of Mas'ud ibn Kilij Arslan, Seljuk Sultan of Turkey and one of his uncle's greatest enemies.[4]

These and other rulers often attacked the crusader states, and more often plotted in order to weaken them. The Emperor of Byzantium, though a Christian ruler, maintained a delicate balance of power with his Moslem neighbours and was careful not to allow the crusader states to become powerful enough to upset this balance. To the north lay Armenian Cilicia, of vital importance for the overland route from Europe but ready to create alliances with the crusaders' enemies when necessary. Also to the north were the Seljuks of Mas'ud, and to the north-east the lands of the Danishmend emir Mohammed Ibn Ghazi—the chief power in Asia Minor. Several important Moslem rulers permanently encroached on crusader lands from the cities of Aleppo, Damascus, and Homs, which were only a short distant from major castles and cities of the four states. Further east the Seljuks of Baghdad and the Fatimids of Fustat were ready to take advantage of any weakness, while the Sultan of Egypt constantly threatened the southern frontier of the Kingdom of Jerusalem.

The Templars were forced to operate within this complex web of shifting alliances in order to develop and consolidate their own power. It is therefore not surprising that in one of their earliest recorded actions they were allied to Emperor John of Constantinople and the troops of the Count of Edessa against the interests of the Kingdom of Jerusalem. It might be argued in the light of later accusations of treachery that the kind of idealism inspired by a man like St Bernard had necessarily to be modified in the rough and tumble of life in the East.

It appears that the first military actions in which the Templars engaged were in the north of the Holy Land—far from their nominal task of guarding the pilgrim road from Jaffa to Jerusalem. Riley-Smith has argued that the Order may have come into possession of the important March of Amanus in the Principality of Antioch as early as 1131; at the latest, the Templars held Amanus in 1137, before any military activity in the Holy Land is recorded.[5] This March consisted of a massif just north of Antioch which constitutes a natural barrier between the city and the province of Cilicia, or Asia Minor, to the north. It was created in order to control the two roads which led through the Syrian Gates to the city of Antioch. King Fulk of Jerusalem, Baldwin II's successor, travelled north to Antioch in 1131 and may have granted the March to the Templars in that year. Five years later Count Raymond of Poitiers arrived in the Holy Land to marry Constance, heiress to Antioch.* His first task was to recover Cilicia and he immediately engaged in a campaign which lasted from April 1136 into 1137. If the Templars did not already possess the March, it is likely that they came into possession of it during Raymond's campaign. The powerful stronghold of Baghras lay in the March of Amanus, together with the minor Templar castles of Roche Roussel and Darbsak.

Baghras, which is now in Turkey, was vital for the defence of Antioch but also desired by Moslem forces as a safeguard against Armenian advances from the north. It passed in and out of Templar hands constantly: they held it in 1156, but from 1160 to 1161 it was a fief of the Prince of Antioch; from 1175 it was held by the Templars as their northern headquarters until Saladin took it in 1188; it was again in Templar hands from 1216 to 1268, but they lost it after that date and were themselves responsible for burning the castle in 1283.[6] In fact the story of Baghras, even in this bare form, vividly illustrates the frequent changes in those turbulent years, and the difficulty of listing Templar possessions at any given moment in their history.

That the Templars were themselves caught up in this political web is illustrated by the following incidents. In 1137 the Emperor John of Constantinople advanced into Cilicia and then laid siege to the city

---

* Raymond arrived from England, where he had been the guest of Henry I, whose daughter had recently married Fulk's son Geoffrey.

of Antioch on 29 August. In March of the following year he moved into Antioch itself accompanied by troops of the Prince of Antioch and the Count of Edessa, and *a contingent of Templars*,[7] presumably from the March of Amanus. They appear to have participated in the Emperor's entire spring campaign of that year, in which his army reached Aleppo without taking the strongly defended city and besieged Shaizur from 28 April to 21 May 1138. Yet their role was even more ambiguous during John's sortie to Antioch in 1142: on 25 September of that year he arrived at the Templar castle of Baghras and demanded that Raymond should give up Antioch.[8] If Riley-Smith's hypothesis that Raymond had given Baghras to the Templars is correct—and it is plausible in the context of other castles given to the Hospitallers on the southern frontier of the Kingdom of Jerusalem—then the Templars were indeed in an ambiguous situation. When the Emperor John sent an embassy to Jerusalem to treat with Fulk, the King of Jerusalem chose Geoffrey, Abbot of the Temple, to carry his reply to the Emperor.* For the Templars it was perhaps fortunate that John died in April 1143, before their position became impossible to sustain.

The history of the Order in the East is extremely hazy in this period, and in fact one of their earliest recorded actions appears to have been a humiliating defeat. During a campaign of Fulk in Gilead, Runciman relates, 'a band of Moslems managed to cross the Jordan close to its junction with the Dead Sea and to raid Judea, where they lured to its destruction by the tactics of a feigned retreat a company of Templar knights sent against them'.[9] It was indeed some time before the Templars and other knights present in the Holy Land developed tactics to counteract those of the Moslems and the Seljuk Turks, who each employed means of warfare different from those to which European knights had been accustomed. The Templars made good use of these early experiences and later became the military strategists of the kings and crusaders who fought in the Holy Land.

Before considering the tactics and weapons used by the Templars, we may ask what became of their original vocation as protectors of Jerusalem-bound pilgrims. When they appear in history they are already

* It is interesting in the light of accusations of ignorance made against the Templars that Runciman describes Geoffrey as 'a good Greek scholar' (*History of the Crusades*, II, p. 224).

part of the crusading states' regular military forces, while their original function seems to have been forgotten. It is a curious fact that their first castle was on the northern frontier, four hundred miles from the Jaffa-Jerusalem road, while the earliest castles on the southern frontier were neither entrusted to nor constructed by the Templars: Ibelin, built by King Fulk of Jerusalem ten miles south-west of Lydda, was entrusted to Balian, brother of the Viscount of Chartres, who was to guard the roads from Ascalon to Jaffa, and to Ramleh; Blancheregarde was built south of Ibelin to guard the road from Ascalon to Jerusalem, and was placed in the hands of the baron Arnulf; a further castle, called Bethgibelin, was built to command the road from Ascalon to Hebron and was given to the Hospitallers. This latter castle was built after Patriarch William of Jerusalem had organized a campaign against bandits on the Jaffa-Jerusalem road.[10] The first Templar castle in the south of the Latin Kingdom of Jerusalem was Gaza, which was rebuilt, fortified, and entrusted to the Templars in 1149–50 as a base for reprisals against Ascalon.[11] Somewhere along the line, between Hugues' original inspiration and the expansion of the Order under Robert de Craon, the Templars had completely changed character. It is as a fully-fledged crusading order that we first hear of notable Templar successes.

The Second Crusade and Louis VII of France

The most exposed of the crusader states had always been the County of Edessa, vulnerable on three sides far to the north-east of the Holy Land, astride the Euphrates with the city of Edessa almost at its eastern extremity. After a four-week siege in November 1144, Imad ed-din Zengi, son of the ex-governor of Aleppo, self-appointed champion of Islam against the Franks, took the city. The Moslem forces, with Kurds and Turcomans from the upper Tigris in support, entered Edessa on Christmas Eve, and Zengi immediately set about executing the entire Frankish population. Zengi was the atabeg or governor of Mosul for the Seljuk prince Alp Arslan, but after this triumph against Edessa was made King and Conqueror by the Caliph himself. 'The news of the fall of Edessa reverberated throughout the world. To the Moslems it brought new hope. A Christian state that had intruded into their midst had been destroyed, and the Franks restricted to the lands by the Mediterranean. The roads from Mosul to Aleppo were now cleared of the enemy, and there was no longer a Christian wedge driven between the Turks of Iran and the Turks of Anatolia.'[12] The loss of Edessa was a traumatic shock for the Christians of Western Europe, and with hindsight appears as the first step towards the ultimate disintegration of the crusading states—a mere half-century after the hard-won conquest.

Messages were dispatched to Pope Eugenius III, whose immediate action was to set about organizing a new crusade. The Pope's choice for leader fell upon Louis VII, who had always supported Eugenius and retained as his religious advisor Bernard of Clairvaux, the Pope's own spiritual mentor. Here again a network whose focal point was St Bernard enters the story of the Templars. The Second Crusade was preached to a vast audience by St Bernard himself at Vézélay on 31 March 1146, and he then travelled widely through northern Europe pressing the cause: he preached the crusade in Burgundy, Lorraine, Flanders, Germany, and Eastern France, and supervised the arrangements for the departure, perhaps with the assistance of the Templars. It was to be the largest of all the crusades, with French, German, English, and Italian contingents fighting in the East, as well as against the Moors of the Iberian peninsula and the Wends of northern Germany and East Saxony.[13]

Whatever may have been their role in the initial organization, the Second Crusade was important for the Knights Templars for three reasons. In early April of 1147, Pope Eugenius III travelled from Rome to meet Louis VII of France at Dijon; he then continued north to Clairvaux, where he met Bernard on 6 April. Two weeks later he moved to the abbey of St Denis for the Easter period, remaining in Paris until early June.[14] It was presumably during this six-week period of residence in Paris that the pope attended the General Chapter of the Knights Templars, and awarded them the privilege of wearing the red cross on their mantles. King Louis departed from St Denis on 8 June, travelling eastwards for the departure of the crusade that was scheduled to start from Metz a few days later. He was accompanied by Everard de Barres, Master of the Temple, with a regiment of Templar recruits destined for the Holy Land. Their participation was to lead the Order to its first notable military exploit; furthermore, the importance of the Order and respect accorded to its Master were demonstrated when Everard de Barres was sent ahead by Louis to negotiate the passage of his army through Constantinople.[15]

The third factor of great interest is that this crusade appears to be the first occasion on which the Knights Templars emerge as international financiers. Louis VII, like the leaders of all the crusades, found the enterprise more expensive than he had thought. When in Syria he needed to contract a loan in order to complete his campaign, repayable upon his return to France. The Templars were able to satisfy his immediate needs.[16] Thus, during that important crusade, sponsored by the Templars' own spiritual patron, Bernard of Clairvaux, the twin functions of permanent fighting force at the service of the Holy Land and financiers to the royal courts of Europe came simultaneously to the fore.

But their military role in the Second Crusade, testifying to an unusual degree of training and discipline amidst such undisciplined troops, is perhaps the most striking and vital factor. Before the departure of the crusade, Louis had enacted a series of laws to ensure peace between the competing factions of his army; but it seems that the rigours of the journey together with innate antagonism and the temptations placed before them were too much for many of the crusaders. Moreover, the whole enterprise was marked by a fatal lack of coordination between the army of Louis and that of Conrad Hohenstaufen, which preceded Louis along the overland route to the East. Constant pillaging and the harassing tactics of the Turks along the curving route south from Constantinople further weakened the discipline of troops whose loyalty was to their own lords. Conrad's army was routed and decimated before reaching the Holy Land, and when its survivors staggered back to Constantinople the French army was frightened into even greater disorder. In this mass of disparate and demoralized forces, with rivers swollen with winter rain and insufficient supplies for a body of perhaps twenty thousand men, the Templars alone maintained strict discipline.

On the leg of the march from Ephesus to Adalia,* when the army's supplies were reduced to horsemeat and bread baked in the ashes of camp-fires, their role was vital. Odo of Deuil, who travelled with the crusaders as official chronicler to Louis VII, describes the situation as follows:

Against them [i.e. the harassing Moslems] the Templars and the Master of the Temple, Lord Everard of Barres, who should be revered for his piety and who furnished the army an honourable example, saved their own possessions

---

* Now Antalya, and in the twelfth century still forty days overland journey from Antioch.

wisely and alertly and protected those of other people as courageously as possible. Now the king liked the example which they set and was glad to imitate it, and he wanted the army to be influenced in that direction, for he knew that, even if extreme hunger should weaken them, unity of spirit would also strengthen them in their weakness. By common consent, therefore, it was decided that during this dangerous period all should establish fraternity with the Templars, rich and poor taking oath that they would not flee the field and that they would obey in every respect the officers assigned to them by the Templars. Thus they were given a commander named Gilbert, and he was given associates, to each of whom he should assign fifty knights.[17]

Thus ordered and inspired the army continued on its journey, and although when they arrived in Antioch in late spring only half of the original number were present, the saving of that half of the army was largely due to the discipline and example of the Templars. For the first time, in the spring of 1148, the Order of the Temple emerges as having played a decisive part in an important military action. But even that success was limited by the disastrous overall failure of the Second Crusade, which was ultimately 'brought to nothing by its leaders, with their truculence, their ignorance and their ineffectual folly'.[18]

The Templar Knight in Action

The French *Rule* provides the basis of a detailed description of a Templar Knight, supported by surviving illustrations of the Templars in battle. The knight may have three horses and one esquire, plus a fourth horse at the discretion of the Master. His armour is listed as follows: a mail helmet (*haubers*), protection for the legs, at first sack-cloth but later mail (*chauces de fer*), and a helmet (*heaume*) or light hat covering the top of the head (*chapeau de fer*). In addition he wore pieces of armour designed to protect shoulders and feet (*jupeau d'armer, espalliers, soliers d'armer*), while his armour was completed by a triangular body-shield whose vertical sides were slightly curved (*escu*).

His principal weapon was a straight two-sided sword (*espée*), with as secondary weapons a lance and a Turkish mace (*mace turquese*)—an iron head with projecting spikes. In addition each knight was to be armed with three knives: a long dagger worn to the left of the belt, a small pocket knife, and a very short knife with long blade (*1 d'armes, 1 de pain taillier,* and *1 canivet*).[19]

Twelfth-century battle tactics were founded upon a preliminary mounted attack of knights armed with lances. The knight held reins and shield in his left hand and used his right hand to hold the lance, either rigid under his arm or wielding it with a swinging thrust. The charge was carried out at the horse's maximum speed, and the lance might also be thrown like a javelin under certain circumstances. If the lance were broken or lost, then the knight continued to fight with his sword. But even with the greatest discipline, this charge remained a combined charge of individual knights rather than a precisely controlled charge, and depended for its success on the force of impact. Thus, although the Frankish charge was feared throughout the East it required great discipline and skilled timing in order to have its greatest effect. [20]

Yet against Turkish Seljuk tactics it seems that the greatest weapon in the hands of the Templars was in fact their discipline, rigidly controlled by the *Rule*. The fundamental weapon of Turkish armies was the mounted archer, quicker and more flexible than Frankish knights as the result of ligher weapons and armour, combined with the pace of their horses. This created severe problems for European knights trained to attack a stationary force awaiting their charge. Increased mobility enabled the Turks to base their tactics upon four main features:

1. They remained at a discreet distance from a body of Frankish knights, and could choose at will their moment of attack or retreat if the Franks appeared to be preparing an attack.

2. One of their favourite tactical weapons was the feigned retreat, sometimes lasting days, in which they used a small body of men as bait for the eager Franks.

3. They usually attacked the flank or rear of the enemy, a tactic for which European experience was useless. The enemy was therefore either outflanked or completely encircled.

4. They forced the Franks to fight on the march, whereas they would have preferred to marshal and fight in order.

These unusual tactics caused a great deal of trouble, as on Louis VII's march through Cilicia to Antioch. Coupled with the ability of Turkish horsemen to use their bows from the saddle without stopping or dismounting, thereby killing valuable horses on the march as well as soldiers, they necessitated a new response on the part of the crusaders. [21]

The major answer was discipline, which was always difficult under enemy provocation, since to resist the temptation to fight back 'demands severe restraint of normal human instincts'. [22] It was their defence against constant harassing on the march which led to the Templars' success in the Second Crusade. Thenceforth the knights of both the Temple and the Hospital were often used as rear-guards on the march, for against such tactics the rear-guard became the element of most importance in an army on the march. The *Rule* firmly established that no knight could leave the formation without permission (§162), the only exception made being when a knight requested permission to test his horse and harness with a short gallop (§162). Another circumstance under which a Templar could leave his squadron was to rescue a Christian in dire danger of death at the hands of a Moslem (§163). Otherwise any breach of these orders could lead to a Templar being deprived of his habit, and Smail observes that 'the very existence of such penalties proves to some extent the difficulty of enforcing the rule'.[23]

Together with this extreme and essential discipline, the quality for which the Templars were most renowned was their courage—even on the numerous occasions on which they lost a battle. Moslem chroniclers emphasize this fact. Ibn Wasil's description of the Mamelukes of Malik as-Sahih, who routed the Franks and captured Louis IX of France in 1250, as the 'Templars of Islam' testifies to the esteem in which the Order was held by its enemies.[24] Earlier, after the battle of Safouriyad in 1187, Ibn-Alatyr had commented: 'It was a signal victory for the Moslems, because the Templars and the Hospitallers were, so to speak, the fiery heart of France.'[25] The most celebrated account of their courage was provided by Jacques de Vitry:

Thus they became so terrible to the enemies of Christ's faith that one of them sued to chase a thousand, and two of them ten thousand; when they were called to arms, they did not ask how many of the enemy there were, but where they were. They were lions in war, and gentle as lambs at home; in the field they were fierce soldiers, in church they were like hermits or monks; they were harsh and savage to the enemies of Christ, but kindly and gracious to Christians.[26]

It is interesting that he also stresses the importance of their discipline, and its role in establishing the reputation of the Templars:

Now, seeing that religious zeal cannot be kept up without strict discipline, these wise and devout men from the beginning safeguarded themselves and provided for the good government of their successors in determining in nowise to disregard or leave unpunished the negligences and trespasses of their delinquent brethren . . . [27]

This neatly summarizes the two essential qualities, discipline and courage, which remained the recognized attributes of the Knights Templars notwithstanding their rather meagre record of military success.

Templar Castles in the Twelfth Century

Generalized statements about Templar castles are apt to be even more confusing than other generalizations about them: for instance, the greatest of Templar Castles, At'lit or Castle Pilgrim, built to be impregnable and never in fact taken by the Templars' enemies, was not built until 1218. Thus to list the castles or speak generally of their characteristics would be to present a false picture of the situation in the twelfth century. The Templars never held more than ten or so castles at any given moment in their history, far less than the Hospitallers, who already held as many as seven or eight castles by 1160, and at one time or another possessed a total of 56 castles in Latin Syria. [28]

By the middle of the twelfth century the Templars were in possession of perhaps seven castles: in the March of Amanus those of Baghras, Roch Roussel, and Darbsak cited above, plus Gaza in the extreme south of the Kingdom of Jerusalem on the edge of the Sinai desert, which they obtained in 1149, and the castle of Tortosa, where in 1152 the Bishop had 'begged the Templars to take on the guard of the castle to assure his safety and that of the townspeople and to allow the service of God to continue in the cathedral'. [29] In addition they held Ahamant, 'lying beyond Jordan on the borders of Arabia', [30] and Arima in the County of Tripoli. [31] It is interesting to note that the possession of Tortosa was not the result of a siege or battle but the gift of a desperate bishop after the city of Tortosa had been devastated by Nur-ad-Din. The only other important castle held by the Templars in the twelfth century was that of Le Chastellet, near Jacob's Ford; that unfortunate castle, built in 1178, was destroyed by Saladin in 1180 almost as soon as it was completed. The major Templar castles of Beaufort and Safed (Safita), together with At'lit, belong to the substantially different history of the thirteenth century; but of those, Beaufort was only in Templar hands from 1260 to 1268, At'lit from 1218 to 1291, and Safed from 1240 to 1266.

This distinction between the castles of the twelfth century and those of the thirteenth is crucial, for the methods and criteria used in castle building changed dramatically after the Battle of Hattin and consequent Fall of Jerusalem in 1187. The earlier castles fell into two main categories: first, simple castles for attacking purposes, either Byzantine or Moslem castles taken over and modified or new castles built near the coast or on the Eastern frontier to extend Frankish power and open up new trade routes; second, defence castles of ever-increasing complexity and size.[32] * They were small because siege warfare was not yet as sophisticated as it was soon to become, and they were usually simple in structure with towers to provide flanking fire. There is evidence that entire castles were often left ungarrisoned when men were needed to fight elsewhere, and there were none of the immense quantities of supplies or the vegetable gardens and mills of later castles. But they grew more complex as siege weapons rapidly improved.†

R. C. Smail has shown convincingly that stock phrases such as 'guarded the frontier', 'commanded the valley', or 'closed the route' are completely inapplicable to the castles of the Holy Land.[33] There was never a unified system of defence of the crusader states, and the castles served as much as centres of colonization, residence, barracks, administration centres, and police posts as points of attack or ramparts for the defence of conquered territory. In this sense, from the point of view of Templar history, the compounds maintained in major cities such as Jerusalem and Acre were often of far greater importance than the castles. The bishop of Tortosa's 'gift' of the castle of Tortosa brought with it all the churches with parochial rights except five, and half the tithe of the whole diocese; it is likely that similar rights came with the castle of Gaza,[34] and these would have been sufficient justification for acceptance by the Templars without taking into consideration their military value. Tortosa in fact became the administrative centre of the Templars in the County of Tripoli.

Similarly, the distribution of the castles was irrational from any defensive or strategic point of view: there were many inland roads and

* Details of constructions, sites and function of the later Templar castles will be given in Chapter 7.

† A glance at Smail's plan of Crac de Chevaliers will illustrate this fact (cf. Smail, *Crusading Warfare*, p. 248).

mountain passes left unguarded, while castles proliferated along the coast between Haifa and Jaffa. This was a waste of resources since no direct threat was offered while the Franks held undisputed control of the sea routes to and from those ports, and no useful attack could be launched from them. The situation was the same on the eastern frontier:

Throughout the period Damascus was a more important seat of Muslim political power than the towns of the middle Orontes; the defence of the easy routes from that city into the Latin Kingdom was therefore a more urgent and important problem than that of the Homs-Tripoli corridor. A Muslim force marching from Damascus to Banyas was on the main road to Tyre and Sidon, while it could also thrust across upper Jordan to the plain of Acre . . . The entry into the kingdom by way of the Jordan crossing immediately south of Lake Tiberias at al-Sannabra, used during the major invasions of Mawdud and Tughtagin in 1113, and of Saladin in 1182, 1183, and 1187, was virtually undefended.[35]

The importance of these Templar castles was as advance posts offering security, supplies, and water for armies which went out from the major cities to attack incoming invaders. But on the whole, the military function was, paradoxically, of less importance than the other functions enumerated above.

The Castle and Feudal Power

The civil aspect of the castle in twelfth-century Latin Syria, and the extent to which possession of castles led to control of the surrounding territory, rights, income, and services, forms an important part of Templar history and prefigures the rapid rise to wealth of the Order from the middle of the century. Indeed, while at the beginning the two major military orders, Templars and Hospitallers, gained their possessions by conquest, later in the century they tended to *purchase* castles and land, clearly for motives which were not purely military. In this way, the possession of castles led to their permanent integration into the feudal society of the Latin Kingdom and other crusader states. At first the existing castles were built as much for the purpose of *colonizing* the territory around them as for defence. The true importance of the castle and walled city are to be found in the domination by a small ruling class and military élite of the subject peoples of the new colonies; this domination, clearly, was economic rather than military.

The feudal structure of the crusader states was based upon the ruler giving land to his vassals as fiefs, the holders of which were required to provided well-armed forces upon demand. But an important shift in this structure occurred in the mid-twelfth century, after the military successes of Imad ed-din Zengi and his son Nur ad-Din. There were two major problems for the crusading states: the unification of Moslem Syria, which rendered defence of the states more difficult; and the gradual impoverishment of feudal tenants as the result of almost continuous campaigns. This made it necessary to bolster military strength with extra-feudal manpower, which both the Templars and the Hospitallers were ready to provide. It was at this moment that their real power was created, beginning with the grant of Bait Jibrin to the Hospitallers in 1137.

Far from strengthening the crusader states, as might have been expected, this policy gradually weakened them as feudal entities, for reasons which Smail has explained as follows:

These concessions made to the knights were transfers not only of property but of power. Feudal government in Latin Syria was progressively weakened, not because lords and vassals failed to achieve a satisfactory relationship, but because lands, castles, powers and rights over men had continually to be conceded to Orders which were not wholly part of the feudal structure. In the special conditions of Syria the landholding feudal knighthood lacked the resources to discharge its duties to society in war and government, and the well endowed orders had increasingly to take its place.[36]

Thus Gaza, for example, was not only a castle, but a feudal lordship, and large tracts of land passed into the hands of the orders together with leases and fiefs. From 1142 the possessions of the Hospital in the County of Tripoli almost constituted an independent principality.[37] The essentially urban, monetary economy of the Latin Kingdom also gave rise to the granting of cash fiefs in the place of land. The Templars possessed Bedouin pasture rights which were paid in horses, camels, and sheep, and even owned entire Bedouin tribes.[38] That situation is directly in line with the feudal ownership of serfs. The Templar compounds became effectively independent ecclesiastical lordships, with autonomous markets created within them.[39]

As their feudal power increased, the Masters of the military orders became significant political figures without whose advice important decisions could not be taken. Power—deriving from economic rather than military strength—necessarily implied an interest in domestic politics: by 1186 the Master of the Temple, the Master of the Hospital, and the Patriarch of Jerusalem each held a key to the crown jewels,[40] a symbol of their authority within the Kingdom. When Baldwin IV died at the age of twenty-four in 1185, the Templars and Hospitallers were given the custody of royal castles during the regency of Raymond of Tripoli.[41] This single fact is sufficient testimony of the status of the orders as feudal lords and guarantors for the crown.

But in this new power lay the seeds of discontent, and the roots of the arrogance which slowly gained them powerful enemies within the Church—notably William of Tyre. The main problem was the much-flaunted independence of the military orders, and the fact that they never rendered the full services which they should have done as feudal lords and vassals to—among others—the King of Jerusalem. Again, Smail has described this situation vividly:

They rendered military aid not as tenants owing service to a feudal overlord, but as powerful international Orders which became progressively more free of feudal control in Syria. This progress towards freedom is reflected in the terms on which they acquired the castles. They used occasions of grant or sale to negotiate special privileges. They won the *right to negotiate* their own truces with the Muslim, independently of the feudal prince, and to be *exempt* from the normal custom of dividing spoils of war. Although these charters are in the form of a grant from a feudal prince to the Orders, they read like treatises between *equal and independent powers.*[42]

With the full support of a series of influential popes, untrammelled freedom of action in the Holy Land, and the backing of vast sums of money now pouring in from European possessions and donations, the power of the Templars was immense in the late twelfth century. Nor did they ever endear themselves to the local ecclesiastical hierarchy, although the Patriarch of Jerusalem had possibly been the inspiration behind the foundation of their order.

This breathless description of their headquarters in Jerusalem at the height of their power about 1172, written by the German pilgrim Theoderich, will give some idea of the regal splendour in which the Master and his immediate entourage then lived:

Next comes, on the south, the palace of Solomon, which is oblong, and supported by columns within like a church, and at the end is round like

1. Richerenches (northern Provence): main entrance to the well-preserved commanderie, still with its four walls, each 200 metres long.

2. Richerenches: ramparts, showing the beginning of the vault of the Temple, to the right of the restored church.

3. Richerenches: detail of the Temple, with the arches giving some idea of how impressive the building must have been.

4. Richerenches: side wall of the Temple.

5. Gréoux-les-Bains (north of Aix-en-Provence): the largest surviving Templar castle, presently being restored, dominating the valley it controlled.

6. Gréoux-les-Bains: corner tower.

7. Gréoux-les-Bains: internal courtyard.

8. Gréoux-les-Bains: entrance to the commanderie beneath the castle.

9. S. Maria del Ponte (Tione, Abruzzi, Italy): commanderie on the crusader route through Italy from Perugia to Sipcnto (port of departure), preserving its original form with a house built into the walls.

10. S. Maria del Ponte: south entrance, beside the heavily restored church in illustration 9. Note the similarity in style to that in illustration 8.

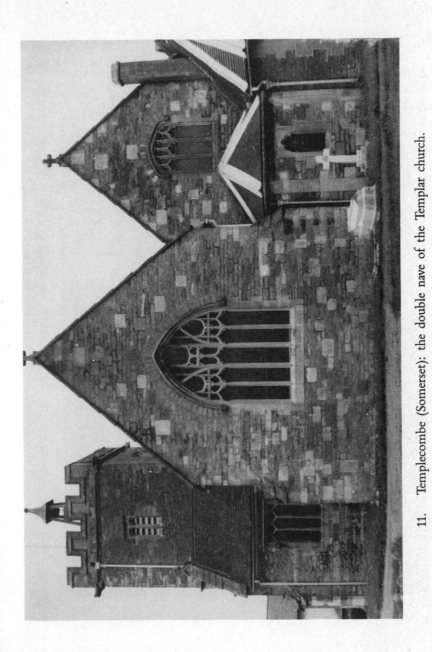

11. Templecombe (Somerset): the double nave of the Templar church.

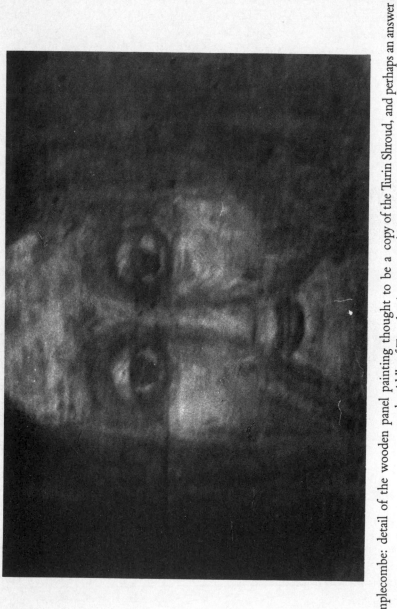

12. Templecombe: detail of the wooden panel painting thought to be a copy of the Turin Shroud, and perhaps an answer to the riddle of Templar image-worship.

a sanctuary and covered by a great round dome, so that, as I have said, it resembles a church. This building, with all its appurtenances, has passed into the hands of the Knights Templar, who dwell in it and in the other buildings connected with it, having many magazines of arms, clothing, and food in it, and are ever on the watch to guard and protect the country. They have below them stables for horses built by King Solomon himself in the days of old, adjoining the palace, a wondrous and intricate building resting on piers and containing an endless complication of arches and vaults, which stable, we declare according to our reckoning, could take in ten thousand horses with their grooms. No man could send an arrow from one end of their building to the other, either lengthways or crossways, at one shot with a Balearic bow. Above it abounds with rooms, solar chambers, and buildings suitable for all manner of uses. Those who walk upon the roof of it find an abundance of gardens, courtyards, ante-chambers, vestibules, and rain-water cisterns; while down below it contains a wonderful number of baths, storehouses, granaries, and magazines for the storage of wood and all other needful provisions. On another side of the palace, that is to say, on the western side, the Templars have erected a new building. I could give the measurements of its height, length, and breadth of its cellars, refectories, staircases, and roof, rising with a high pitch, unlike the flat roofs of that country; but even if I did so, my hearers would hardly be able to believe me. They have built a new cloister there in addition to the old one which they had in another part of the building. Moreover, they are laying the foundations of a new church of wonderful size and workmanship in this place, by the side of the great court. It is not easy for anyone to gain an idea of the power and wealth of the Templars—for they and the Hospitallers have taken possession of almost all the cities and villages with which Jerusalem was once enriched, which were destroyed by the Romans, and have built castles everywhere and filled them with garrisons, besides the very many and, indeed, numberless estates which they are well known to possess in other lands.[43]

The vast stables, endless rooms and new buildings that the Templars were constructing in the 1170s illustrate both their feudal power and their wealth in the Holy Land at that time.

Within fifty years the original idea of an 'Order of Poor Knights' set up to guard helpless pilgrims had been surpassed. It is salutary to reflect what power the Templars might have gained in Latin Syria had it not been for the fall of Jerusalem at the hands of Saladin fifteen years later.

Military Action 1147-87: The Holy Land

From the moment of their success in King Louis' crusade, the Templars participated in most military actions, campaigns, and sieges in Latin Syria. Their role was often important, but equally often controversial; it must also be remembered that they were involved in compromising defeats and suffered heavy losses during this period. In this section we shall review some of their most important actions in the Holy Land up to the Battle of Hattin.

In the light of their later history, and frequent charges made against them, it is fascinating to read that accusations of cupidity were already being launched against the Templars in the decade after the Second Crusade. Few large-scale offensive campaigns were attempted in the middle years of the twelfth century, and the first—a campaign against Damascus—resulted in failure because even the large army assembled with the extra forces of the Second Crusade present in the Holy Land was unable to besiege successfully that great and well-defended city.[44] It was perhaps this lack of opportunity to exploit their privileges concerning plunder which enticed the Templars, or encouraged their enemies to believe that they had been enticed.

The armies were invited to an assembly in Acre, presided over by Baldwin, the Patriarch Fulcher and Kings Louis and Conrad, together with the Archbishops of Caesarea and Nazareth, the Master of the Temple, the Master of the Hospital, and other leading nobles and ecclesiastics of the Kingdom of Jerusalem and the Crusade. At this assembly, held on 24 June 1148, the decision was made to attack Damascus.[45] The precise role of Robert de Craon in the debate, and of his Order in the ensuing campaign, are unknown. But exactly a month later the forces of King Baldwin, with a Templar contingent led by their Master, arrived at the gates of Damascus and camped on the edge of the gardens and orchards that surrounded the city.

The result of this massive action, with an army estimated as 'at least 50,000' commanded by Baldwin, Louis and Conrad,[46] is typical of the frequent stalemate in the warfare of Latin Syria: whereas in 1126 and 1129 the army of Damascus had left the city and fought the Christian army on the plains, this time the Moslems dared not issue from the safety of their city to challenge Baldwin's army in the field. Yet the Christian army itself was unable to mount a successful siege.[47] The city was reinforced by troops sent by Nur ad-Din from

Aleppo, and under constant harassment the Franks were forced to retreat from their positions in the gardens within three days of their arrival. Runciman describes the retreat as follows:

On 27 July the whole army moved to the plain outside the east wall. It was a disastrous decision, for the new site lacked water and faced the strongest section of the wall; and Damascene sally parties could now move more freely about the orchards. Indeed, many of the Frankish soldiers believed that the Palestine barons who advised the Kings must have been bribed by Unur to suggest it. For with the move the last chance of their taking Damascus vanished.[48]

Raymond of Antioch faced similar accusations. The great army disintegrated amidst rumours of bribery and treachery, and the planned sequel of a combined attack on Ascalon never took place.[49] The Templars were also accused of betraying the army and accepting bribes, although there is no authoritative evidence to show that they did so. It is only with the hindsight of events a few years later that these accusations against the Templars appear to ring true. There are many indications that the brothers often put the safety, prestige, and wealth of their own Order beyond all other considerations. This clearly nurtured an attitude which was bound in turn to breed distrust and hatred regardless of the truth or falsity of such accusations.

In the following year, 1149-50, however, the Templars received praise from one of their most vehement and outspoken critics, William of Tyre, who at this point in his *History* was discussing events of which he had direct knowledge. At this period the castle and lordship of Gaza, ten miles south of Ascalon, were put in charge of the Templars as the result of the policy of strengthening the frontier castles and increasing the Frankish hold over the southern part of the Kingdom of Jerusalem. From the beginning of the history of the Kingdom, the Moslem town and stronghold of Ascalon had been a perpetual menace, as we have seen. The rebuilding, fortification, and assignment of Gaza to the Templars was the first step in a strategy aimed towards the eventual elimination of this threat. Here at last is an indication of the Templars pursuing their original task:

Again and again they have vigorously assaulted Ascalon, sometimes openly and again by attacks from ambush. As a result, those enemies who formerly overran and desolated the whole region and made themselves dreaded by the Christians, now consider themselves most fortunate if, by entreaties or money, they can obtain a temporary peace and permission to dwell quietly within their walls. [50]

The success of this policy swayed the balance of power in the region and the strategically important castle was first isolated, and then taken. It is interesting to see the Templars of Gaza applying, in their use of harassment and the ambush as an offensive weapon, the tactics used against them earlier by the Seljuk Turks. This is a significant indication of their gradual adaptation to Eastern means of warfare.

Yet Ascalon was the scene of one of the greatest and most effective criticisms made against the Order just three years later. On 25 January 1153 the whole army of the Kingdom of Jerusalem, led by Baldwin III and the new Master of the Temple, Bernard de Tremelay, appeared before the walls of Ascalon with siege weapons and began a blockade that lasted for months. The city was provisioned and re-armed by those ships sent by the Egyptians which evaded the small Christian fleet. One night in July a siege tower being used against the walls was set alight by Moslem troops who came out of the fortress; it fell against the walls of the city and caused a breach to open in the walls. By chance, the Templars were stationed at this point. Next morning forty knights entered the breach, as William of Tyre relates:

But Bernard de Tremelay, the Master of the Templars, and his brethren had reached there much before the rest; he held the opening and allowed none but his own men to enter. It was charged that he kept the rest back in order that his own people, being the first to enter, might obtain the greater and richer portion of the spoils and plunder . . . Through cupidity they refused to allow their comrades to share in the booty, therefore they alone justly suffered peril of death. About forty entered, but the rest were not able to follow. [51]

The Templar action, however courageous, was useless: the breach was soon sealed, and while the Templar corpses were hung from the walls of the citadel their heads were sent as trophies to the Caliph in Cairo. [52] Ascalon fell on 22 August 1153, about a week after the Templars entered the fortuitous breach, so they could not claim credit for the eventual victory. Neither, ironically, could they take a share of the considerable booty.

This flouting of royal orders, and of the right of other knights, rulers, and orders to share the potential spoils, clearly made the Knights Templar vulnerable to attacks such as that of the Archbishop of Tyre. But more important was the fact that such independent behaviour led in the long term to the weakening of the Kingdom. Lack of control of military operations by the secular rulers was to become one of its most devastating weaknesses within a few decades.[53]

Yet still nobody, not even William of Tyre, doubted the courage of the Templars in what seems to have been almost suicidal folly. They were criticized, but still admired and feared. The decade brought other tribulations for Masters of the Temple. When King Baldwin III's army was ambushed at Jacob's Ford in June 1157 by the forces of Nur ad-Din, the Master of the Temple, Bertrand de Blancfort, was captured with most of Baldwin's knights, while the King himself made a fortuitous escape and managed to reach Acre.[54] Sometimes the knights were severely punished, as in 1165 or 1166 when twelve Templars were hanged by the King of Jerusalem for losing a fortress to Shirkuh by surrendering to him. This castle, according to William of Tyre, lay 'beyond Jordan on the borders of Arabia'[55] and was presumably Ahamant.

Criticism, though, alternated with notable political and military success. In 1168 the Templars repeatedly refused to join a military expedition to take Egypt, perhaps out of sectarian jealousy at a project heartily supported by the then Master of the Hospital. Two years later, in 1171, they played a vital role in the defence of the Kingdom against an unexpected advance from Egypt by Saladin: they accompanied King Amalric, brother of the late Baldwin III, in the relief of Daron, and then defended Gaza against Saladin, who soon retired to Egypt as mysteriously as he had come.[56] In 1177 the Templars stationed at Gaza made a vital contribution to Baldwin IV's victory over Saladin at Mont Gisard,[57] which postponed the loss of the Kingdom for a decade.

These victories were more than counterbalanced, however, by the loss of Le Chastellet. Saladin undermined its outer defences within a year of its completion, digging under the walls and providing temporary support for his tunnels with wooden shoring that was later burned.[58] It has been estimated that as many as 80 knights and 750 sergeants died at the fall of Le Chastellet.[59] If these figures are anything like the truth, then it was a disaster for the Order; even if they were much lower, it represented the loss of a strategically important castle—one of the few in Templar hands at that time.

As Saladin's stranglehold on the crusader states tightened in the succeeding years, the Templars came increasingly under fire from their contemporaries. In 1179 the Templar Master Odo of St Amand was blamed for the military disaster at Marj Ayyun.[60] His rashness in ordering an attack which was immediately and effectively countered by Saladin led to the death of many of his men and to his own capture. The sheer force of the attack divided the Christian ranks.[61] Odo was imprisoned, and died in a dungeon in Damascus a year later. Similarly, Gerard of Ridefort was blamed for the massacre at 'Ain Gozeh in 1187, when he led a suicidal attack of ninety Templar knights against a Moslem force near Nazareth. Gerard himself was one of only three survivors after this attack, made in anger and arrogantly against advice to retreat.[62] * Three years later, Saladin was able to pillage the County of Tripoli at his will because both the Templars and the Hospitallers refused to leave their castles for fear that they would then come under siege.[63]

In the last years of the Kingdom of Jerusalem, the Templars conducted themselves with courage and some success. But it is undeniable that for much of the twelfth century their military actions were at best of dubious efficacy, in part as the result of the rashness of their leaders. In making a final judgement on this period, it is difficult not to agree with Lizerand: 'The Templars fought in the Holy Land without great enthusiasm and without great intelligence. But these very ordinary crusaders were good administrators.'[64] It was, as we shall see, their success in administration, finance, and commerce, which underpinned their wealth and reputation.

Military Action 1130-87: Western Europe

The extent and importance of Templar actions in Western Europe are less well documented; but they are perhaps even more fascinating, since they include blatant examples of flouting the strict censures of the Rule against wounding or killing Christians (§235 and 236).

In Spain and Portugal the Templars were as much in the front line as they were in the Holy Land. In Portugal, as early as 1128, Queen Teresa had donated the castle of Soure, on the River Mondego, to the Order.[65] In Spain, recruitment and donations were evidently much influenced by the early membership of Count Raymond Béranger III

---

* See the account on pp. 100-2.

of Barcelona, who took Templar vows on 14 July 1130 and immediately gave the frontier castle of Grancna to the Order. When he died the following year he left his horse Donc and his armour to the Templars.[66] Military action soon followed: about 1134 the Templars gained their first castle in the Kingdom of Castille, Calatrava, as the result of a victory over the Moors,[67] and in the same decade the Order expanded rapidly throughout Aragon and Catalonia as the result of favour shown to them by the rulers in exchange for help in the *reconquista*.[68] The bequest of a third of his kingdom by Alfonso I of Castille may also be understood in this context.

Templar military successes led to large grants of land and houses in Andalucía, Mallorca, and Valencia, while a complex system for division of spoils and computing the value of cash, horses, arms, cities, and castles was evolved.[69] In those regions the Order assumed distinctive local characteristics, such as the keeping of large numbers of bought and captured moorish slaves, as many as forty or fifty in a single convent, together with paid and voluntary free workers, secular clerks, and scribes.[70] As a result of the Templars' huge success throughout Spain, new orders were founded in conscious imitation of them: the Order of Calatrava obtained papal approval in 1164, and that of Santiago in 1175. When lower Extremadura in Andalucía was recaptured from the Moors in the following century, it became almost entirely the property of the Templars and the Orders of Santiago and Alcantara, with over 700,000 acres for each order to be used for sheep and cattle-raising.[71] The Templars were also large landowners in Navarre.

But if their campaigns against the Spanish Moors were perfectly legitimate, the same cannot be said for some of the actions of the English Templars. We have seen that Templar possessions increased rapidly in England during the reign of King Stephen (1135–54), and it seems that he had no scruples about using the Order as a force to supplement his own army. In the state of civil war that lasted in England from 1138 to 1142, between the supporters of King Stephen and those of Empress Matilda of Normandy, the Templars contrived to serve each faction—and win rewards from both King Stephen and Matilda.* They fought for the Empress at the Battle of Standard, where Stephen was

---

* Matilda was the daughter of Fulk of Anjou and thus commanded the respect of the French Templars. Cf. Poole, *Domesday Book*, pp. 131–54.

captured; but Matilda's triumph was brief, and that period saw their rapid growth in south and south-east England and the Midlands as Stephen gained full control.[72]

Beatrice Lees asserts that there was a connection between the siege of Oxford Castle in September–December 1142 and charters issued to the Templars granting them land in Hertfordshire, Oxfordshire, and Bedfordshire. It also seems likely that the series of gifts made by Stephen in Sussex, Oxfordshire, Berkshire, and Wiltshire in 1139, and the gift of the preceptory of Eagle in Lincolnshire—later one of the most important Templar sites in England—were the result of similar agreements. It seems clear that participation in these campaigns was rewarded directly with grants of land, a more blatantly mercenary attitude than that used in the Holy Land. But Poole has pointed out that one of the greatest problems in the history of the period is how Stephen financed his wars; he seems to have 'borrowed extensively from wealthy traders and repaid them in grants of land'.[74] Thus Templar lands may have been obtained either by military actions or as the result of financial aid.

When Henry II, who was the grandson of one King of Jerusalem and nephew of another, and patron of the Templars throughout his long reign (1154–89), went to war against Louis VII, lands were granted in more obvious exchange for favours provided during battle. In 1159 royal charters were issued from the English camp at Vilemur *during* the Toulouse campaign, granting the Templars the site for a mill on the River Fleet in London. The following year William of Hastings, Oto of St Omer, both Templars, and Robert Pirou, Preceptor of Temple Hurst in Yorkshire, witnessed the treaty of peace between the two monarchs.[75] The custody of the castles of Gisors, Néaufle, and Neufchâtel were given to the same three Templar Knights pending the marriage of Henry to Louis' daughter Margaret. It would appear to be a reasonable hypothesis that this was the reason behind the gift of new lands in London and the transfer of the Order from Holborn to the New Temple site in 1161. The scruples of Hugues de Payen and St Bernard were forgotten in England as they had been in the Holy Land. Much later the Bury St Edmunds *Chronicle* states that Adrian le Jay, Master of the Temple in England, died fighting for England against Scotland at the Battle of Falkirk on 22 July 1298.[76]

These activities, military and otherwise, openly flout the *Rule* and the Templars' original mandate. Early criticism against the Order was directed against religious brothers causing bloodshed, and even the ingenuity and rhetorical art of St Bernard in the *De Laude* could go no further than justifying bloodshed in the case of *infidels* and enemies of the Church. The Templar licence to kill with papal approval was limited to Moslems who fought against Christians in the Holy Land. Yet it is undeniable that the Templars engaged in military action against brother Christians, both before and after those clauses were written into the *Rule*. This is a further indication that the Templars took the law, both civil and ecclesiastical, into their own hands, and that the strictures of the *Rule* were not—even in the early years of the Order's history—sacrosanct. The *Rule* was, from the beginning, more the expression of an ideal than a real indication of how the Templars actually conducted themselves.

5

INTERNATIONAL FINANCIERS AND LANDOWNERS

ONE of the most fascinating, and perhaps least appreciated, aspects of the history of the Templars is their widespread and innovative financial activity, although it is a difficult subject to discuss in the absence of a scholarly study of the economic history of the Crusades. The economic effects of the Crusades were manifold and often unexpected, as this passage by a historian of the medieval economy will illustrate:

It will be difficult to say whether their consequence was to augment the flow of gold from Italy and the Levant to the continent of Europe, or on the contrary to drain the continent of its precious metals. Most probably the trickle of gold frequently changed direction, and at times contrary movements cancelled each other out. The occupation of the Holy Land may, to begin with, have brought in booty and ransom, and so must also have done the sack of Constantinople in 1204. On the other hand, ransom sometimes had to be paid and booty yielded. Similarly, crusading expeditions more often than not set up a drain on the western means of payment. The countries which sent them out financed them with levies and taxes; crusading nobles raised funds at home in many and various ways, but mostly in loans on which they could draw abroad. These methods of financing must have helped to mobilize the hoarded reserves of gold and silver, and thus indirectly to quicken the circulation and to influence prices and economic activity in general. Yet they must also have depleted the total supplies of gold in Northern Europe, since they sent precious metals moving away from continental Europe towards Italy and the Levant. Ecclesiastical taxation in support of the Latin Kingdoms, the voyages to the Holy Lands, the military and religious activities of the Templars and the Hospitallers, must all have acted in the same fashion and added to the continental debit balance with Italy and the East.[1]

Although it is difficult to provide definitive evidence of the participation of the Templars in this movement of gold and silver, isolated facts and incidents will give some idea of their importance. They were often the agents for ransom payments and the transfer of funds to the Holy Land for wars, and also provided loans to both crusaders such as Louis VII and pilgrims. More problematical still is the question of whether Templar activities such as the transmission of credit, payment at a distance and tax collecting activities for popes and kings, were 'invented' by them. It seems clear that the appearance of such techniques early in the twelfth century antedates the widespread adoption of them by Italian bankers during that century. Eventually the Italian banks and other secular financiers supplanted the role of the Templars, and have thus come to be seen as innovators when perhaps the techniques they used already existed.

It would be wrong to speak of a purely monetary economy, or even a new monetary economy, coming into existence during the twelfth century, but there seems to be little doubt that in many ways the economy became at that point *predominantly* monetary. In this the Templars were in the vanguard. While other monastic estates in the twelfth century were farmed for the provisions of their inhabitants, the Templar estates 'were administrated primarily with a view to the money revenue which they yielded, rather than to the sustenance which could be derived from them'.[2] Since Carolingian times the monetary unit in common use throughout Europe had been the silver penny (*denarius*), but this unit was replaced in the twelfth century as mints began to appear in the new trading cities and states.[3] In this context it is interesting to note that in the three Italian cities where banking activities developed in the late twelfth century the Templars had already been established by mid-century: in Siena, Lucca (the church of S. Pietro), and Florence (S. Giacomo).[4] It seems likely that the Templars were involved in the great improvements in credit and payment techniques that took place in the twelfth and thirteenth centuries, when the volume of money in circulation was increasing rapidly.

Aiding this shift and involvement of the Templars was the existence of a predominantly urban and monetary economy in the Holy Land, and the success with which the Templars became integrated with it. The crusaders who remained after the First Crusade adopted the monetary economy of gold Arab dinars, Byzantine hyperpera, and silver drachmas, and became expert in a precious-metal economy. Cash fiefs, market tolls, custom duties, merchandise were all part of this economy, and the knights received their feudal income in cash.[5] The Templars soon adjusted to these new ways, adapting their dress, learning the local languages, and even training specialists in Moslem affairs within the Order.[6] The Arab chronicler Usama ibn Munqidh, emir of Shaizar, provides an interesting instance of the extent to which the Templars were adjusted to Eastern life:

When I visited Jerusalem I used to enter the Al-Aqsa mosque, beside which was a small oratory that the Franks had made into a church. Whenever I entered the mosque, where my friends the Templars were installed, they put that little oratory at my disposal so that I could say my prayers in it. One day I entered, said the Allah Akbar and rose to begin my prayers, when a Frank rushed at me, grabbed me and turned my face to the East, saying 'That's how you pray'. Some Templars immediately intervened, seized him and led him away from me, while I returned to finish my prayers. But he, while they were not watching, grabbed me again and turned my face towards the East, repeating: 'That's how you pray'. And the Templars again intervened, led him away and apologized to me saying: 'He's a newcomer, arrived a few days ago from the land of the Franks, and he's never seen anybody pray other than with their face to the East'.[7]

Even with the military defeats we have discussed, by mid-century the Frankish residents had modified their native customs according to Eastern usage. Thus, well established in the urban, monetary economy of the Holy Land, the Templars were ideally placed to anticipate the similar type of economy which was slowly developing in Western Europe, and were ready with techniques to satisfy the demands of clients who required sophisticated banking services.

In agriculture they were also ahead of the general thirteenth-century practice in their emphasis on production for sale, the beginning of what Postan has described as 'more or less capitalistic agriculture on large estates'.[8] This reflected the cash basis of Templar life and their constant aim of creating funds for use in battle against the Moslems. The Templar administration was early prepared to deal with the large influx of cash gifts, and transport funds to the Holy Land when necessary: in 1182 Henry II left 5,000 silver marks to the Order in his will, together with 5,000 for the defence of the Kingdom of Jerusalem;[9] in 1239 the Patriarch of Jerusalem left 16,000 besants to the Templars to be employed in defence of the Holy Land.[10] Since from the beginning papal and other royal allocations placed at their disposition accompanied these legacies, it can be assumed that other cash gifts were common from fairly early in the history of the Templars—perhaps inspired by the generous legacy of Alfonso I of Aragon in the 1130s. Thus the Templars were immediately required to utilize and move large sums of cash. But it is important to stress that forms of mercantile credit were already in use before they rose to prominence. In the eleventh century the *foenus nauticum*, or sealoan, was in widespread use in trade with Latin Syria—whence such products as pepper, brazil-wood, alum, and cotton were already staple imports. The *foenus nauticum* was used by Genoese merchants to make remittances to agents in Syria, raise money on goods to be exported and given as security on the loan, and as a method of securing investment capital. In this type of loan the lender assumed the entire risk 'since payment was contingent upon the safe arrival of the ship and goods or greater part thereof at the destination'.[11] It is also interesting to note that interest was usually 33½ per cent for a round trip of about nine months in the mid-twelfth century, sometimes rising to as much as 50-60 per cent.

The Templars later maintained their own fleet, both for the passage of pilgrims and for commercial purposes, and also for provisioning their own forces in the Holy Land. In 1292 Pope Nicholas IV ordered them to equip twenty galleys in Cypriot waters in order to protect both that island and Armenia.[12] That they were expert in maritime trade and later maintained houses in the key ports of southern Europe is undeniable: in 1275 the Preceptor resident in Brindisi in southern Italy was required by Charles II of Anjou to name a brother to supervise the building of a new lighthouse to make the port safer, a clear indication of the port's importance in the Templar economy.[13] But this combination of financiers, merchants, and shippers is difficult to establish clearly in the twelfth-century history of the Templars, although they were certainly involved on all three fronts. Moreover, there was a recent precedent: in the eleventh century the Christian reconquest of the western Mediterranean by Pisa and Genoa had provided the capital necessary for the early economic ventures of those two cities. From that moment, commercial traffic and pilgrim traffic were closely linked.[14] The consequent increase in wealth of the Templars was channelled into its task in the Holy Land, and into the vast building projects which we have seen illustrated in Theodorich's description of their headquarters in Jerusalem.

The conditions rendering such financial operation possible had only just come into being, and it was possession of the Holy Land which triggered such changes. At the beginning of the twelfth century there was still no international law of trade, and one of the effects of the Crusades was to compel the creation of such laws—rendering sophisticated banking operations possible by providing international guarantees. A historian of the medieval economy has summed up these tentative beginnings of capitalism as follows:

An important creation of the Crusades was the development of business. The Byzantine merchant was a capitalist, as were the merchants and bankers of the Italian cities. So too were the exporters of Venice, Genoa, Marseilles, the Templars and all the religion orders . . .[15]

By becoming the most powerful and innovative of the military orders, and by using the intricate capillary network which the Order possessed throughout Europe, the Templars were able to exploit the new techniques and new wealth to the full. Yet in some ways their rapid rise to great wealth, like that of the Hospitallers and the Cistercians, was coincidental: like all good entrepreneurs, they were in the right place at the right time.

Pilgrim Finance and Pilgrim Traffic

In many ways, the financial operations of the Templars were a rational extension of the Order's original avowed purpose. At least in the early years, the aim of many of their operations was to facilitate pilgrimages to the Holy Land. In fact, one of the earliest documented examples of a Templar financial transaction concerns a loan made so that a certain Petre Desde could undertake a pilgrimage. In 1135 Petre, from Saragoza in Spain, borrowed cash to travel to the Holy Sepulchre in Jerusalem, promising in exchange to leave his 'houses, lands and vineyards and gardens' to the Templars on his death. In exchange, in a singular mortgage formula* which avoided possible charges of usury but was clearly to the benefit of the lender, the Templars were to provide Petre with 50 morabitins for his journey. The most remarkable feature of

---

* Later legitimized by Eugenius III's crusading bull *Quantum praedecessores* (1-12-1145) which gave permission to mortgage property to obtain funds for the journey to the Second Crusade. (Cf. Virginia G. Berry, *The Second Crusade*, in Setton, *History of the Crusades*, vol. I, p. 467).

the deed is the formula which states that the Templars were providing this money out of *charity*, when the Order was in fact accepting the whole of his property in permanent gift in exchange for an immediate advance.*[16]

Another instance which allows a glimpse into the use of loans for pilgrims is given by Forey. A priest at Novillas called Gerald made a donation to the Templars with the condition that they would give him money if he were to become sick, and that they would provide him with a horse if he should decide to go on pilgrimage.[17] Thus the money for such a journey was simply one of the corrodies which were often granted to benefactors of the Order: daily food and drink, a proportion of the produce of the land donated during the benefactor's life, or regular specified measures of wine, cheese, or wheat.[18] In this way, while appearing to offer its services to pilgrims free—safe transport, protection en route, and perhaps accommodation—the Templars soon gained immense wealth even from small benefactors.

These guarantees came at the moment when there was a huge increase in the amount of pilgrim traffic, to sites in Europe—Compostella, Vézelay and Rome—as well as to the Holy Land. The pilgrim traffic became of considerable importance at such ports as Marseilles and the ports of Adriatic Italy, where the Templars were well established:

After the success of the First Crusade, the establishment of the Latin Kingdom of Jerusalem, and the creation of the military orders of religion, organizations for travel to Palestine multiplied. Apart from the Italian communes, notably Venice and Genoa, which possessed hostels in most cities of the Holy Land, the Hospitallers of St John of Jerusalem and the Templars played a prominent role in supervising and facilitating this pilgrim traffic. In fact, the Templars became the great banking agency whose branches in the European capitals, in Jerusalem, and in the majority of Eastern centres handled all manner of exchange transactions with enormous profits from the pilgrim service.[19]

Thus the Templars, following the experiences of the Italian merchant fleets, based much of their business on pilgrim traffic.

The immense profits to be made clearly encouraged competition, and the maritime powers of Barcelona, Marseilles, Genoa, Pisa, Venice,

---

* 'Et dederunt nobis inde illos seniores de Templo Salomonis, *per caritate,* L morabitinos, per facere nostra romeria ad sancti Sepulchri . . . ' [my italics]

and the Adriatic ports all tried to monopolize this business. Limits were eventually set on ships owned by the crusading orders, which were given an advantage by the all-round service they could provide— including finance, the ships, and protection on arrival. From Marseilles, for example, both the Templars and the Hospitallers were allowed a single shipment of pilgrims each year.[20] The all-inclusive service worked for poor and rich alike: while Petre Desde mortgaged his house for the journey, the wealthier 'used a credit system and transmitted their funds to one of the banking houses of Italy or deposited money with the local priory of the Templars or Hospitallers, to be refunded on reaching their destination'.[21]

Deposits

The safety of Templar houses, and the possibility of transferring funds in the event of danger, made them ideal for depositing valuables—not necessarily just money or precious metals. The London Temple, which one writer has described as the 'mediaeval precursor of the Bank of England',[22] was used for deposits of the royal treasure as early as 1185, suggesting that the Order was already by that time a financial power of some importance.[23] The vault may have been in the cellar which can still be seen under the south entrance door of the Temple Church—an architectural feature that does not suggest any other specific function. The Temple in Jerusalem was also used from the beginning as a safe-deposit, and the problems of long-term deposits are well illustrated by the difficulties of the new Bishop of Tiberias in 1198: he found it necessary to bring a lawsuit against the Templars in order to gain possession of a sum of 1,300 besants and some other valuables which his predecessor had deposited with them.[24]

Although in Aragon the banking function was less important than in England and France, the case of the Templar preceptory of Gardeny offers fascinating evidence. At that preceptory there existed a 'house of deposits' in which literally anything could be deposited. While jewellery, documents, and money were the most common deposits, horses, corn, and other agricultural produce could also be left there for safety. Strangest of all, for a modern banker, or client, an owner going abroad could even leave mules or his moorish slaves on deposit, and collect them when he returned home.[25]

Documents surviving from the thirteenth century illustrate more fully the numbers of deposits, and the importance of the 'clients'. In 1204–5 King John of England left the crown jewels at the London Temple for safekeeping—almost as soon as he came into possession of them. His successor Henry III used the Temple widely, and he too deposited the crown jewels in the London vault during the Barons' revolt of 1261. Two years later King Edward forced the Templars to give him the sum of 10,000 esterlin livres which had been deposited by various barons and merchants.[26] Thus it seems that such deposits were fairly normal amongst the emerging merchant classes, and the smaller local commanderies were also used for safe-deposits throughout the thirteenth century. By the end of the century the reputation of Templar vaults was almost legendary, yet it is important to recall that churches and the other religious orders also held safe-deposits. It is rather the other financial operations of the Templars which are distinctive.

Notwithstanding all their precautions, the Templars did occasionally lose money and valuables left on deposit. A document dating from 1255 requesting the return of a quantity of silver suggests that two very ordinary-sounding men—a father and his son—managed to steal the silver from the Templar house at Pisa.[27] Earlier, when Isaac Ducas Comnenus, tyrant of Cyprus and Governor of Cilicia, was captured by the Armenians in 1167, he was sold to the Templars. Andronicus, the ruler of Cyprus, sent the money needed to ransom him; but Isaac used half of this sum to raise a military force in Isauria and cross to Cyprus himself. According to the *Gesta Regis Henrici II,* Isaac paid the other half of his ransom to the Templars—who were then robbed of it by pirates.[28] This anecdote provides an insight into the difficult conditions prevailing in the Holy Land in the twelfth century. But it also shows that even the Templars were not always able to protect their interests—or their capital.

Sequestrations

There are several important cases of sequestration operated by the Templars. These involved the appropriation of the income of a property in order to make payments or satisfy claims against the owner, and their existence demonstrates the faith placed in the Order by rulers or nobles who needed to make international payments with the provision of a satisfactory guarantee.

In 1158, when Henry II of England arranged the marriage of his son Henry to Margaret, daughter of Louis VII of France, some castles were given to the Templars as a guarantee, with the dowry to be paid by them when the marriage was eventually concluded.[29] In 1214, King John desired to promise pensions to certain French barons in order to win their support. Unfortunately, the barons did not trust him, so he deposited at the preceptory of La Rochelle a sum sufficient to pay the pensions for a fixed number of years—which varied from case to case. For instance, 2,500 livres were to be paid annually to Alice, Countess of Angoulême, and a sum of 30,000 livres for five years to Raoul d'Exoudun, the Count of Eu, as an indemnity for the loss of lands in Normandy.[30] Another type of guarantee is demonstrated by the large sums of money paid into the London Temple in 1228 to buy lands for the dowry of Isabel of Scotland.[31]

These few examples from surviving records suffice to demonstrate the role of the Templars as guarantors in important negotiations, as well as their genuinely international status. This role gives an accurate indication of their true strength in the twelfth century, and provides a glimpse of their function as sophisticated international bankers.

Loans and Advances

The function of loan-agents appears very early in the history of the Templars. Even in the 1130s they were acting as moneylenders in Aragon, lending sums of money to persons of all social classes, including the Jewish population.[32] Even within the lifetime of Hugues de Payen, moneylending was seen as part of Templar duties. Perhaps this was simply because they were recognized as possessing large cash reserves and were pressed to provide such services. It is impossible to know how or when the Templars entered into such activities, or if indeed there was ever a concerted decision. The surprising feature is their open flouting of Church rules against usury.

The contemporary attitude towards money and moneylending derived from a series of authoritative pronouncements against avarice, which during the late eleventh century replaced pride as the chief Christian vice.[32] Peter Damian had attacked avarice as 'the root of all evil', while St Bernard himself described an avaricious man as 'like hell'.[33] L. K. Little observes that 'the increasingly common presence of usurers in towns from the eleventh century onwards inspired a wealth of moral condemnations of moneylending that had accumulated since the time of Moses'.[34] It was condemned by the Third Lateran Council of 1179 and by almost all contemporary writers: avarice and moneylending were seen to be symptoms of the moral decadence of urban life and were at the root of such movements of voluntary poverty as the Waldensians and Franciscans towards the end of the twelfth and beginning of the thirteenth century. The crisis derived from medieval man's unease and practical difficulty in the long process of adaptation to the profit economy, and the principal scapegoat for this hatred was the Jewish community.

St Bernard explicitly identified the whole money trade with the Jews and attacked them virulently. In a letter he wrote: 'We are pained to observe that where there are no Jews, Christian moneylenders "Jew" or "Judaise", worse than the Jews, if indeed these men may be called Christians, and not rather baptised Jews.'[35] It is ironic that the Order inspired and sustained by St Bernard should be amongst the greatest moneylenders of Christendom—even within his lifetime, as the example of Aragon given above demonstrates.

To be sure, sale-credits and loans were common in medieval trade, though perhaps not institutionalized at the time of St Bernard. Without such loans, commerce would often have been impossible. Yet, perhaps as the result of Church strictures against usury, interest payments were usually disguised. The 'loan by sale' was one such method: 'Loans of money between merchant and merchant were sometimes disguised in the shape of ordinary sales.'[36] Postan also argues that other kinds of mediaeval loan were often unrecorded or even 'misrecorded'.

Forey explains how the Templars managed to conceal interest payments, usually on the basis of a deduction for expenses which in fact equalled an interest payment:

The sums allowed to the Templars for expenses could easily hide an extra payment, especially when the Order was assigned a fixed proportion of revenues for this purpose. In some other cases it is possible that interest was deducted from a loan at the time when the money was lent, so that the amount mentioned in the instrument of debt would represent the sum loaned, but not the actual amount received by the borrower.[37] *

* The interest was also disguised in additional payments made by the borrower *pro recompensacione dampnorum, interesse, et expensis* included in existing bonds (cf. Ferris, *Relations of Templars to English Crown*, p. 15).

Although for obvious reasons few documents can be found to substantiate the claim, he asserts that in Aragon the 'rate and custom of the Temple' was 10 per cent per annum, which was approximately half the interest charged by Jewish moneylenders.[38]

Thus, incredibly in the light of the proximity of St Bernard to the Templars, moneylending became one of their major financial services. In Spain the Order was virtually the only institutional moneylender, since Tuscan bankers were banned by James I. In Barcelona both the King and his nobles and merchants were obliged to go to the Temple when they needed funds.[39] In France the Templars were bankers to the royal house for well over a century, while both King John and King Henry III of England had recourse to Templar funds on several occasions. Even a rich and important monastery like Cluny sometimes found itself short of cash, and in 1216 was forced to borrow 1,000 silver marks from the Temple—with the guarantee of the Countess of Champaigne. In the East, Baldwin II of Constantinople gave the True Cross as guarantee for a loan from the Templars in Latin Syria in 1240; a parallel case in France is that of Count Eudes of Nevers, who died in 1266 with a 3,000 besants debt to the Templars which was discharged by his executors.[40]

An example of a commercial loan given by the Templars at Famagusta in Cyprus on 13 December 1300 is given here to illustrate the formula, although it is much later than the loans mentioned earlier in this section. We can see the guarantee specified, and the payment deducted for services:

In the name of the Lord, amen. I, Master Thomas, physician, resident of Famagusta, acknowledge and publicly recognize to you, Sanç Pérez of Sant Marti, receiving this acknowledgement and stipulation on behalf of the noble count, Lord Bernat Guillem of Emprença, that I have had and have received from you and Bernat Marquet, captain of the ship named Saint Nicholas, which is in the port of Famagusta, 8,000 *modii* of grain, according to the *modius* of Cyprus, belonging to the said noble count, and that you, jointly with the said Bernat, have consigned them to me as a security for those 16,350 silver deniers Tournois of France which we state that the aforementioned noble count has received in loan from Master Theodore, my brother, physician of the Temple . . . And this grain I promise you, in the said name, to sell and to send the proceeds wherever it pleases the aforementioned noble count or his accredited messenger, with the exception, however, that I or my said brother are to be allowed to obtain full payment concerning the said amount of money out of the bezants which will be collected from the said grain, according as it is sold. And in regard to that grain we state that it is registered with the customs office of Famagusta. Also, on the other hand, I acknowledge that I have had and received from you, said Sanç and from said Bernat Marquet, in the said name of aforementioned noble count, in my keeping and trust 3,006 *modii* of grain according to the said *modius*, and in addition thirty jars of Catalonian oil belonging to the aforementioned noble count . . . And out of that oil, then, I am to be allowed to obtain full payment of 229½ white bezants for the expenses incurred by me.[41]

The sophistication and completeness of Templar banking activities are stressed by Master Thomas' declaration that the money raised on loan can be sent 'wherever it pleases the aforementioned noble count'. These examples illustrate yet another of the inherent contradictions within this 'poor' Order, whose brothers seem to have openly flouted both their *Rule* and Christian practice just as much as they obeyed them.

Transmittal of Money

The loan to the Count of Emprença could be paid wherever he wished. Such operations were another of the everyday financial services offered by the Templars: the 'mandate', 'letter of payment', or 'tratta', in modern terms a bill of trade, was, in Postan's words, 'the most cosmopolitan of all diplomatic inventions of the later Middle Ages'.[42] Yet while he gives the earliest example in England as occurring in 1260, the Templars were transmitting money between their commanderies long before this. At least as early as 1148 Abbot Suger of Saint Denis sent money to Louis VII during the Second Crusade by means of the Templars.[43]

But while capital transfers to the Holy Land from Western Europe became more frequent in the following century, the financing of the Crusades was not the only use made of the transmission system. Henry II of France provided a pension to his daughter which was payable at the Templar commandery of Sainte-Vaubourg, near Rouen, where she would have to travel regularly to collect her money.[44] A surviving document shows that in 1248 Henry III of England made a payment to Thomas of Savoy and Amadeus, Count of Savoy, through the London Temple.[45] He also used the Order's financial services to distribute pensions, and the Temple customarily acted as debt collectors and payment agents for clients such as Kings, Popes, great secular lords and merchants; two examples are Alphonse, Count of Poitiers and the mother of St Louis.[46] The Order performed a further important service in collecting debts and tithes. When crusader taxes were introduced in England in 1166, and again in 1185 and 1188, based on income and the value of movable property for a three-year period, with the exemption of horses, arms, and clothing essential to a knight,[47] it was the Templars—together with the Hospitallers—who were responsible for collection. The latter tax, of 1188, was known as the 'Saladin tithe', to be collected in each parish; the work was again shared by the Templars and the Hospitallers. One unexpected consequence was that a certain Templar called Gilbert of Ogerston embezzled most of the money he had collected. He later confessed to the new Master of England, Geoffrey Fitz Stephen, and was punished for his action with 'fetters . . . and diverse pains'.[48]

As collectors of papal taxes, which were then transmitted to the Holy Land, the Templars became powerful during the pontificate of Innocent III (1198–1216). In 1202 he ordered that one-fiftieth of revenues of certain abbeys and religious orders should be set aside for the needs of the Holy Land and were to be sent directly to the Paris Temple.[49] In 1208 he directed that the alms of the Cistercians plus one-fortieth of the deposits of the Bishop of Paris at the Paris Temple should be sent to the Holy Land for the use of the Patriarch of Jerusalem and the Masters of the Temple and the Hospital in that city.[50] Four years later, the same pope sent the sub-deacon Pierre Marc to collect the dues of the Church in southern France: he was instructed to pay the receipts to commanders of the Templar houses of Provence, Montpellier, Saint-Gilles, and Arles, who would then send the money on to the Paris Temple.[51] Other sums, tenths, twentieths and fiftieths, destined for the Holy Land throughout the Latin occupation of Jerusalem flowed through the major Templar banking centres of London and Paris.

In Spain, where the Order's role was often quite different and geared to the particular needs of the local situation, the Templars also became important tax collectors. Innocent III ordered the Jews and Mudejars of Valencia to pay all their taxes to the Templar Master, who was to use these funds towards 'liberating the realm from mortgages'.[52] In 1220 James I of Aragon nominated the Templar William as bailiff-general in Catalonia, and another Templar brother was given the same position in Aragon. These Templars had total responsibility for supervising and collecting revenues and income in James's realm, and for discharging debts and mortgages.[53]

Papal and Royal Bankers

The number and importance of these financial operations indicate how the Templars became the bankers of powerful popes and monarchs in the two centuries of their existence. The Popes also used other banks, but as far as activities in the Holy Land were concerned—whether new crusades or miscellaneous payments for the battle against Saladin— the Templars were the main bankers to the Holy See. Delisle concludes: 'It is therefore no exaggeration to say that the treasury of the Temple was throughout the thirteenth century the cashier's office where the financial resources destined to the crusades and the various needs of the Holy Land were centralized and administered.'[54]

Two examples will suffice. In 1198 Innocent III wrote to the Templar Master Gilbert Erail sending funds for the use of Christians in the East; at the same time he excused himself for not being able to send a larger sum.[55] In 1219 his successor, Honorious III, sent funds to the Master, then William of Chartres, for him to dispense 'either in galleys, or in other equipment, according to the prudence of the Papal Legate, the Bishop of Albano'.[56] But it seems that Delisle's 'thoughout' is slightly exaggerated, for it has been argued that during the thirteenth century lay bankers supplanted the Templars in papal banking services: 'Although papal revenues had been deposited with the Templars into the early 1200s—for example, the Languedoc hearth tax raised during the Albigensian Crusade in 1212—the Tuscans had taken this business by mid-century.'[57] This assertion is confirmed by a general decline in relations between the papacy and the Templars after the pontificates of Innocent III and Honorius III.* But a further observation is made by the same historian: 'Equally important was the fact that great quantities of specie no longer had to be transported. A reason for this was that, imitating the earlier methods of the Templars and Hospitallers, merchants and bankers had devised a variety of paper transfers.' Here the emphasis is clearly on the Templars as innovators, and it is they— more than the Hospitallers—who led the way in banking activities. It is undeniable that the Templars in Latin Syria effectively acted as

_____
* i.e. after 1227.

papal agents, through whom papal subsidies made their way to the Holy Land and information returned to Rome.[58]

Since the Templars were in a sense a papal creation, and administratively were directly responsible to the Holy See, their importance as papal bankers and agents is comprehensible. What is perhaps more interesting and less to be expected was their function as royal bankers, especially to the kings of France and England—where the two greatest Temples outside the Holy Land were established, in Paris and London.

We have already seen the role of the Templars in Louis VII's crusade, as well as examples of royal banking activity. Later, these services became practically indispensable to the French throne: from the time of Philip Augustus (1180–1223) to Philippe le Bel (1285–1314) the Paris Temple was literally the centre of financial administration in France. It offered a complete financial service, administering finances and collecting taxes, transmitting money, controlling debts, and paying pensions.[59] The great French nobles and merchants were clearly encouraged by the confidence of the monarchy and used the services of the Temple to a similar extent. Financially, the Paris Temple was far more important than its counterpart in London, and remained so into the first decade of the fourteenth century.

Delisle provides a detailed example of the services offered by the Paris Temple for Phillippe le Bel in the year 1287 (the *Compte de la Chandeleur*). It consists of 290 articles, which Delisle in his introduction to the accounts divides into 11 main chapters. This abbreviated list of the main chapters will give some idea of the completeness of Templar services:

1. Résumé of expenditure on individual accounts of Templar houses.
2. Résumé of expenditure.
3. Résumé of expenditure for Navarre.
4. Account of receipts taken by the Temple.
5. Account of payments made by the Temple for the 'hotêl du roi'.
6. Accounts for rents, pensions, gratuities, and pledges assigned by the King on the Temple.
7. Account of large expenses charged on the Temple.
8. Account of sums paid by the Temple for Navarre.

9. State of periods of respite granted to various debtors for discharging their debts.

10. Detailed account of reimbursements that the Templars had to make on debts incurred by the King in Normandy.

11. Account of advances made to soldiers in the King's service in Navarre.

It is clear from this reduction of the 290 articles that the Templars provided a complete banking service for the king such as no other banker, even the commercial banks then beginning to flourish in Italy, could perform at that time. The immense network of Templar houses and commanderies throughout France rendered these operations possible.*

In England, the Templars were from the first favoured by Henry II and King Stephen; but charters and privileges were also conferred upon them by Richard I, John, Henry III, and Edward I. These grants included exemption from both local and national taxation, freedom from toll and passage dues, freedom from attending local courts, the right to hold their own courts and receive the profits, and freedom from exactions of money and supplies under the pretext of scutage, forest laws, or the temporary needs of the King.[60] But their role was by no means generally accepted, and the Templars often found it difficult to obtain these exemptions in practice—hence the need for successive kings to repeat the privileges so frequently. Perkins gives the details of a long series of disputes between the Templars and the burghers of Bristol.[61]

The English Templars were particularly valuable for the capital that their estates produced, both from able management of local products and the considerable income derived from churches which they owned. One such church, at Rothele in Leicestershire, brought an average net income of £76 1s. 1d. per year between 1308 and 1313.[62] In addition, the English Templars sometimes farmed the revenues of other churches in the hope of making a profit and let their own farms and manors advantageously when possible. It has been calculated that at the time of the Order's dissolution the total annual value of Templar lands in

* See the complete list of Templar houses in France given by Leonard in *Introduction au Cartulaire*, pp. 30–173.

England—based on receipts—was about £4,720; Templar lands in Ireland at the same time were valued at £411 11s. 7d.; no figures are available for the three Templar houses in Scotland mentioned in surviving records (Blantrodok, Culthur, and Templiston).[63] This income, plus sums raised in tax collections, served as the base for Templar banking activities in England.

Although in the twelfth century the English exchequer was at Westminster, the king employed several treasuries, in the Tower of London, at Winchester, and in the New Temple. Eleanor Ferris cites a fragment of an exchequer receipt roll for 1185 which mentions the Westminster exchequer and suggests the function of the Temple in this system: 'From funds received there, the treasury at Winchester was replenished, while the balance was deposited in the Temple.'[64] Records exist of many kinds of taxes which were paid into the Temple and either accredited there to royal accounts or transferred to the exchequer, including carucage, fractional grants of movables, tallage of London and of the Jews, the Irish treasure, queen's gold, and feudal dues.[65] While the role of the London Temple was of less importance than that of its Paris equivalent, it seems to have been for over a century an integral part of the English government's financial system.

The Templar financial administrators must have kept detailed records, since their manifold activities would have demanded an elaborate book-keeping system. In fact brothers were often employed on financial commissions and on boards for auditing accounts. In 1294 the Preceptor and the Treasurer of the London Temple constituted two-thirds of a three-man committee formed to adjust the conversion from old to new money. Ferris concludes that '. . . it seems to have been customary to employ Templars in matters of financial administration which involved skill, accuracy, and honesty throughout the thirteenth century.'[66]

But the Templars were often more than mere royal bankers. The political and social power of the Masters was often of equal importance. When King John died, his son Henry was only nine years old. He was crowned on 28 October 1216 in the royal castle of Gloucester by Peter des Roches, the Bishop of Winchester, becoming king of a country half-controlled by Louis of France—including London—with no organized government and no exchequer. Baronial rebels held most of the ports on the southern coast. The child-king was well received, however, even by the rebels, and the long reign of Henry III was of vital importance for the formation of English institutions. To supervise the early years a council of the most powerful leaders was created, based upon the executors chosen by King John: the Papal Legate; the bishops of Winchester, Chichester, and Worcester; the Master of the Temple; the Earl Marshall of England; the Earls of Chester and Derby; and four other powerful secular lords.[67] The guiding spirit was William the Marshall, a close personal friend of the Master of the Temple, who attended him at his death; the Marshall was buried in the round church of the Temple in 1219.[68] One of the most significant acts of these two friends had been to raise 10,000 marks, about £7,000, as a peace payment to Louis. The sum was, naturally, deposited at the Paris Temple.

Throughout his reign, therefore, Henry III was indebted to the Templars and often turned to the Master for guidance. In 1259, during discussions about the vitally important Provisions of Westminster, which modified the common law and made long-lasting legislative provisions, the Parliament actually met and worked *inside* the London Temple.[69] Thus the position of Master of the Temple, as head of a great religious house and banking service, granted him a privileged status. Lees argues that official positions within the Order were carefully filled with men of good family and powerful local connections, who would naturally already form part of the hierarchy. But they were never great nobles or landowners, so it would appear that the immense prestige the Templar Masters had during Henry's reign was derived from their rank within the Order rather than from their feudal status. The prestige of the Order is demonstrated by the fact that at one stage Henry himself intended to be buried in the Temple.[71]

Farmers and Landowners

Templar wealth derived from their land. It was in the management and administration of their estates that the Order was truly exceptional and pioneering. Farms and manors throughout Europe generated vast sums of cash, beyond the produce which served the Order, for their activities in the Holy Land. It was obviously far more convenient to send money to the Holy Land from northern Europe than to send food, although grain and fodder for horses were transported from Apulia, where Charles II of Anjou later exempted grain exported by the Order to Cyprus and Syria from taxes.[72]

The Chronicler of St Albans, Matthew Paris, asserted towards the end of the thirteenth century that:

The Templars in Christendom have nine thousand manors, but the Hospitallers nineteen [thousand], besides the emoluments and various revenues arising from their brotherhoods, and from procurations, all of which are increased by their privileges. And of these, every manor can furnish, without grievance, one soldier, well armed and fully equipped, for the succour of the Holy Land, even with all things which appertain to the full equipment of a soldier.[73]

While allowing for the probably inflated figures, this explains how the possession of manors was conceived: their task was to finance the Templar knights, together with the equipment, horses, and men necessary for the successful implementation of their role. But even in Matthew Paris' estimate, it is important to notice that the possessions of the Hospitallers are said to be more than twice those of their rivals. Estimates of huge Templar wealth and treasures are largely unfounded and exaggerated: in Aquitaine, where the Templars were as prosperous as anywhere, a computation of 1300 gives their wealth as 6,000 livres— equal to that of the Hospitallers, but only half the sum attributed to the Cistercian Order.[74] This proportion seems to be reflected elsewhere in Europe, and a reliable historian has asserted that at the moment of the trial 'the value of the Templars' movable property was much less than we might expect'.[75] Regarding both land and movable property, the Order was not thought to have become less wealthy in the thirteenth century.

The Templars came into the possession of their estates in four main ways. The first, and most obvious, was by donation, whether as direct gifts from royalty and nobility or in the form of benefactions which guaranteed the continued availability of cash or sustenance until the donor's death. Second, the Templars, especially in Spain, gained large tracts of land by conquest or as the result of grants made after military actions; this also clearly applied to the gift of castles such as Tortosa in the Holy Land. Third, perhaps less to be expected, the Templars also purchased land. This could be either as a means of investing cash produced by other sources or as part of an attempt to extend estates by buying adjoining lots of land. This tended to be a development in the later phase of the Order's history. As was the case with most monastic orders, the early enthusiasm which resulted in mass donations slowly diminished: by the late twelfth century in Aragon, for example, there are more records of sales of land than of donations.[76]

Last of all, surprising and at the same time fascinating, was the possession of land by reclamation. This was extremely important in Lincolnshire and Yorkshire, where in the thirteenth century the Templars reclaimed substantial areas of fen and marshland for agricultural use, especially around Temple Brewer (Lincs, founded 1195) and Temple Newsam (Yorks, founded 1181).[77] It is noteworthy in this context, and testifies to the efficacy of the management techniques of the Order, that the computation of annual values of property at the time of their trial made by Clarence Perkins shows Yorkshire to be by far the wealthiest county in Templar terms, and Lincolnshire second—with four times the income of the next-ranking counties of Essex, Gloucestershire, Leicestershire, Oxfordshire, and Warwickshire.[78] The concentration of many of the greatest English preceptories and estates in those two counties exemplifies the success of their policy of reclamation.

We possess a particularly accurate record of Templar estates in England at the end of the twelfth century. As the result of the appointment of Geoffrey Fitz Stephen to the Mastership of the Bailiwick of England, and perhaps to avoid future disputes by constituting a reliable record, an *inquisitio* or inquiry similar in scope to the Domesday book was made in England.* The possessions of the Order were listed under seven headings: donors of lands, possessor of lands, churches, mills, assized lands, demesne lands, and assized rents. Rents were to be fixed by agreement, which enabled the administration to have precise guidelines and also underlined the importance of fixed money rents in the Templar economy. The inquiry is unfortunately incomplete, partly because such returns as those of East Anglia arrived too late for inclusion, but also because the Sussex Templars were in dispute with local clergy and made no returns. But for the rest of the country, the returns offer an accurate picture of Templar possessions and administration in 1185.

The usual terminology for the *domus* or Templar 'house' was *templum* or *le tempil*,[80] but there were in fact different types of rural economy gathered for convenience under this common usage. The *domus*,

---

* Possessions at the time of their suppression may be judged from Knowles and Hadcock, *Mediaeval Religious Houses*, pp. 234-9 and Perkins, *The Wealth of the Knights Templars*, p. 253. Local information may be found in the relevant volumes of the Victoria County History, extensively cited as VCH in the references to this section.

modelled on manorial husbandry, was the basic administrative unit whose main types were:

1. The small royal manor (e.g. Finchingfield in Essex).
2. Manors of 'widespread honour' (e.g. Cressing in Essex and Cowley in Oxfordshire).
3. Great fiefs (Clare in Hertfordshire, Ferrers, Pevenel, and Mowbray).
4. Lesser foundations (Harcourt, Braose, Basset, Deyncourt, and Vilers).
5. Ecclesiastical estates (the benefactions of the Archbishop of Canterbury).
6. Scattered unmanorialized holdings in Lincolnshire, including reclaimed land. [81]

The *domus* and preceptory were often small,* and various forms of agricultural usage included the gardens of Kent, the cornfields of Essex, the western and northern pastures, the marshlands of the north-east, forests and hills. These properties frequently changed hands, while much of the land was let to tenants for standardized rents. Many holdings were in fact distant from Templar houses: for example, the Order owned between two and four acres in the small Somerset village of Drayton, near Langport, for which the Bristol preceptory received twelve pence annual rent. [82]

Many donations to the Order were also small, those to the preceptory at Temple Cressing in Essex being usually of between one and five acres. Tenancies were correspondingly fragmented, so that Cressing had a total of about 160 tenants. [83] A typical small Templar tenant was a certain Roger Janitor, who held three tofts in New Street from the London Temple, with a messuage on the Leicester fee, a joint share in 'Thurolds' Land' in Hackney, and a stall or booth rented at sixpence a year. [84] Thus the overall possessions could be broken up into large numbers of surprisingly small holdings. The London Temple owned the advowsons of the churches of St Clement Danes and the chapel of the Holy Innocents in the Strand; houses on the north bank of

---

* For instance the preceptory at Temple Cowton in Yorkshire consisted, in 1308, of a hall, chamber, chapel, kitchen, brewhouse, and smithy (*Victoria County History, Yorkshire*, Vol. II, p. 259).

the Thames, in Holborn; meadows in Hackney, Low Leyton, and Tottenham; land in Southwark and Bermondsey; a mill on the River Fleet, and some rented mills in Southwark. The Order may have built New Street, which later became Chancery Lane, together with the New Temple and both land and houses on each side of the street. Tenants and rentpayers included St Giles in the Fields, the Canons of St Paul's, and market-stall holders in the City. [85] The new round church, which still stands today with its penitential cell and later nave, was nearing completion at the time of the 1185 inquest. It was dedicated in that year by Heraclitus, the Patriarch of Jerusalem, who was temporarily in England. [86]

Some Templar houses had specialized functions. The preceptory of Denney in Cambridgeshire, part of which is extant, was a hospital for sick and superannuated brothers. The original priory, belonging to the monks of nearby Ely, passed into Templar hands in 1170 and may indeed have been purchased with the specific aim of creating a hospital. The already existing monastic buildings were ideally suited for such a purpose, which conformed with paragraphs 60 and 61 of the *Rule* ordering that care must be taken of sick and elderly brethren. When the fraternity at Denney was arrested in 1308, all but two 'must have been elderly, 1 was insane and 2 were crippled by age and infirmity'. [87] The only other preceptory in England used as an infirmary and home for retired brothers was that at Eagle, in Lincolnshire, founded by King Stephen. [88]

The important Somerset preceptory of Templecombe, where parts of the *domus* and the church are still intact, was granted to the Order in 1185 by Serlo Fitz Odo, a descendent of Odo the Bishop of Bayeux and half-brother to William the Conqueror. The grant involved half the manor, *Combe Templariorum*, while the other part, *Combe Abbatissa*, never formed part of their property. This preceptory appears to have been used as a recruiting and training centre for the English branch of the Order. [89] The beautiful wood-panel painting of Christ in the church at Templecombe, thought by some to be a copy of the Turin Shroud, probably illustrates the importance of Templecombe in the Templar hierarchy.*

Very little is known about the Kent preceptory at Ewell, just north

* See Illustration. 12.

of Dover on the route to Canterbury, but its proximity to the major channel port of medieval times would suggest a vital role as a staging post. An incident substantiating such a hypothesis occurred in 1205, when King John made his submission to Pope Innocent III there.[91] Its function does not seem to have been agricultural, since the preceptory possessed no more than 49 acres. This was a relatively small proportion of the 1,000 acres held by the Order in Kent, mainly belonging to the *domus* at Strood.[92]

In Sussex the most important possession was at Saddlecombe, north-west of Brighton, which was granted by Geoffrey de Say in 1228. Evidence exists of an unexpected use of that preceptory: 'A remarkable document entered amongst the Saddlecombe deeds, and therefore possibly relating to this preceptory, is a letter from a certain Archbishop Azo requesting the master of the Temple in England to receive Joan, the aged wife of Sir Richard Chaldese, who had taken the oath of chastity and wished to submit herself to the rule of the Temple.'[93] It is not known whether this extraordinary request was granted by the vehemently misogynistic Order, but it nevertheless represents an interesting insight to the multiple functions of a Templar preceptory—at the very least as this was conceived by contemporaries.

However, the main function remained that of raising and producing cash to sustain military activities. The greatest reserves in England came from Yorkshire, which became so important in later years that a Chief Preceptor or Master was appointed exclusively for that county and its ten houses—including Flaxfleet, perhaps the richest of all English properties.[94] Elsewhere in the country the bigger preceptories often extended their jurisdiction and influence over county borders: for instance, property in Hampshire and Berkshire was managed from the Oxfordshire preceptory at Sandford-on-Thames in the second part of the thirteenth century.[95]

Manpower for these estates was provided by an army of lay brothers, servants and salaried agricultural workers. At a preceptory with large demesne lands such as Lydley in Shropshire—important as the result of its site near Watling Street—the normal residents consisted in 1273 of the preceptor and two serving brothers. There were no knights present and the preceptor himself was therefore in all likelihood a sergeant, as was often the case.[96] Other servants and workers were not necessarily recorded. The small numbers of Templars found in other

English possessions suggest both a depletion of military manpower towards the end of the Order's history and a small permanent force of *Knights* Templars in England. Outside London the presence of knights would in fact be superfluous, and most administrative functions were carried out by sergeants or specialized lay clerks.

Matthew Paris's explanation of the function of Templar manors in Europe was certainly accurate, even though he may have exaggerated the number. These possessions, and the huge army of non-knightly workers, served a single purpose: 'The Templars employed farmers and agricultural labourers, shepherds and millers, gardeners and artisans, but over all they exercised the same central control, directed by the same motive, the increase of the common revenue and the financing of the Holy War.'[97] It was the gradual decline of the 'Holy War', especially after the fall of Jerusalem in 1187, that lay at the root of the Templars' long and agonizing death-throes.

SALADIN AND THE FALL OF JERUSALEM

THE Moslem leader mainly responsible for the débâcle of the Kingdom of Jerusalem, hero of the anti-crusade and sworn enemy of the Templars, was Saladin—whose full name was Ṣalāḥ-ad-Dīn Yūsuf ibn-Aiyūb, or 'Righteousness of the Faith, Joseph son of Job'. Born in 1138 in the city of Baalbek—east of Beirut near the modern frontier with Syria— where his father was the Governor, he spent the first twenty-four years of his life studying the Koran, Arabic, rhetoric, poetry, and indulging in the sports and pastimes suitable for the scion of such a prominent family: hunting, riding, chess, and polo. Later his father, Job, 'Najm-al-Dīn' or 'Star of the Faith', was made the military commander of the city for Nur-al-Dīn, while Saladin's uncle, Shirkūh, was a general in the Sunnite king's army. As the third great anticrusader, Saladin himself became the successor to Nur-al-Dīn, and the latter's father Zengi, who had scored the first important victory over the crusading Franks at Edessa in 1144.[1]

Saladin's military experience was gained on campaigns with his uncle Shirkūh in the years 1164-9; in the latter year Shirkūh became vizier to the Caliph al-'Adid in Cairo. The holder of that office was generally known as the 'Sultan' and when Shirkūh died soon after his promotion, Ṣalāḥ took his place. From that moment he began a rapid rise to power. Within two years he overthrew al-'Adid and became ruler of Egypt; he also began to initiate drastic changes in the Fatimid Shi-ite army, for he himself, of Kurdish origin, was a member of the orthodox Sunni faith. What is most interesting in his career is the fact that he was from the beginning of his 'sultanate' fully conscious of a mission as the successor to Nur-al-Dīn. The concept of Holy War, *jihād*, as the often-cited diploma of investiture as vizier emphasizes, was part of his policy as early as 1169. Saladin is perceived as the embodiment and prime instigator of *jihād*:

As for the holy war, thou art the nursling of its milk and the child of its bosom. Gird up therefore the shanks of spears to meet it and plunge on its service into a sea of swordpoints . . . until God give the victory which the Commander of the Faithful hopeth to be laid up for thy days and to be the witness for thee when thou shalt stand in his presence.[2]

This prophetic passage informs Saladin's battles and campaigns of the next twenty years. He first consolidated his power as a ruler of the Moslem world, then slowly strangled the crusading states using a strategy against which they could offer little resistance. Saladin was by all accounts a man of simple tastes, with no interest in personal wealth or power, whose life was dedicated to the idea of *jihād*. He died barely leaving enough to pay funeral expenses. It is perhaps for this reason that his name is still evoked and that he is the most popular historical figure among the Arabs. His tomb in Damascus is today the object of pilgrimage.

In 1174 Saladin took Damascus and in the following year managed to supplant Nur-al-Dīn's son al-Malik al-Salih, who had opposed his leadership but was routed at his northern stronghold at Hamah. Saladin became effectively ruler of Egypt, Nubia, al-Maghrib, Arabia, Palestine, and Syria. Then, from Damascus and from Cairo, he began to operate a crushing pincer movement against the Christian states. In 1177 he took Ascalon with an army of 26,000 men and moved on to al-Ramlah: here the Franks were led by the Templars from Sidon, together with forces from the frontier castle of al-Karak led by Reginald of Chatillon. An attack against Saladin using these troops and led by the leper King Baldwin IV threw Saladin's army into confusion. This battle, at Mont Gisard, was one of the most humiliating defeats of Saladin's military career: his men were without food and water and constantly harassed by Frankish troops as they withdrew raggedly into Egypt.[3]

He never forgot that lesson, which was to serve him well in a situation almost exactly the reverse at Hattin. In 1179 his first revenge was obtained against the newly-constructed Templar castle at Jacob's Ford. With auxiliary forces of Turkomans and siege troops he besieged the Templar stronghold for six days, after which the castle was stormed. Seven hundred prisoners were taken. The castle had been carefully undermined by sappers who had dug tunnels and then burned the shoring, but Saladin was not satisfied: 'In spite of the heat and the stench of dead bodies, Saladin would not leave until the last stone had been razed.'[4]

In 1182 he finally conquered Mosul, which had been the last stronghold of Izz-al-Din, Caliph al-'Adid's brother, and in the following year took Aleppo. From that moment the destiny of the Frankish Kingdoms was in fact sealed. We have seen in an earlier chapter that the Christian forces were able to establish themselves in Latin Syria partly as the result of the fragmentary composition of Moslem states and minor emirates and the lack of a coordinated Moslem policy. Saladin's success cancelled that weakness and from about 1183 he began to use the title 'Sultan of Islam and the Moslems'. The Franks were then surrounded by a single Moslem power whose leader was dedicated to *jihād* and the reconquest of territory captured by the knights of the First Crusade.

The Battle of Nazareth

The destruction of the Templar castle at Jacob's Ford was part of Saladin's strategy of removing unguarded pawns from the board: his army was never strong enough to attack such Frankish strongholds as Tripoli or Tyre, but his actions show how he gradually dismantled and weakened the defences upon which the crusading knights depended.[5] An example of this strategy occurred on 1 May 1187 near Nazareth, only weeks before the battle of Hattin, severely weakening the Templars and taking Christian forces by surprise.

Whereas the Moslems had for decades lacked a single leader, now Christian forces were divided into two contesting factions. When the leper King Baldwin IV was no longer able to move and command his forces he appointed his sister's husband, Guy de Lusignan, as *bailli* for the Kingdom of Jerusalem. Guy was sustained by most of the recently-arrived knights in the Kingdom and by his friend Gerard de Rideford—Master of the Templars since 1185. The opposing faction was led by Raymond of Tripoli, Baldwin's cousin and one of the most powerful feudal barons in the Kingdom. In 1185, when the twenty-four-year-old Baldwin's body was rendered useless by his leprosy and he knew that death was near, Raymond of Tripoli was chosen to act as regent over his nine-year-old nephew and successor Baldwin V. The following year, Baldwin V himself died and Raymond was again usurped by Guy de Lusignan, who made himself the first Lusignan King of Jerusalem.[6] The political uncertainty and constant disputes afflicted the Franks at their moment of greatest external peril, and it has been argued that the downfall of Jerusalem can be directly traced to the existence of opposing factions among the local barons.[7]

The Templars were in the front line both militarily and politically, as illustrated by an incident deriving from Raymond's controversial position which led to the decimation of a contingent of the Order just as their full strength was to be required. Raymond of Tripoli's continuing possession of the lordship of Tiberias, on the west coast of the Sea of Galilee and on the main route south from Damascus, necessitated a satisfactory *modus vivendi* with Saladin once Jacob's Ford was in Moslem hands.* Even when the hot-headed Reginald of Karak in the south of the Kingdom of Jerusalem attacked a pilgrim caravan travelling from Cairo to Damascus at the beginning of 1187, Raymond was forced to maintain an uneasy truce with Saladin—who had sworn to lead a *jihād* against the Kingdom of Jerusalem and kill Reginald with his own hands. At the end of April that year two parallel series of events combined to provoke a tragic loss for the Temple.

King Guy had sent a mission to Tiberias to negotiate a reconciliation with Raymond, whose co-operation would be indispensable in the forthcoming weeks as Saladin prepared to attack the Christian forces. For some inexplicable reason Gerard de Ridefort, the Templar Master and most bitter enemy of Raymond, was included in this embassy. It travelled north, stopping at Nablus, the castle of Balian of Ibelin, leader of the embassy, and the Templar castle of al-Fūlah (or La Fève). While this small force was en route, al-Afdal, a son of Saladin, asked for permission to cross Raymond of Tripoli's land—as stipulated by an agreement between Raymond and his father. The Count gave permission for him to enter his territory the next day, 1 May, on condition that al-Afdal's force should return no later than the following evening. When Gerard de Ridefort learned of this raiding party he immediately summoned ninety Templar knights encamped a few miles away under the command of the Marshal of the Temple, James of Mailly, and prepared to meet al-Afdal with the addition of this extra force.

De Ridefort was determined to have battle, so when Christian forces came upon the Moslem raiding party the next day at the Spring

* Ibn al-Athir says that the barons accused him of having become a Moslem, otherwise such an arrangement would have been impossible (in Gabrieli, *Storici arabi*, p. 118).

of Cresson near Nazareth he at once ordered an attack. Both the Master of the Hospital, Roger of Moulins, and James of Mailly argued against attacking an obviously superior force; but Gerard de Ridefort, perhaps prompted into even greater determination by taunts against him, insisted and led a downhill charge against al-Afdal. It was a suicidal charge, made in ire rather than with intelligent strategy. The Master of the Hospital, the Marshal of the Temple, and all but two or three of the Templar knights were killed. Miraculously, Gerard himself survived and, badly wounded, retreated to Nazareth. Thus, as a result of foolishness and intestine squabbling, a good proportion of the best knights available was lost. The deep feeling of hatred between Raymond of Tripoli and Gerard de Ridefort was exacerbated by this incident. Moreover, the truce achieved between King Guy and Raymond after the battle was small compensation for such a psychological and moral defeat just as Saladin was gathering his forces for a full-scale attack on the Kingdom of Jerusalem. [8]

Once again it is interesting to note how the person of the Master of the Temple was largely responsible for a disastrous defeat. Although he must have deeply regretted his action, and the death of so many Templar knights (including the third-ranking official of the Order), it was his obstinate determination to attack at all costs against the advice of his peers which caused the débâcle. The chronicler Ernoul, Balian's squire, who was present and whose account forms the basis of modern versions, was forthright in blaming the defeat on 'the pride of the Master of the Temple'. [9] Ambroise relates that the losses 'caused the Temple grievous pain'. [10] For their part, obviously, the Moslems exalted in this 'success': al-Afdal had gained an even greater victory than his mission would have done had he continued into the territory of Acre as his father had wished. They particularly relished the death of Roger of Moulins, whose bravery was recognized and feared. Ibn Al-Athir concludes: 'It was a great victory, since the Templars and the Hospitallers constituted the strength of the Franks, so that the good news was spread everywhere.' [11]

Hattin

The Horns of Hattin are a double hill guarding a pass through the northern ridge of the mountains between Tiberias and the road from

Acre, to the west. Baldwin describes the area as follows:

Between Ṣuffūriyah and Lake Tiberias, some fifteen miles to the east, the terrain was high and plateaulike with rock swells and small depressions and almost no water during the summer. This barren area was bounded on the east and north by a curving range of hills whose northern and eastern slopes descended sharply, well below the level of the plateau to the lake shore. Thus, the hills which would appear steep and high to a person standing to the north and east would seem only a low ridge from the viewpoint of the rugged plateau to the west and south.[12]

The main east-west road, built by the Romans, is known as the Darb al-Hawarnah and links the Jordan fords, the Sea of Galilee, and the Mediterranean coast. To the east, at Tiberias, lay Saladin, accompanied by 12,000 knights with 'regular provisions and military salary',[13] well aware of the difficulties of terrain; to the west, at the Al-Qastad springs near Sephoria, was King Guy's army, with 1,200 knights and 15–18,000 Turcopoles and infantry.[14]

Saladin had taken Tiberias without great difficulty on 2 July with only a small part of his forces, while Raymond was at Acre with King Guy and the Christian army. In Acre the antagonism between Raymond of Tripoli and Gerard de Ridefort gave rise to a series of fatal errors: Raymond argued that it would be foolish to attack the Moslems in summer heat and that they should allow Saladin to take the initiative; Gerard accused him of cowardice and persuaded King Guy to order the march from Acre inland to Sephoria. Since there was ample pasturage for the horses of the army, and also sufficient water supplies, he argued it would be possible to wait there in safety for Saladin's next move.

Raymond countered that it would be disastrous to march across the barren land between Acre and Tiberias in mid-July. He understood Moslem tactics and Ibn al-Athir credits him with understanding Saladin's strategy. Raymond argued that 'If Saladin takes Tiberias, he will not be able to remain there, and when he has left it and gone we shall retake the city; if he wishes to remain he can only do so with all his forces, which will not accept being far from their families and villages for long.'[15] He knew the Moslem predilection for seasonal campaigns and that Saladin's men would wish to return to their homes for the harvest. All historians agree that Raymond's advice was sound, that it was courting disaster to leave good pastures and water to attack an enemy at least equal in number and in a good strategic position.* It seems that most of the men present also agreed, since many of them knew the country as well as Raymond. But one important person disagreed: Gerard de Ridefort argued—on the basis of the events preceding the Battle of Nazareth—that Raymond was a traitor and that Tiberias was only a few miles away. By insinuating that in refusing to act King Guy would be perceived by his enemies as a coward, he managed to overturn the decision taken only a short time before and obtain the order to attack Saladin's army at Tiberias. [16]

Although King Guy's decision and Gerard de Ridefort's advice have often been criticized, the arguments used made a certain amount of sense in the light of the events of the recent past. Raymond had refused homage at Guy's coronation the previous year; he had close diplomatic relations with Saladin, and, most important of all, he was supporting the kind of plan that had disgraced Guy four years earlier. [17] Guy was on his first campaign as King of Jerusalem, and it is easy to see how the Templar Master's argument that he could not ignore the plea for help from Raymond's wife, still inside the citadel of Tiberias, would appeal to the king's sense of honour. A further convincing factor, given his friendship with Gerard de Ridefort, was the threat of withdrawing Templar support. What, he must have thought, would be the strength of the military forces of the Kingdom if they were deprived of the Templar contingent? [18]

The Christian army left its camp at Sephoria on the morning of Friday 3 July, ironically providing the Moslems with an additional psychological stimulus, since Friday, the Moslem's holy day, was Saladin's favourite day for military engagements. The immediate objective was to relieve Tiberias, but from the beginning the Templar rearguard was harassed by the usual Moslem tactics of skirmishers firing bows at the gallop. Saladin received news of the advance during dawn prayers

* Smail notes that the accounts of Raymond's speech are not completely reliable because 'contemporary versions of them were written down after the subsequent catastrophe, and it is probable that some of the chroniclers concerned succumbed to the temptation of presenting Raymond as a prophet.' (Smail, *Crusading Warfare*, p. 191; cf. Baldwin, *Raymond of Tripoli*, pp. 96–135). On the complex matter of Christian and Moslem sources for an account of the battle see Prawer, *Crusading Institutions,* pp. 484–7 and Runciman, *History of the Crusades*, II, Appendix II, pp. 486–91.

in Tiberias and immediately left to join the bulk of his forces at Kafr Sabt; by noon he was with his army, watching from above the Christian army's move towards Tiberias.[19] Guy's army reached the spring at Turan, about a third of the distance from Sephoria to Tiberias, and was faced with an important decision: they could either halt and camp at Turan where there was water, or they could continue the advance towards Tiberias, which lay nine miles ahead. Two routes were available, one of which passed close to Saladin's main body of troops; a northern route across what appeared to be a ridge and down to the village of Hattin, where there were further springs, was the best available. From his position the land looked favourable to Guy, who perceived the steep hills as a low ridge. He decided to advance towards Tiberias.

As soon as the Christian army left Turan, Saladin sent two wings of his army to flank the Christians, take the spring and block a possible retreat. Thus King Guy's army, unable to reach Tiberias because of Saladin's main body of men blocking the route, and cut off from any possible retreat, was forced to make camp for the night without a water supply—after a long and hot afternoon during which they had been unable to water their horses.[20] They made camp surrounded by Saladin's army, taunted by cries of 'God is Great!' and the evident joy of the Moslems. Soldiers who left the camp in search of water for their unbearable thirst were picked off by Moslem snipers. In the Moslem camp, things were different: water was brought up from the Sea of Galilee, arrows were distributed and seventy dromedaries with reserve supplies were stationed among the troops. Saladin spent the night preparing for the victory which he confidently expected the following day.[21] 'In spite of his success and the apparently hopeless position of the Franks, he still took care to see that skirmishers were detailed by name from each squadron.'[22] Fires were started in the scrub around the Christian camp to irritate the Christian soldiers' thirst with smoke.

On the morning of 4 July, at about nine o'clock, the Christian army broke camp and began to move towards the springs of Hattin. Thirsty and tired they had to advance into the hot rising sun, whose brilliance dazzled them.[23] The first to come under attack from Saladin were the Templars in the rearguard. They fought vigorously but unaided and their counter-attack failed.[24] The infantry collapsed under the main thrust of Saladin's attack: thirsty and exhausted even before engaging in battle, they broke ranks and rushed up one of the two hills that formed the 'horns' of Hattin. The knights remained at the foot of the hill, surrounded by brush-wood fires that the Moslems had started, with visibility drastically reduced. It is generally agreed that the knights fought heroically against overwhelming odds without the support of their infantry; but after vicious fighting King Guy and the knights themselves retreated to the top of the hill, with the Bishop of Acre bearing the True Cross. Late in the afternoon, Saladin launched his final attack, which decimated the Christian army, leaving thousands dead together with most of the horses; thousands more were captured. Imad ad-Din gives a particularly gory description of the battlefield, with every conceivable kind of wound and dismemberment vividly portrayed.[25] The Moslems took the royal tent and the True Cross, and at that moment Saladin knew that the battle was finally over. The cream of the military forces of the Kingdom of Jerusalem, gathered from castles and garrisons throughout the crusader states, had been destroyed.[26]

Several contemporary accounts of the battle exist. The jongleur Ambroise related that:

> The Master of the Temple died*
> Amid the raging battle-tide.
> 'Twas he who said the noble word
> Learned in the good school of the Lord
> When at this onslaught, timid folk
> And fearless folk as well, bespoke
> Him thus: 'Come, sire, come, leave the fight,'
> And had he willed to, well he might
> Have come.† 'May God forbid,' said he,
> 'That elsewhere I may ever be,
> Or any man ever upbraid
> The Temple, that I fled afraid.'
> He fled not, rather perished thus,
> Born down by Turks too numerous.[27]

Moslem sources again emphasize Templar courage. Ibn al-Athir, who based his version on the information gleaned from Saladin's son al-Afdal, recounts that the Templar prisoners taken were to be executed

---

* Poetic licence: he was spared at the request of King Guy and died two years later.

† A clear reference to the flight of Raymond from the battlefield.

on Saladin's orders because they were 'among the most warlike of all the Franks'.[28] Similarly Ibn al-Qalānisi said that it was Saladin's custom to massacre Templars and Hospitallers because of the evident hatred they had for the Moslems.[29] *

Saladin's wrath was first extended to Reginald of Karak, whom he had vowed to kill with his own hands. Many of the other knights were ransomed, as was customary in twelfth-century warfare. But special treatment was reserved for the Templars and the Hospitallers taken prisoner, some two hundred altogether. Imad ad-Din recounts the grisly episode:

Two days after the victory, the Sultan gathered the Templar and Hospitaller prisoners, and said: 'I will purify the earth of these two impure races.' He then assigned fifty dinars to each man who brought a prisoner, and immediately the army brought forward hundreds. He ordered them to be decapitated, preferring to kill them than to enslave them . . . Some cleaved in a clean cut, and were thanked; some slackened and failed; and some caused laughter, and others took their place. You saw who mocked and who killed, who talked and who acted: how many vows were fulfilled, how many praises acquired, and perpetual prizes obtained with the blood that was made to run, and pious works adjudicated with the neck of him who was beheaded! How many blades tinged with blood for a desired victory, how many lances brandished against a lion captured by him, how many illnesses cured by rendering infirm a Templar . . .[30]

Even in the midst of Ibn ad-Din's rhetoric, this reference testifies to the courage of the Templars as recognized by their enemies. Yet their renowned valour had rarely been matched by success in the field, and now may even have contributed to the defeat of the kingdom; for at the Battle of Hattin, the Christian army was annihilated as a fighting force.

The Fall of Jerusalem

King Guy had ordered a general mobilization of the armed forces available in the Holy Land, perhaps as many as twenty thousand men. As Prawer

* But Jacques de Vitry, writing not long afterwards and close to the Templars, says: 'After much slaughter, Guy de Lusignan, King of Jerusalem, and the Grand Master of the Templars, with many others of greater degree, were led away captive and fled cowardly before the face of their pursuers.' (*History of Jerusalem*, p. 201.)

points out, it was ironically the huge success of this mobilization, which facilitated Saladin's task once the army had been defeated at Hattin.[31] Castles, ports, garrisons, and even Jerusalem had been left unguarded. The peaceful occupation of Jerusalem, which was of no strategic importance, would be a vital factor in underlining the sincerity of the religious motivation of his whole campaign: 'It had been the focal point in his efforts to win support and it had to be recovered before he could fairly test whether or not he had finally won his point.'[32]

The task was facilitated by the lack of defences. Sir Hamilton Gibb observes that after Hattin the 'subsequent crumbling of the inner defences of Jerusalem and Antioch demonstrate rather the fundamental weakness of the Crusading states than the military genius of the conquerors, a point emphasized by the fact that many of them fell to small detached forces.'[33] For eighty years the crusaders and colonists had lived in a precarious state of false security, their strength deriving not from the courage of the military orders and skill of their commanders, but from the disunity of the Moslems.

By mid-September 1187 Saladin had taken Acre, Nablus, Jaffa, Toron, Sidon, Beirut, and Ascalon. On 20 September his army camped before Jerusalem and began to attack the north and north-west walls—knowing that there was only a handful of knights in the city to resist his siege. By 29 September the walls of Jerusalem were breached. After negotiations with Balian of Ibelin, commanding the city together with the Patriarch Heraclitus (who had consecrated the New Temple in London two years earlier), Jerusalem fell to Saladin on 2 October 1187. The Christians inside the city were ransomed for 30,000 dinars, avoiding a repeat of the slaughter at Hattin.[34]

Once the remaining Templar contingent had left the city with other refugees, Saladin ordered the buildings of Jerusalem to be restored to their original condition. Foremost amongst these was the al-Aqsa mosque: 'The Templars had erected constructions for their habitation to the west of al-Aqsa, with granaries and latrines* and other necessary services, incorporating part of al-Aqsa in their buildings; the area was

---

* Imad ad-Din confirms this. If it is true, then the fact of having built latrines in the *mihrab* (the niche facing Mecca to which the faithful face when praying) may well have been an act of deliberate sacrilege (cf. Imad ad-Din, in Gabrieli, *Storici Arabi*, pp. 161–5).

restored to its pristine condition. The Sultan ordered that the Mosque and the Rock were cleaned of all filth, and it was done.'[35] Thus all signs of the Templar occupation were eradicated, and their departure from the holy city symbolically marked by Saladin's attendance at prayers in the mosque the following Friday. As he had dismantled Jacob's Ford stone by stone, so he cleansed Jerusalem of the presence of his hated enemies.

The following twelve months were marked by a list of conquests as Saladin picked off targets almost at will.[36] But one of the last conquests is of interest in the history of the Templars, who still maintained the castles in the march of Amanus which they had possessed since the 1130s. After a month of constant action that began on 2 July 1188 with the sack of Tortosa—where Saladin failed to take the Templar castle and so retreated, as was his custom—his forces rested for a few days in the vicinity of Antioch. That city was protected by the three Templar castles of Darbsak, Baghras, and al-Qusair, and on 2 September Saladin implemented his strategy by laying siege to Darbsak. A breach was soon made in the wall, but Ibn Shahhad recounts the way in which the Templars prevented Saladin from taking the castle by acting as a human wall, 'each stepping in his comrade's place'.[37] This heroic defence continued for fourteen days, while most other cities and castles had capitulated to Saladin much more quickly.

Again, therefore, the courage of the Templars was stressed; but in this case that courage was in a sense compromised by an unusual development. Having resisted for two weeks, the garrison asked for quarter: the Templars gave up their stores, grain, and weapons and reluctantly agreed to pay a heavy ransom, which had to be taken from their treasury. This measure, after the suicidal attack of Nazareth and the bravery on the battlefield at Hattin, suggests both consciousness of their weakness and perhaps despair. Even Ibn Shaddad remarked that the payment of a ransom by the Templars was something that was 'unheard of'.[38]

This was one of the last actions in the two-year campaign of Saladin against the crusader states. Jerusalem was again in Moslem hands, and the once glorious military orders were decimated and at least to a certain extent tainted with failure and defeat. The entire Kingdom of Jerusalem had been taken with the exception of the impregnable fortress of Belfort and the city of Tyre. The principality of Antioch was reduced to the city of Antioch—retained by its ruler Bohemond as the result of a truce with Saladin—and the castle of al-Marqab. In the County of Tripoli only a single tower in Tortosa, the two small Templar castles of Castel Blanc and Castel Ruge (Qala'at Yahmur), the impregnable Hospitaller fortress of Krak des Chevaliers, and the city of Tripoli were still in Christian hands.

The Templars emerge from this with little credit: Templar courage was never doubted, but it was often misplaced. If the Order's total strength in Latin Syria had indeed been the 600 knights cited earlier, then half that number was lost in a matter of weeks: 60 at Nazareth and 230 at Hattin.[39] Others were lost at Darbsak and the minor battles of Saladin's campaign. While the Order was at its peak in the West as a financial power and landowner, at the close of the twelfth century the Templars in the Holy Land were a broken and disheartened band of men.

TEMPLARS IN THE
HOLY LAND 1187–1292

THE years immediately following the Battle of Hattin constituted the blackest period of the middle years of Templar history. Drastically reduced in numbers, and lacking experienced leadership since their Master Gerard de Ridefort was Saladin's prisoner, they were intimately involved in the internal political struggle that divided the remaining crusader towns. As soon as Gerard was released, he was recaptured and killed; furthermore, the Order suffered more losses, and a disastrous setback to their pride in Cyprus. It was only with the renewed support given them by Innocent III—who became pope in 1198—and the efforts of the two successors to Gerard de Ridefort, that the Templars began to recover something of their lost prestige in the Holy Land.

As in the case of the fall of Edessa in 1144, the immediate consequence of the loss of Jerusalem was the stimulation of interest in the idea of a new crusade. Already, at the 1184 Council of Verona, Frederick Barbarossa and Pope Lucius III had discussed a new crusade; and in the following year Baldwin IV—just before his death—appealed to Henry II of England to lead a crusade. But after the events of 1187 the demand was more pressing. Letters, messengers, and returning knights rapidly spread the news of the fall of Jerusalem throughout Western Europe. News of the disaster was said to have killed Pope Urban II, already a sick man, while his successor Gregory VIII sent the Archbishop of Tyre and Henry of Albano on missions to the European monarchs to persuade them to take the cross: the first response was from Frederick Barbarossa, while Philip Augustus of France and Henry II of England interrupted their on-going desultory war to agree on a joint crusade.*

---

* It was then, from Le Mans, that Henry ordered the levying of the 'Saladin tithe' mentioned in Chapter 5.

Henry's son Richard, soon to succeed him, immediately took a crusading vow. [1] The nature of the news encouraged popular enthusiasm for holy war, and tens of thousands of European soldiers were mentally prepared for the great crusades that were about to take place. Such interest was sustained by propaganda pictures: Conrad of Montserrat, whose unexpected arrival had saved Tyre at the moment of capitulation to Saladin, sent a picture of an Arab horse defecating in the temple of Jerusalem, while other pictures showed Christ being beaten by Arabs. These brash efforts whipped up popular support. [2]

Conrad's leadership had retained Tyre for the Franks, and in 1188 Henry II gave 30,000 marks to the Templars and the Hospitallers to improve the City's defences. Tripoli was saved by the prompt response of William II of Sicily, 'William the Good', who was married to Joan, daughter of Henry II and sister to Richard. He also provisioned and reinforced Tyre and Antioch; had he not died in 1189 the Sicilian forces would have played an important part in the new crusade. [3]

Frederick Barbarossa, who had desired to go on a new crusade since his participation in the Second Crusade, left Ratisbon on 11 May 1189 with an army estimated at 100,000 men. His progress through the Balkans was hampered by the usual problems of bad roads, hot climate and marauders, but was further complicated by difficult relations with the Byzantine Emperor Isaac—which almost degenerated into full-scale war. In Anatolia, the Seljuks forced Frederick's army to a series of battles and constrained it to use the hardest of routes through barren mountain areas. Frederick's journey ended in tragedy: within sight of the city of Seleucia, which offered respite among the friendly Armenians, he was drowned while seeking refreshment from the climate in the River Saleph. [4] His army, already seriously depleted, disintegrated in the following months, and thus what had appeared to be a mighty crusade ended in what Runciman describes aptly as a 'grim fiasco'. [5] The Arabs considered his death a gift of God. [6]

Philip Augustus and Richard I were compelled by mutual distrust to travel to the Holy Land at the same time, although not exactly together. After several spontaneous crusades of Danish, Flemish, and English ships in 1189, Richard and Philip planned their departure. Large numbers of barons from all over Europe arrived in Palestine that summer. [7] In the meantime, events in the Holy Land had led towards a new, and surprising, action. Renewed discord between the barons, who were crammed together against their will in the city of Tyre, led to disputes between the established parties. The greater part of the nobles accepted Conrad of Montferrat, who had saved Tyre from Saladin's advance, as their natural leader,* while King Guy, supported by the Templars, was compelled to seek another city in which he could exert his full authority as King. Thus, in what might have seemed a suicidal move, in 1189 he laid siege to Acre.

This two-year siege was disastrous for the Templars. When Guy's army launched an attack against Saladin's position on 4 October 1189 the Order suffered heavy losses amongst its knights. At first the Frankish army seemed to have put Saladin's forces to flight, and even the Moslems thought that the battle was lost.[8] But as they chased fugitives Saladin charged them. While his own centre had collapsed, Saladin had regrouped his men behind the lines and led the attack against the Franks. Ibn al-Athir describes his victory:

Thus the swords of the Believers surrounded them on all sides, and no one fled but most of them were killed while the remainder were taken prisoner; amongst these, the Master of the Templars, who Saladin had captured and then released, and who now, again in his hands, he had killed.[9]

According to the Arab chronicler ten thousand[†] Christians died in that battle—mostly knights, since the infantry had not managed to join them in battle. Saladin ordered a retreat of some three miles 'in fear that the smell of corpses would cause his men harm'.[10] It was a further blow to the power and prestige of the Templars, whose Master had now been captured by Saladin twice in two years.

Richard I, Cyprus, and the Templars

On his way from Messina to Acre, Richard of England and his fleet made an enforced landing on Rhodes, where the king spent ten days apparently recovering from a bout of sea-sickness. Several other ships, however, carrying Queen Joan of Sicily and Princess Berengaria of Navarre—who was bethrothed to Richard—were driven towards Cyprus.

---

* Bahà'ad Din describes him as the shrewdest and strongest of the Franks, and attributes to him the responsibility of 'exciting the crowds' to come on the new crusade (in Gabrieli, *Storici Arabi*, p. 203).

† Bahà'ad-Din estimated slightly less than 7,000 (Gabrieli, *Storici Arabi*, p. 191).

These ships, including the treasure-ship, were wrecked off Limassol and prisoners and booty taken by the men of the self-styled Emperor Isaac Comnenus. Isaac refused to give up his booty, and after a feigned attempt to pay homage to Richard fled into the island's interior.

Richard, together with King Guy—who had come from Palestine to meet him in Cyprus—other nobles, and most of the important Templar officers, sacked the ports of Cyprus and took the castles of Famagusta and Nicosia. By the end of May that year Richard had conquered the island of Cyprus, which had not been among his objectives, and obtained a huge booty which helped finance his expedition to the Holy Land. As soon as the island was safely controlled, Richard set sail for Tyre where he arrived after a single day's voyage; thence he sailed to Acre, and joined the recently-arrived Philip Augustus in the siege to that city. After two years' siege, the Garrison had almost no food and the European kings' arrival was a sufficient boost to bring about the end of the operation. On 12 July 1191 Acre surrendered: Richard and Philip divided the city, Richard making his quarters in the Templar house.[11]

Once in Acre, with the manifold problems and intrigues concerning French and German crusaders, the possession of Cyprus seemed to Richard of less importance. Although it was a fertile source of potential supplies and possible refuge, his garrison on the island had informed him of incipient unrest. He was very close to the Templars' new Grand Master, Robert de Sablé, and negotiated the sale of Cyprus to the Order. The price was a hundred thousand gold dinars ('besanz sarazineis'),[12] which represented a genuine bargain for the Order, since only forty thousand were to be paid in cash, and the rest in instalments payable from the island's revenues.[13]

But the ownership created unexpected problems. The chronicler of the *Continuation* of William of Tyre says that the Templars wanted 'to treat the people of the island of Cyprus as they would the people of a castle in the land of Jerusalem. They wished to ransom, beat and maltreat them, and wished to control the island of Cyprus by a guard of twenty brothers.'[14] A legend recounts that the castle of Buffavento was built by a noble lady in order to take refuge from the Templars, who tyrannized the people during the year that they held the island.[15]

A plot was hatched to surprise and massacre the Templars and their commander in Cyprus, Arnaut de Bouchart, to take place on the Saturday of Holy Week in 1192—when the Knights would least expect such an attack. Arnaut de Bouchart learned of the revolt in advance and was able to retreat to the castle of Nicosia, with 14 brethren, 29 other mounted men and 74 foot-soldiers. It was not a particularly strong castle and they possessed limited supplies of food; they were trapped inside by a rowdy mob demanding their blood, with no way of summoning immediate help. Once again, the Templars were saved by their foolhardy courage:

Hearing this, Bouchart suggested that, rather than starve like cowards, the little company should make a sally and meet their death like men. On Easter Sunday morning, therefore, having heard mass, they sallied forth, completely surprising the Greeks, who never suspected so small a force of so audacious an enterprise. The Latins slew the Greeks indiscriminately like sheep; a number of Greeks who sought asylum in a church were massacred; the mounted Templars rode through the town spitting on their lances everyone they could reach; the streets ran with blood, which found its ways to the water-course at the bridge of the Seneschal (Lodron), whence the water carried it to the bridge of the Pillory; there a great stone was afterwards set up in memory of the slaughter. The Templars rode through the land, sacking the villages and spreading desolation, for the population of both cities and villages fled to the mountains. [16]

The acquisition of Cyprus had not been fortunate, and this popular rebellion represents ambiguous evidence of the Templars' attitude towards their possessions. They were masters once again, albeit temporarily, of a hostile island. They already possessed some land on the island granted by Amaury, who had received the gift of a ruby in exchange, [17] but Arnaut de Bouchart fled to Acre, where he explained the events 'to the master and to the convent', [18] and the Templars agreed that they should no longer attempt to hold the island.

We may assume that the 'remarkable understanding' [19] that existed between Robert de Sablé and King Richard ensured that the Templars played an important part in the campaigns that he undertook in his two years in the Holy Land. The Templars fought either on the King's right or in the vanguard at the Battle of Arsuf on 7 September 1191, when Richard demonstrated that Saladin could be beaten. [20] The Master's knowledge of eastern tactics and customs must have been valuable to the crusading king, and de Sablé might even have been behind the remarkable proposition made by Richard to offer his sister

Joan, widow of William of Sicily, in marriage to al-'Adil (or Saphadin), the brother of Saladin, in order that they should rule together over Jerusalem.[21] His role is suggested by the terms of a proposed truce involving the marriage settlement: as part of the complex agreement, Saladin was to return properties which he had taken from the military orders. Clearly Saladin refused this condition, together with the other proposals.[22]

After twice arriving within twelve miles of Jerusalem and then retreating, retaking Acre from Saladin and aiding his nephew Henry, Count of Champaigne, to supplant Guy de Lusignan by marrying the widow of the assassinated Contrad of Montferrat and thus to claim the title of King of Jerusalem, Richard eventually came to terms with Saladin on 2 September 1192. A five-year peace treaty was signed by Saladin and sworn on Richard's behalf by Henry of Champagne, Balian of Ibelin, and the Masters of the Temple and the Hospital. The coastal cities south to Jaffa were to remain in Christian hands, pilgrims were to be allowed to visit Jerusalem, and the citadel of Ascalon was to be demolished. Richard himself never went to Jerusalem, but the 'mere presence of Richard and his host through 1191 may well have prevented Saladin from reaping the full fruits of his victory at Hattin'.[23] Throughout his campaign, his friendship with the Templars was witnessed by important events, not least the controversial sale of Cyprus. Finally, with his approval, the island was in turn sold to Guy de Lusignan, who was conveniently removed from the internal hostilities of Palestine so that Richard's nephew could rule without discord.[24]

Yet this was not the last incident concerning Richard and the Templars. When at last the treaty was signed he could plan his return to England—where his brother John was gradually usurping Richard's position. But the journey was fraught with danger. According to Ernoul, Richard appealed for assistance to the Master of the Temple in the following terms:

Sire, I well know that I am not loved by everybody and it is well known that I do not like the sea, and I know that I shall not arrive in that place without being killed or captured. If you please, for God's sake, you will instruct your brother knights and your brother sergeants, who will come with me in a ship, and when we have arrived, will lead me, as if I were a Templar, to my country.[25]

The Master agreed and Richard travelled to Europe disguised as a Templar knight, as an interesting confirmation of his close relationship to the Order. His fear of being captured by the Emperor Isaac Angelus led him to this subterfuge, and also led to a popular identification between King Richard and the Templars.

Unfortunately the aid of the Templars was to no avail. The king was involved in several adventures with pirates, storms, and a dramatic landing on the coast of Istria in northern Yugoslavia. He was too well known to travel incognito, was recognized and captured near Vienna, and imprisoned by Duke Leopold of Austria.[25] While it is fascinating that he should put his life in the hands of the Templars, it is also noteworthy that even they were unable at that time to guarantee the safe passage of the king from Acre to England.

Revival of Templar Power in the East

The Templars had been directly responsible to the Holy See since the protection of Pope Eugenius III, but while the last years of the twelfth century had seen a series of short-lived and weak pontificates the turn of the century was marked by the advent of one of the most ambitious and successful of all popes, Innocent III (1198-1216). Gifted with a brilliant legal mind, he was zealous and austere in his ways; one of his many books, De Contemptu Mundi, written before his election to Rome, recalls St Bernard in the way in which he attacks pride and sensuality. The iron will and extreme spirituality for which he was renowned are also reminiscent of the founder of the Cistercians. Innocent's ambitions were not personal: he conceived as a political ideal the creation of a feudal state based upon the supreme power of the Church, a regale sacerdotium in which the pope would represent the summit of a hierarchy of vassal states depending directly or indirectly on the Church through its empire.[26] This theocratic ideal, and the tenacity with which Innocent pursued it throughout his pontificate, represent the high watermark of the power of the medieval Roman Church.

It was natural that such a pope should perceive in the Knights Templars an instrument for the implementation of his design. From the beginning of his pontificate his policy was twofold: to liberate Jerusalem and to combat heresy, especially Catharism. These aims were repeated in his letter convoking the bishops to the Fourth Lateran Council of 1215, in which he wrote that 'Two things are above all dear to me, the liberation of the Holy Land and the reform of the Universal Church.'[27] In this persistent desire to reverse the defeat in Hattin and its consequences he often turned to the Templars for guidance, support, and their ability to transmit and control papal funds for war in the East. We have seen examples of his use of the Order for the collection of papal taxes destined for the Holy Land, and Delisle's conclusion that the 'treasury of the Templars was the bank where the financial resources destined for the crusades'[28] were collected and administered was certainly valid during Innocent's pontificate. Innocent once referred to the Templars as 'the beloved brothers of the militia of the Temple',[29] and promulgated fifty bulls on their behalf—including frequent repetitions of Omne datum optimum. Melville asserts that Innocent thought of the Templars as a kind of pontificial militia,[30] and it was at this time that three successive Masters (Philippe de Plessiez, 1201-9, William of Chartres, 1210-19, and Pedro de Montaigu, 1209-32) consolidated and managed to extend the Templars' power in the Holy Land. The next pope, Honorius III (1216-27), in many ways continued the policies of his predecessor and aided this process of revival.

Several other factors facilitated this development. Changes of rule and dynasty at Acre, Antioch and in neighbouring Latin states enabled the Templars to consolidate their power base by means of diplomatic manoeuvres and carefully-constructed alliances; even the birth of a new military order, the Teutonic Knights, was not sufficient to fill the existing power vacuum. Furthermore, after the conquest of Cyprus (1191) and Constantinople (1204), and the consequent establishment of Latin settlements throughout Greece, knights in Europe who might once have ventured to the Holy Land to seek land and wealth preferred these nearer and less difficult territories. From about 1205 the only new knights who established themselves in the Holy Land were members of the military orders. The fragmentary crusades which followed the deaths of the Holy Roman Emperor Henry VI and Richard I of England were fatally weakened by the same power vacuum and diversionary conquests. Jacques de Vitry states that the military orders were the only knights who managed to avoid the corruption and indolence that afflicted Christians in the East: while the Moslems were militarily weak after the death of Saladin, and concentrated on commerce, the orders were able to expand.[31] Thus they were able to build new and enlarged fortresses and became even more important than they had been in the delicate balance of power along the narrow coastal strip now left in crusader hands.

Evidence of this can be seen in a period of castle building and rebuilding that began towards the end of Innocent's pontificate.* After the battle of Hattin only Tortosa had remained in Templar possession, and the strategy behind castle building had changed dramatically. Saladin's campaigns had demonstrated that the small twelfth-century attacking and colonizing castles of the castrum type were impotent in large-scale warfare, while the great fortress of Krak des Chevaliers had withstood all attempts to take it. New siege techniques demanded the construction of castles which adopted the more sophisticated Eastern architectural features. Massive ramparts were developed to resist ever more powerful mangonels, which catapulted rocks of up to 150 kilograms at castle walls from a safe distance; wall towers were increased in number and double enceinte castles became more common in defence against sapping and undermining techniques; these features also offered greater protection against the belfry, an iron-plated wooden tower which could be moved near to a castle wall and from which a drawbridge could be lowered to allow attackers to run straight onto the castle ramparts. Wall towers with firing positions to cover previously dead ground were introduced. Fortified 'bent gates', with which anyone entering the outer gate had to make a sharp turn towards an inner gate, also became regular features.[32] 'Atlit and Safed also had moats.

When the Templars again came into possession of Baghras in 1216, as the result of their support for Bohemond of Antioch and Patriarch Albert of Jerusalem against Leo of Armenia, it was immediately reinforced. After this work was carried out Baghras remained in Templar hands until 1268, the longest continuous period of ownership.[33] In fact the re-acquisition marked the beginning of a period of almost independent rule in the Amanus march.[34] Now, rather than constantly attending upon the King of Jerusalem and the Lords of the other crusader states, the Templars went their own way as feudal overlords.

* In the early years of the century Azor (Casel des Plains) was rebuilt. In 1216 Baghras was strengthened, and 'Atlit (Castle Pilgrim) was built from 1217–18. In 1232 Habonim-Carfarlet, five miles south of 'Atlit, was bought by the Templars. In 1240 the great spur castle of Safed was started, while Tsipori was built in c.1250 and Beaufort in 1260.

The most important Templar castle built during this brief period of revival was 'Atlit (Chastiau Pèlerin or Castle Pilgrim), situated on the only promontory on the coastline between Jaffa and Haifa. It represents both the quintessence of the new policy of castle building and, ironically, the beginning of the end of the attempt to colonize Palestine. It was started in the winter of 1217–18 on the site of an earlier watch tower, known as Destroit, built by the Templars to protect pilgrims on the route to Jerusalem from the coast.[35] The chronicler Oliver of Padeborn, who describes its construction in great detail, relates that the 'chief use of these buildings is to enable the Templars to escape from the sinfulness and filth that fill the city of Acre'.[36] But its defensive character, open to attack from land only on one side, is immediately obvious both from the site and from its plan. It was built with the experience of the sieges of Acre and Tyre in mind, and the Templars understood that a castle provisioned and strengthened with reserves from the sea could hold out indefinitely against the land-bound armies of the Moslems. 'Atlit marks an important shift in crusader mentality, and was in fact never taken by the Moslems. The other great thirteenth-century spur castles of the Templars, Safed and Beaufort, were also based on the concept that huge walls could take the place of manpower.

While the great Hospitaller castles of Krak and Marqab, and the Templar castle of Safed, were strengthened in the thirteenth century by the addition of a second enceinte,* 'Atlit—and also Tortosa, built on a similar site—still had a single enceinte. But in the case of 'Atlit and Tortosa this single wall rose virtually from the sea. 'Atlit was surrounded on three sides by the sea, and on the fourth side the rugged natural cliff was strengthened by an ingenious scheme of defence based on a fosse, bailey, and three towers;† it was built by skilful engineers who put into practice all the Templars' experience of the twelfth century.

The entrance was through the towers, which had two outer gates, one with portcullis and one without, so that together with an inner

* Chastel Blanc and Chateau Ruge, inland from Tortosa, are other examples of Templar castles with a double enceinte.

† Beaufort was similarly defended by a 300-metre precipice on its eastern and northern sides, so that attack was only feasible from west and south (Smail, *Crusading Warfare*, p. 221). Use of natural features was of particular value in such rugged terrain.

gate they formed a dog-legged or bent entrance of traditional oriental type.[37]* Between the towers the bailey wall was six metres thick, with 'almost as great a relief over the counterscarp as it could have without blocking the command of the great towers over the terreplein outside'.[38] Thus, an approaching enemy at the edge of the six-metre deep sheer-sided fosse would be faced by the bailey wall twenty-five metres away, and would be under defensive fire from at least four arrow slits at any given point.[39] It is thought that the fosse could be flooded with sea water. The towers commanded the fosse perfectly, and also offered a view across the plain as far as Mount Carmel, so that observers would be able to see approaching dust clouds for at least seven to eight miles up and down the coast. The area was rich in fish, salt, wood, oils, vines, grain, and fruit and was therefore of great value beyond its strategic significance.[40] It also had a good natural harbour.

The builders' skill was considered by C. N. Johns, who excavated the site in the 1930s, to have been exceptional. It offered a near-perfect defence to landward, while the castle could be provisioned from the sea—where the Franks, with the assistance of the great merchant fleets of Pisa, Genoa, and Venice, maintained command for most of the thirteenth century. The one surviving tower stands thirty-four metres high, and has two barrel-vaulted halls as high as the two lower floors. This tower was connected to the other towers by an internal corridor, offering excellent communications amongst the defenders.[41] 'Atlit, with its enormous food stores, fresh water supply and gardens, could sustain a force of several thousand people,† knights and the necessary servants. With its ten-sided chapel and rib-vaulted great hall, it was fit for receiving and providing hospitality for royalty, high clergy, and the great secular lords who visited the Templars: in 1251, Queen Margaret of Provence, wife of Louis IX of France, stayed there while her husband was on crusade, and gave birth to a child inside the walls of 'Atlit.[42]

Two years after it was completed, 'Atlit was attacked by Al-Mu'azzam, ruler of Damascus. The Sultan laid siege to the castle with

---

* Tortosa, also encircled on three sides by the sea, had a more normal single bent entrance.

† In 1220 the garrison numbered 4,000 (Benvenisti *Crusaders in the Holy Land*, p. 177).

sophisticated weapons such as a trebuchet (an extremely accurate device for hurling rocks by counterpoise), three petraries, and four mangons or slings. But the castle was well-protected against the most feared of siege tactics, the undermining of defence walls, since its foundations were under sea-level. The garrison of 300 Templars, supervised by Pedro de Montaigu, the Grand Master, resisted all attacks and managed to put the trebuchet and one petrary out of action. After a month of siege, the Sultan was forced to abandon his attack, having lost as many as three emirs and 200 mamlukes.[43] In 1229 Frederick II of Hohenstaufen was forced by 'Atlit's strength to desist from an attempt to take the castle from the Templars, and it was only lost when the Order evacuated the site after the fall of Acre in 1291. Burchand of Mount Sion, who visited 'Atlit in 1280, did not exaggerate when he wrote that it was '. . . the most strongly fortified of all the places ever held by the Christians. It stands in the deep sea, and is fenced with walls and outworks, and such strong barbicans and towers that the whole world ought not to be able to take it'.[44] The ruins of 'Atlit remain today as the greatest monument to Templar power in the Holy Land.

The importance of the new fortress was recognized during one of the first major offensive actions which the Franks carried out in the thirteenth century. Just as it was reaching completion in 1218 fresh crusading forces were gathering in Acre; Ibn al-Athir refers to a 'new apparition' of the Franks after a long absence.[45] In May of that year King John of Brienne and the army of what is generally known as the Fifth Crusade with a large number of German, Frisian, and Italian crusaders,* stopped at 'Atlit en route from Acre to their destination at Damietta, on the Nile delta. It is interesting that 'Atlit was already regarded as the most important port of call south of Acre. A contingent of Templars including the Master William of Chartres sailed with the crusading army to join them in their planned assault on al-Adid, the ageing son of Saladin, at Damietta. Again the new fortress can be

---

* A fascinating insight into Templar influence is provided by the case of Andrew II of Hungary, who had sailed with the crusaders from Europe but had then returned in January 1218. If Andrew should not return it had been agreed that the Kingdom of Croatia and Dalmatia was to be governed by Pons of the Cross, Master of the Hungarian Templars (Cf. Van Cleve, *The Fifth Crusade*, in Setton (Ed.) *History of the Crusades*, II, p. 387).

seen to represent a revival of Templar power, especially since the expedition against Damietta had already been proposed by the Templar and Hospitaller masters the previous year but abandoned for lack of adequate manpower.[46] The army touched for a few hours at 'Atlit while extra supplies and Templar knights were taken on board; then they sailed directly for Damietta, where William of Chartres stepped ashore with John of Brienne, Duke Leopold VI of Austria, and the Master of the Hospital.

The city of Damietta was considered a vital spearhead for control of the Near East, and as a base for further attacks on the kingdom of the Sultan al-Adid. If Damietta and Alexandria were taken, the leaders of the crusade believed it might even be possible to negotiate an exchange with Jerusalem. The army landed on the west bank of the Nile opposite Damietta, and prepared to attack the city and simultaneously defend its own camp by digging a moat and building a defensive wall.

Damietta was a well-fortified and defended city, with as many as eighty thousand people present when the crusading army arrived. The first attacks were made against a chain-tower in the Nile: a chain and pontoon-bridge between this tower and Damietta gave the Moslems control over river traffic by blocking the only navigable channel. But the tower was heavily fortified and resisted these initial attacks; at the same time, an attack led by a force of 70–80 ships failed to dent the city's defences. Thus began a siege which lasted from 27 May 1218 to the eventual taking of the abandoned city on 5 November 1219. The Templars played an important role amidst a large and often undisciplined army: one Templar attempt to take Damietta by charging the city in a large ship ended with the scuttling of their ship beneath the walls;[47] on another occasion, Templar forces overwhelmed Moslem troops who came out from the city;[48] again, only the combined forces of the Templars and the Hospitallers in support of John of Brienne prevented the destruction of the Christian army.[49] Most important of all, in the light of several not entirely successful masters, was the skilful leadership and tactical sense of the new Master Pedro de Montaigu, who succeeded William of Chartres after his death on the Damietta campaign.[50] His leadership clearly helped to maintain morale amongst the Templars while other elements of the army floundered.[51]

The long siege was maintained in vain, for Damietta was evacuated after an eight-year truce was negotiated with the Moslems. Promised extra forces from Europe never materialized, and what was nearly a triumph ended in failure. The Holy Land had not been retaken by either conquest or negotiation; Damietta was not to serve as a spearhead for attacking Egypt; and although Jerusalem was at one stage offered in the terms of truce, it was not accepted. But on this occasion the Templars were not to blame. From the departure from 'Atlit to the sacking of Damietta, which provided an enormous quantity of booty, their reputation for great valour was maintained. They lost one Grand Master, but gained another who was to play a vital part in Templar history in the next decade. Their role in part created a rejuvenated prestige which helped to alleviate the memories of the failures and losses the Order had suffered under Saladin.

The Templars and the Crusade of Frederick II

Frederick II of Hohenstaufen (1197–1250), Holy Roman Emperor and King of Sicily, had long promised to go on a crusade. It is possible that Jerusalem would have been taken had he joined the large army of Crusaders at Damietta in 1218 or 1219. But from the beginning his motives were of less pristine nature than most great crusaders. After a failed expedition to northern Italy from his kingdom in Sicily in 1226, he sought Pope Honorius III's support against the Lombard communes which had resisted him. His aim had been to 'reform the political status of the Empire'[52] by bringing the independent Lombard League within his own power; to oppose them, he used the strategy of emphasizing his obligation to lead a crusade—and thus the need to remove obstacles to the carrying out of such a crusade—in order to gain Honorius' approval. It was at this time that Frederick began to regard the Pope as a temporal rival, rather than as a spiritual leader. Thus from the beginning, his crusade was political in inspiration.

Honorius III was succeeded in March 1227 by Gregory IX, nephew of Innocent III, who launched a policy of world dominion by the Church. Gregory 'saw in Frederick's long-standing obligation to undertake a crusade the supreme opportunity for crippling, if not destroying, the Hohenstaufen menace'.[53] When Frederick eventually departed in September of that year, and almost immediately returned, Gregory did not believe that sickness had been the reason and excommunicated the Emperor. But it seems that he had also been engaged in a series of actions in Sicily against the Templars and other landowners loyal to the Holy See.[54] When Frederick did leave on 26 June 1228, Gregory actually sent an army against his kingdom in Sicily; even stranger was the paradoxical fact of an excommunicated Emperor leading a crusade.*

This anomaly resulted in even stranger consequences. When Frederick arrived at Acre on 7 September 1228 with a fleet of forty ships and several hundred German and Sicilian knights, he was welcomed with enthusiasm by the Templars and Hospitallers—as the result of his vow to fight the Saracens for two years. But soon afterwards a letter reached them from Gregory, ordering them to play no part in Frederick's crusading activities.[55] And the Templars' enthusiasm was already matched by concern: under Frederick's patronage the Teutonic Knights were rapidly growing to equal them in possessions and power, and it seems that Thomas of Acerra, the Emperor's representative in Syria, was charged with the specific duty of curbing the power of the Templars.[56] Their growing concern was increased by a second excommunication of Frederick II, who was accused by the Pope of setting out for a crusade without waiting for absolution from the first excommunication. This made it difficult for the Templars, under direct papal patronage, to support Frederick—notwithstanding the paradoxical command of the second paragraph of their *Rule* to associate with excommunicated knights where possible. The situation led to bizarre results: on the march south to Jaffa, the Templar contingent marched under Pedro de Montaigu *one day's journey behind* Frederick—in order to avoid accusations that they marched *with* him.[57]

The crusade of Frederick was anomalous in other ways. The Emperor spoke perfect Arabic, having been brought up in an Islam-influenced court in Palermo; he himself kept a harem in Sicily, and Pope Gregory was irritated by Frederick's Arab ways and lifestyle. The Arab chronicler Ibn Wasil states that Frederick was 'friend to philosophy, logic and medicine, and favourable towards the Moslems'.[58] He engaged in scholarly exchanges on mathematical problems with the Moslem leaders,

---

* Excommunication was not exceptional in such cases, and was as much a sign of disapproval as a real punishment. Frederick's uncle Philip of Swabia had been excommunicated by Innocent III, and the Doge Dandolo and the whole Venetian fleet was excommunicated after the sack of Zara on their way to the Fourth Crusade.

and his proposals of truce found favour with the Sultan as the result of the natural sympathy that existed between them. He cultivated a profound friendship with Fakhr ad-Din, son of the Sultan of Egypt, and maintained diplomatic and friendly contact with the descendants of the Sultan until the end of his life. These personal relationships resulted in the greatest anomaly of all: Frederick II actually negotiated the return of Jerusalem to Christian hands, succeeding where numerous crusades and attempts at negotiation had failed. The treaty was signed on 18 February 1229.

It must have seemed to the Templars that they were to bear the brunt of Frederick's concessions: the terms of the treaty specified that the Moslems were to retain Al-Ḥaram ash-Sharif, and the enclosure containing the mosque of Omar and the Temple of Solomon—although Christians were to have access to the Temple for prayers.[59] The enemies of Frederick complained that the treaty had been made without mention of Church, Christianity, or pilgrims. The Templars were understandably furious that the Temple, their former headquarters, should remain in Moslem hands. In the words of Thomas Van Cleve:

It was a tenet of their faith, the *raison d'être* of their order, that they were to fight unremittingly against the 'infidel'. The acceptance of Frederick's terms would impose upon them peaceful relations with the Moslems for at least ten years. Already they had experienced hardships and suffered disease and privations in winning control of fortified places from which they could pursue the conquest. Now, at a single stroke, a Christian emperor, notoriously friendly with Moslems, had set their achievements at naught, ignored their rights, perhaps, indeed, pledged himself to prevent their further conquests.[60]

The Templars needed holy war to survive, and this is the first sign of the unease which the lack of conflict with the Moslems created in the Order. On 17 March 1229 Frederick II was crowned King of Jerusalem, and it must have appeared to some of them even then that their future was in serious doubt.

Whilst at Jerusalem Frederick visited the mosque of al-Aqsa, former headquarters of the Templars, and if the account of Sibt Ibn al-Giawzi is to be believed, feelings between the Emperor and the Templars were running high. This chronicle, rich in interesting details of Frederick's visit to Jerusalem, relates that Frederick 'stayed in Jerusalem no longer than two nights, and then returned to Jaffa, fearing that the Templars wished to kill him'.[61] The subsequent attempt on Frederick's part to assault 'Atlit, and the Templars' role in the Patriarch Gerold's plan to take Jerusalem in the name of the Pope with their help, testify to the difficult relations between the two sides.

Yet the Templars were far too opportunistic, and the Master too expert a diplomat, for such concerns to disturb their long-term perspective. Sooner or later, Frederick would have to return to the West and the problems of his kingdom there, while the Templars could afford to wait. Thus at the last possible moment before total rupture the Templars seem to have volunteered to assist in the reconstruction of Jerusalem. Van Cleve attributes this change to their opportunism and argues that it represented a 'belated recognition by both the Orders and the Patriarch Gerold that the achievement of Frederick II was something which might be made to redound to their own advantage, especially after the Emperor's departure which they believed to be imminent'.[62] But their involvement with Gerold's plans had already compromised the Templars in Frederick's mind. The Emperor held a meeting in Acre at which he condemned the supporters of Gerold and especially the Templars. They were branded as traitors, expelled from the city of Acre, and the streets leading to their compound were guarded by the Emperor's troops. His last act before leaving the Holy land on 1 June 1229 was to ship or destroy all available arms so that the Patriarch and the Templars could not make use of them.[63] He also helped the Teutonic Knights to redeem the land around their castle at Montfort, dominating Acre, as a further countermeasure against the Templars.[64]

This persecution continued in Italy. Arriving with extraordinary speed, so that even the Pope was not informed for a further month, Frederick began the reconquest of his kingdom with the help of loyal German troops. By the end of 1229 he had succeeded. These operations included the confiscation of Templar property in the Kingdom of Sicily, but the Pope was able to negotiate compensation payments as part of general concessions made by the Emperor in 1230. The tension continued, however, and when Gregory IX was led to excommunicate Frederick yet again in 1239, the accusations and complaints included his action ten years before on returning from the Holy Land. Eleven of the sixteen complaints listed concerned Frederick's alleged misdeeds in the Kingdom of Sicily; one of them dealt specifically with his despoiling of the Templars and Hospitallers. [65]

Thus the relations between Frederick II and the Templars were continuously turbulent over a long period of time, deriving perhaps from his support for the Teutonic Knights but also exacerbated by his open attacks on Templar prestige and power. Many other secular leaders may have felt as Frederick about the Templars, but none was powerful enough to act as he did. Papal support was in this case of inestimable value to the Order, and it is true that—as they had forseen—once Frederick had left the Holy Land their situation there soon returned to its previous status. Most important of all was the fact that the Templars had never been as powerful in Italy, especially the Kingdom of Sicily, as in France and England, where Frederick's political influence was negligible. Henry III of England was an ally and correspondent of Frederick, and gave his sister Isabella in marriage to the Emperor; but he was at the same time fervently loyal to the Templars.

Military Actions: 1229-91

This defiance of the Emperor Frederick II represents a recovery of prestige and power by the Templars after the disasters of the last decade of the twelfth century. In the 1230s the Order reassumed part of its original purpose, and began the shipping of both pilgrims and merchandise to the Holy Land from Marseilles. [66] In 1240, as the result of a truce between Richard of Cornwall, Henry III's crusading brother, and the Sultan of Damascus, they received Safed again, although they violated the treaty which gave it to them by attacking Hebron two years later. [67] In the same year they were secure enough to openly attack the Teutonic Knights, burning their church at Acre while the Genoese fleet laid siege to the Hospital compound there. [68] In 1252 the Grand Master Thomas Berard provided safe conduct for twenty-six people from Malta to Tripoli in order to judge a contestation with the Prince; Berard's order, 'by the grace of God humble Master of the Knights of the Temple', demonstrates their international power as guarantors. [69] Their renewed power is also shown by the grant of the fiefs of Belfort and Sidon, which passed to the Templars in 1260, when the secular lords decided that they could no longer maintain their defence. [70] Immense reserves of men and money in Western Europe enabled them to accept such responsibilities as the burden of maintaining fortresses in Latin Syria, which had become intolerable for local barons who could no longer rely on the taxes that their eleventh-century predecessors collected.

But it was also in this period that the most open abuses of Templar power occurred, and chroniclers spoke openly of their part in losing cities, castles, and even in weakening commerce between Tyre, Acre and the West, as the result of feuding between the military orders and Italian merchant colonies. The power of the Templars and the Hospital increased in the presence of a Moslem power vacuum. After the death of Saladin, Moslem power had been divided amongst the sons and nephews of the great anti-crusader, and by the mid-thirteenth century internecine squabbles and rivalry had virtually negated the advantages obtained by Saladin. Minor truces governed the delicate balance of military power in the Holy Land, and the Templars were always prepared to break them when there was an obvious advantage to be gained. From Saladin's death in 1192 to about 1260, they were able to steadily increase, or recover, their dominions and power. But after 1260, the last of the great Arab anti-crusaders, Baybars, reunited the Moslem forces as Saladin and Nur-ad Din had done before him. Then, once again, the frailty of the Latin Kingdom of Jerusalem was demonstrated, and Templar power declined dramatically for the remainder of the century.

But before Baybars came to power, what a recent historian has described as the 'last whole-hearted effort of Christendom against the infidel'[71] took place under the banner of Louis IX of France. It was also the first time since the crusade of Louis VII that the Templars were largely responsible for the financing of a crusade.* Yet in some ways their pride and arrogance had created the need for the crusade: as the result of a broken treaty the Sultan turned to the Khorezmian bands of northern Syria for assistance. The result of the alliance was that the Khorezmians took Jerusalem on 11 July 1243, and in a battle at Gaza the following year between the Khorezmians with their Egyptian allies and the Franks and Damascenes, the latter force was virtually annihilated. The Templars suffered terrible losses second only to those at Hattin, the Master Armand de Peragors was taken prisoner, and the crusading efforts of twenty years were rendered vain.[72]

* Much of the finance came from the old Kingdom of Burgundy, traditionally a Templar stronghold (Joseph R. Strayer, *The Crusades of Louis IX*, in Setton (ed.), *History of the Crusades*, II, p. 490).

Louis IX did not take the cross in 1244 as the result of the defeat at Gaza, but this disaster certainly aided him in finding men, arms, and finance for his first crusade. The organization of the fleet that took Louis and his army to the Holy Land was carried out by Renaud de Vichiers, who was then Templar Preceptor in France and later became Master there—partly as the result of his close personal relationship with the King. Louis departed from the specially-constructed fortress of Aigues-Mortes in the Camargue, and landed at Damietta on 5 June 1249 after a long pause in Cyprus awaiting further troops from Europe. Templars from Acre joined his forces there, and provided a crucial part of the advance guard for Louis' failed attack on Cairo. [73] When Louis himself was captured by the Saracens he turned to the Templars for assistance in paying the huge ransom they demanded for him, and this episode provides an insight into Templar thinking—and pride. They were willing to provide cash for the king's ransom provided they were as a result freed from any blame in the failure of the crusade. [74]

This aspect of their activity confirms the criticism we shall later review, but throughout the four continuous years that Louis IX spent in the Holy Land the Templars remained advisers to the King, participating in all his military and diplomatic activities. He made his base at 'Atlit, where, as we have seen, his Queen gave birth to a child in 1251. Ironically, this long sojourn in the Holy Land, and the Templars' assistance, were not only to no avail but indirectly caused the end of crusader power in the East. Once the French King had left, no other well-organized crusade ever set sail for the Holy Land. Louis himself led a tail-end crusade against the Emir of Tunisia in 1270, but that was the result of the Emir's support for the enemies of his brother, Charles of Anjou. In 1272 Edward I of England travelled to the Holy Land, but his journey had no significant military consequences; since his expropriation of funds deposited at the London Temple in 1263, [75] the Templars had no reason to look upon the English king with sympathy.

The defeat of Louis' army indirectly led to the establishment of the Mamluke sultanate which eventually destroyed all crusader power in the Holy Land and came to include Egypt, Palestine, Syria, areas of the upper Euphrates valley, south-eastern Anatolia, Hejaz, the northern Sudan, and Cyrenaica. [76] These Mamlukes, or slaves, had figured prominently in the campaigns of Saladin, and later came to supplant the Aiyūbid dynasty founded by Saladin himself. When Tūrān-Shāh, the last Aiyūbid ruler of Egypt was murdered in May 1250, the Mamlukes made Aybeg the Turkoman commander-in-chief to prevent the possibility of a counter-attack by Christian forces to release King Louis. Shajar ad-Durr, a slave wife from the harem of Tūrān-Shāh, married Aybeg in order to legitimize his claim to power, and then abdicated in his favour to avoid possible criticism of a female ruler.[77] This was the beginning of the first Mamluke dynasty.*

Ten years later Baybars, general to the Mamluke Kutuz, murdered his Sultan and usurped the Mamluke throne, in October 1260. He was a brave and decisive military leader who had earlier in the same year defeated the Mongol Ilkan Hulegu in a pitched battle at Ain Julat near Nazareth, thus liberating Damascus from the fear of Mongol invasion. Baybars was to remain Sultan until 1277, and become the last of the great series of anti-crusaders. He gained the honorific title Malik al-Zahir, or 'The Victorious King', and his exploits survived in story-tellers' romances in Egypt into this century.[78] Cairo became the seat of Islam under Baybars, who quickly consolidated his empire in a series of moves which demonstrated his speed of action, resolution, courage, shrewdness, and determination.[79] It was this consolidation, with the strengthening of fortresses in Syria, and the organization of estuaries by the new watchtowers, and the organization of communications between Damascus and Cairo, which provided for Islam the ideal conditions for dealing a series of crushing blows against the Christian crusaders in the East.

From 1265 Baybars launched a vigorous military offensive against the crusaders. He took Caesarea, Haifa, and Arsuf and razed their fortifications to the ground. In the following year he personally besieged the Templar castle of Safed. The siege began on 7 July 1266 and the garrison capitulated eighteen days later. The loss was disastrous for the recently-renewed Templar power, since as many as 160 villages and 10,000 peasants were dependent on Safed. The Templars themselves, 'demoralised and paralysed by their suspicions', were betrayed by Syrian Christians. Baybars beheaded all of them.[80] Evidence of the fact that Templars did not always take the rearguard in crusader formations

* There were two Mamluke dynasties: the Bahri (River) Mamlukes (1250–1390) and the Burji (Tower) Mamlukes (1382–1517).

is provided by Baybars' tactics in the following year: according to the *Gestes de Chiprois* he attempted to surprise the garrison of Acre by carrying the captured Templar and Hospitaller banners in front of his troops. [81] In 1268 the Templars lost Beaufort to Baybars after a ten-day siege, and after the fall of Antioch in the same year they abandoned Baghras and Roche Roussel in the Amanus march. [82] In 1271 Baybars took the Templar fortress of Chastel Blanc, and also the great Hospitaller castle of Krak des Chevaliers. [83] When he died in 1277, the crusader state was further decimated and Templar possessions once again greatly reduced. Their only strong castle was the impregnable 'Atlit, which Baybars had unsuccessfully attacked on his way into Syria in 1265.

The military power of the Templars was virtually nullified by the successful campaigns of Baybars, and if the kingdom was falling apart they were at least partly responsible. In 1282 they were forced to accept the terms of a truce with Sultan al-Malik al-Mansur in order to preserve their possessions at Tortosa, which had thus far survived Baybars' onslaughts. Qalawun, as al-Malik is usually known, signed this treaty with Guillaume de Beaujeu, Grand Master of the Templars, to last for ten years. The unequal truce, by which the Templars were bound not to attack any of the Sultan's possessions—including the recently-lost Safed—gained them the single and virtually useless guarantee of peace in Tortosa. These terms, accepted by the Grand Master, effectively cancelled the Templars' role in the East, since they were reduced to inaction. [84] Qalawun himself continued the erosion strategy of Baybars, taking Tripoli in 1289. By that date the crusader state was reduced to the territory of Acre, with two remaining Templar positions outside Acre, at Tortosa and 'Atlit.

The Fall of Acre

The inhabitants of Tripoli and other cities lost in the preceding decades were concentrated in Acre, together with as many as 2–3,000 knights, 18,000 foot soldiers, and 2–3,000 squires, sergeants, and turcopoles. [85] Already in 1289 a Templar brother named Hertrand and the Hospitaller Pierre d'Hèzquam had been sent to Rome to implore papal support and finance in the defence of the last Christian city in the Holy Land against what must have seemed for some years an imminent attack. [86] Guillaume de Beaujeu and the greatest part of the Templar forces remaining in the East were present at Acre in 1291 when the expected siege began.

Al-Ashraf, Qalawun's son, completed the task that had been initiated by Baybars and continued by his own father. He left Egypt on 6 March 1291 with forces far superior* to those awaiting his approach in Acre and arrived before the city on 5 April with a hundred siege guns, including one famous Christian mangonel taken from the Hospitaller fortress of Krak des Chevaliers.[87] The siege began the following day, with mangonels and petraries hurling rocks at the city walls and engineers working constantly to fill the moat and undermine the city's defences. At the same time archers attacked the Christians defending the ramparts of Acre. At first the Christian forces were sustained by supplies and aid from the sea, which they still controlled. The chronicler Abu L-Fidà, who was himself present, describes how the Moslems were attacked with arrows from ships standing off-shore equipped with wooden towers protected by buffalo skin.[88]

During the siege the Templars fought valiantly, always at the heart of the action. On 15 April they made an evening sortie beyond the city walls into the Moslem camp, but suffered heavy losses as knights tripped over guy-ropes in the gloom.[89] The next day the Moslems launched a major attack against St Anthony's Gate, one of the main landward gates to the north-east. It was a ferocious battle, in which by common consent only the extraordinary bravery of the Templars and Hospitallers saved the city. Guillaume de Beaujeu was mortally wounded in the right shoulder, and died in the Templar compound, to which some brothers had carried him.[90] Immediately after this ominous battle the evacuation of Acre began with the use of Venetian ships, although there were far too few for the huge crowd of prospective refugees.

On Friday 18 April, Sultan al-Ashraf took Acre. The chronicler known as the 'Templar of Tyre', who was probably a clerk on the staff of the Grand Master, describes the beginning of the Moslems' general assault:

When Friday came, before dawn broke, the beating of giant drums was heard, and to this sound, so loud and horrible, the Saracens attacked the city of Acre on all sides. The place where they made their first entry was the Accursed

* Benvenisti suggests 66,000 horse and 160,000 foot soldiers against 14,000 infantry and 800 knights in Acre (*Crusaders in the Holy Land*, p. 91).

Tower,* which they took. They came on foot, in numbers past counting: first those who bore great high shields, and after them throwers of 'Greek fire', then dart throwers and those who shot feathered arrows, so thickly that it was as if rain was falling from the sky.[91]

The only surviving Christian stronghold was the Templar castle, which stood to the south-west of the city protected on two sides by the sea. For a week the Templars who had retreated there with citizens of Acre held out against the impossible odds.† The Sultan at length made an offer to the Templar commander, Peter de Sevrey, Marshal of the Order. The Templars would be allowed to retire to Cyprus with all the people inside their fortress on condition that they surrendered the building. They accepted: the Sultan's battle standard was raised above the fortress, and Mamluke soldiers entered in order to control the operation. But they began sacking and pillaging, and raping women and girls inside the fortress. In immediate retaliation the Templars killed the Mamlukes, closed the gates of their fortress, and increased their resistance to al-Ashraf.[92] Their situation was, however, desperate: al-Ashraf's offer to safe conduct was repeated and Peter de Sevrey, having no realistic alternative, left the fortress to discuss terms with the Sultan. He and his escort were immediately beheaded and the fortress then subjected to a frontal assault by two thousand Mamlukes, who entered a breach created in the wall by the Sultan's sappers. A handful of Templars survived, but with the loss of their fortress Acre had capitulated totally to the Sultan, who set about the systematic destruction of its markets, towers, and fortifications. Even the harbour was blocked with stones and rubble.

Thus, as the pilgrim Ludolph von Sachen relates, 'on the twelfth day of the month of May, the most noble and glorious city of Acre, the flower, chief and pride of all the cities of the east, was taken. The people of all the other cities, to wit, Jaffa, Tyre, Sidon and Ascalon, when they heard this, left all their property behind and fled to Cyprus.'[93]

* On the extreme north-eastern point of the city's defences, near St Anthony's Gate. The name derives from the siege of 1190–1, when the crusaders under Conrad de Montferrat retook Acre from Saladin.
† The Templar castle had once been the palace and castle of al-Afdal, Saladin's son and Governor of Fatimid Acre, who had provoked the Battle of Nazareth.

After nearly two hundred years of precarious co-habitation with fragmented Moslem forces, the Holy Land was lost.

The Templars never fought a major battle again after the siege of Acre. Surviving Templar castles in the Holy Land lacked sufficient garrisons to defend them, since all available fighting men had been sent to the defence of Acre. On 3 August 1291 the castle of Tortosa surrendered, and on 14 August 'Atlit was evacuated and left to the Sultan's army, so that, in the words of Abu L-Fidà', 'all Syria and the coastal zone were purified of the Frankish presence'.[94] The Templars now held a single castle in the East: Ruad, safely sited on an island two miles off the coast from Tortosa. It remained in Templar hands until 1303, when that last, tiny possession was in turn evacuated. But the new Templar Grand Master Theobald Gaudin had managed to escape from Acre with the treasure and relics of the Order, finding refuge in Cyprus.[95]

When Gaudin died two years later Jacques de Molay, who had joined the order at Beaune in 1265,[96] became the last Grand Master. That same year the Templars equipped six galleys at Venice for the protection of the island of Cyprus and in 1294 de Molay travelled to Europe to attempt to make up for losses sustained at Acre.[97] In 1295 Pope Boniface VIII granted the Order the same privileges for Cyprus that it had held in Latin Syria. The Templars now held extensive estates throughout Cyprus—especially near Lemesos, but also estates with fortresses at Gastria, Kolossi, Yermasoyia, and Khirokitia. Boniface admired their participation in the defence of Acre, and urged the King of Cyprus to treat them with favour in view of their great sufferings for the Holy Land. A second bull asked Edward I to allow the Templars to export supplies needed in Cyprus.[98]

But these were at best palliative measures. With the loss of Acre the Templars had lost their power and role in the East. The glory of Acre added lustre to their tarnished reputation, but it was too late to save the Order. In view of their role in the military operations of the previous century the judgement of the French biographer of Philippe Le Bel that the Templars were 'more heroic than efficacious, courageous but undisciplined',[99] seems fair. La Monte echoes this sentiment, and also emphasizes the ironical fact that much of the glory later attributed to the Templars derived from this last great defeat when he states that the 'magnificent but futile heroism of the Templars in the last desperate stand at Acre in 1291 has always remained a monument to the glory and valor of the Order'.[100] In the light of their real military achievement, with the flattery of literature and gloss of legend cast aside, the Templars must be judged as having failed.

8

CRITICISM AND DECLINE

THE original motivation of Hugues de Payen sustained the Order of the Temple for a relatively short time. An internal metamorphosis was imposed by the Order's unexpected and overwhelming success, ever-increasing momentum, and papal privileges, and it was perhaps even transmuted into a different kind of order against the will of its founders. It may be that rapid institutionalization was sufficient in itself to modify the original concept beyond recognition.

The privileges and independence from local ecclesiastical authorities resulting from the bull *Omne Datum Optimum* seem to have caused initial resentment against the Order. As early as 1154 the Patriarch of Jerusalem complained about the abuse of privileges by the Templars, who in response shot arrows at his door. This and other similar manifestations of arrogance clearly conditioned the attitude of the Templars' most vociferous opponent in the twelfth century, William of Tyre, whose view probably represents the feeling of the clergy as a whole in the Holy Land. It is worth noting that he recognized the shift away from the original concept, implying that he approved of the Order as it had been originally conceived but not as it had become in his own lifetime:

For a long time they kept intact their noble purpose and carried out their profession wisely enough. At length, however, they began to neglect 'humility, the guardian of all the virtues, which, voluntarily sitting in the lowest place, runs no risk of a fall'. They withdrew from the patriarch of Jerusalem, from whom they had received the establishment of their order and their first privileges, and refused him the obedience which their predecessors had shown him. To the churches of God also they became very troublesome, for they drew away from their tithes and first fruits and unjustly disturbed their possessions.[1]

In this passage, relatively free of vituperation, his account fits the facts remarkably well.

William of Tyre was not alone in his feelings about the Templars, although he is the only person to stress the change in their character. They never endeared themselves to the local hierarchy, whether secular or ecclesiastical, in the Holy Land—although at the time of foundation the Patriarch had probably perceived the Order as providing support for his own position.[2] In 1160 Pope Alexander III issued a bull restraining people from pulling Templars from their horses, treating them dishonestly, or abusing them.[3] This suggests that popular feeling matched ecclesiastical disdain. Amalric I was constantly in conflict with the Templars: we have seen that in 1166 he executed twelve knights for treachery, and in 1174 he considered expelling the Order from the Holy Land after the murder of Ismaili ambassadors who had been sent to him.[4] Five years later abuses of their privileges were discussed at the Third Lateran Council, where William of Tyre voiced the concerns of the clergy in the East in his diatribe against the Order.

A more surprising and prophetic early criticism came from the pen of the Cistercian Abbot Isaac of Étoile, who writes of:

this dreadful new military order that someone has rather pleasantly called the order of the fifth gospel was founded for the purpose of forcing infidels to accept the faith at the point of the sword. Its members consider that they have every right to attack anyone not confessing Christ's name, leaving him destitute, whereas if they themselves are killed while thus unjustly attacking the pagans, they are called martyrs for the faith . . . We do not maintain that all they do is wrong, but we do insist that what they are doing can be an occasion for future evils.[5]

Thus from the earliest years of the Templars' existence, at least from the dramatic change in the character of the Order that occurred in the 1130s, regular and powerful criticism was launched against them. The history of the Templars can be viewed in terms of the mounting vehemence and authority of these criticisms, culminating in the series of trials which led to their suppression. The trials were by no means a bolt from the blue, but an inevitable consequence of two centuries of criticism. Yet, on the other hand, as Edward J. Martin wrote in his study of the trial, 'no body of men could have supported these privileges without unpopularity . . .'.[6]

Towards the end of the twelfth century the criticism was

concentrated on the two cardinal sins of pride and avarice. Pope Innocent III in a letter of 13 September 1207 formally condemned the pride of the Templars. [7] Later the chronicler Matthew Paris constantly referred to problems caused by the overbearing pride of the Order, [8] and when Richard of Cornwall recaptured Ascalon in 1242 the fortress was deliberately not given to the Order because of their excessive pride. [9]

Similarly, after humbly functioning as guardians of the pilgrim routes in the Holy Land, the Templars quickly became a byword for avarice. We have seen William of Tyre's criticism for the behaviour at the siege of Ascalon of the Grand Master Bernard de Tremelay, who allowed only his own men to enter a breach in order 'to obtain the greater and richer portion of the spoils and plunder'. It seems that the extensive tax exemptions and privileges were not sufficient for the Order, and that they became more avaricious as their wealth increased. It is ironic that they should so quickly have reached a status which so blatantly contradicted the precepts of St Bernard, and criticisms of their avarice gained added point from the development of movements of voluntary poverty at the beginning of the thirteenth century. Innocent III berated them for their avarice a year after he had issued the papal bull which effectively founded the Mendicant Orders.

Papal Criticism

As papal bankers and as a religious order subordinate to the Pope, the Templars were protected against direct papal criticism—especially during the pontificate of Eugenius III, ex-monk at Clairvaux. Yet some popes, such as Innocent III, were ready to attack the Order when necessary whilst at the same time using their services for the transport of funds to the Holy Land. Already at the 1179 Lateran Council, during the pontificate of Alexander III, the Order had been severely censured, presumably with the tacit consent of the pope. As the result of the attack against the Templars led by William of Tyre, they were formally accused of weakening episcopal authority by encouraging brothers to enjoy privileges to which they were not entitled: burying the excommunicated and improperly admitting them to the sacraments of the church, collecting alms in churches more than the once a year consented, and improperly receiving churches from lay persons. [11]

The privileges repeatedly granted to the Templars with the bull *Omne Datum Optimum* led to further papal rebukes, especially the right to grant burial within their own cemeteries beyond diocesan control. As early as 1144, an instance of this abuse occurred at the London Temple: Geoffroi de Mandeville, the Count of Essex, who had been excommunicated, was received into the Order on his deathbed and then buried in the cemetery of the Old Temple. While this apparently obeyed the commandment of the controversial second paragraph of the Templar Rule, it antagonized the bishops. In 1175 Pope Alexander III issued a strong statement against the burial of excommunicated persons in the cemeteries of the Templars and Hospitallers in England.[12]

The most severe attack against the Templars was that launched by Innocent III in 1207 and then continued by his successor Honorius III—although both relied upon the services of the Order when necessary. In his violent denunciation of Templar practices, Innocent again stressed the controversial burial of excommunicated bodies in their cemeteries, and the title given to the bull by scribes, 'On Templar Pride',* suggests the general tone of its content. According to Innocent it was inordinate pride which led them to abuse the privileges granted to them by his predecessors. But their recruitment policies also came under fire: anyone prepared to pay two or three pence (denarii) a year could be admitted to the Order, and could thus buy himself a guarantee against burial as an excommunicate. He also accused them of lack of respect for papal legates, apostasy from God, and scandalizing the Church. Apart from excommunicates, he argued, usurers and adulterers were also buried in Templar cemeteries.[13] This was indeed a violent denunciation from a man who only nine years earlier had written of the Templars as 'our dearly beloved brothers . . .'. In suggesting that the Templars yielded to the doctrine of demons in giving their cross to anybody, Innocent's bull provided the basis for many of the accusations levelled against them a hundred years later.[14]

Popular feeling against the abuses of the Templars increased throughout the thirteenth century, to the extent that Clement IV (1265-8) again reprimanded them and suggested that they display greater humility and mildness. Etienne de Sissi, Marshal of the Order, had been excommunicated and only after a lengthy controversy was the excommunication rescinded: in a letter announcing his decision, Clement reminded the Templars that they were dependent upon the papacy,

* De Insolentia Templariorum.

and that without papal support they would have no defence against the hostility of bishops and secular princes. He accused them of mendacity, of recruiting brothers and serving brothers for money, and criticized them for the possession of their immense fortune and their pride.[15] Shortly after this Gregory X (1271–6) accused the Master Thomas Berard of unspecified depravations.[16] Financial gain and usury seem to have occupied an ever more prominent part of Templar policy during the thirteenth century. In Aragon, they granted rights and revenues to both individuals and communities, therefore passing on rights which they themselves had received in donation for other motives. This was the cause of a later, forceful criticism by Boniface VIII in 1297: 'It has come to our hearing that not only the beloved sons the preceptor and brothers of the house of the Temple of Jerusalem in Aragon and Catalonia but also their predecessors have granted tithes, lands, houses, meadows, pastures, woods, mills, rights, jurisdictions and certain other goods of that house . . . to the grave harm of the same house . . .'[17] What was perceived by Boniface as 'grave harm' was clearly considered beneficial by the Templars themselves.

These few examples will suffice to illustrate that the Templars had frequently come under fire from successive popes for their policies and activities. It was not in the last few years of their existence, after the fall of Acre, that the Roman hierarchy suddenly became aware of their vices and faults. Within a generation of the death of their spiritual patron, St Bernard, they were already drawing frequent censure, which increased in direct proportion to their power and wealth, regardless of success or failure in the Holy Land.

Weakness, Failure, and Treachery

Other factors that contributed to the eventual downfall of the Templars also made their appearance early in the Order's history. Certain defects built into its recruitment procedures and administrative methods appear to have had more important consequences as the Order matured and expanded through two centuries. The Templars from the beginning tended to attract and recruit knights from the minor nobility, often poor knights or second sons who could not afford to pay their own crusading expenses. The consequence of this policy was a mediocrity which has often been noted by historians of the Order. Knights were usually illiterate or semi-literate, and it would indeed hardly be expected that literacy should play an important part in the everyday life of the Order. Forey provides a list of books in an inventory of possessions at the Templar house of Corbins in 1229, a list which may have been fairly typical. Perhaps more convincing than the number of volumes is the content and proportion: of sixteen volumes, twelve were religious service books, two were books of sermons, and two were lives of the saints. [18] This reflects the monastic status of the Templars, and suggests that it was the clergy within the Order who were most literate. It must also be remembered, however, as we have seen, that in the East many Templars were conversant in Arabic and acted as ambassadors and interpreters; similarly, the financial experts, originators of Templar accounting methods, must have attained a certain degree of literacy. Yet the clergy, interpreters, and accountants were a tiny minority. Unfortunately, the surviving documents do not permit us to form a clearer picture of Templar activities, but if the serving brothers and entire staff of Templar houses are included, it would appear likely that the level of literacy was low. Their lack of understanding of the political situation, and consequent inability to defuse criticism and thus forestall their impending doom, are amongst the strongest condemnations that can be made of the Order's hierarchy.

A second weakening factor derived from the administrative organization of the Order—paradoxically that same international structure which had made it wealthy and powerful. Central administration was carried out by chapters-general held in Jerusalem, where the most important business was discussed; in individual houses the local commander was responsible for the organization of weekly chapters in which local business was discussed and decisions made. Such an organization sounds excellent in theory, but was severely weakened by frequent changes in personnel: a policy of rotation of senior members of the Order hindered efficient administration by not allowing them to remain in a single preceptory or *domus* long enough to understand the local situation. There are many cases where the local administration must have been carried out by completely unprepared serving brothers, perhaps for a considerable length of time. [19] As the Order became less and less a knightly order, this weakness was aggravated, and it is likely that the fullest possible benefits were not derived from the Order's vast possessions.

These administrative weaknesses were also exacerbated by the negative political and propagandistic effects of frequent military failure. In the survey of military activities in the Holy Land we have noted several defeats with heavy human losses: it is sufficient to recall the disaster at Ascalon in 1244, when only five Templars survived from a force of 290. The Templars were not successful militarily: even their acclaimed—and nostalgically recalled—heroism derived from desperate resistance in defeat. But with the resources and privileges at their command, it might reasonably have been expected that they would attain greater military success. Failure generated administrative instability, which in turn contributed negatively to the Order's military organization and preparation for campaigns in the Holy Land. It was a vicious circle that drew ever tighter; behind the façade of strength was an incurable tendency to ineptitude which derived from the paradox inherent in the ideology behind the Order and the dramatic difference between the Templars in the West and the Templars in the East.

Such problems were perhaps the real cause of numerous instances of apparent treachery to the crusading ideal, synthesized in accusations of selfish conduct or cowardice. Matthew Paris voiced this feeling when he wrote of the underachievement of the Templars, after commenting on the Order's great wealth and its theoretical capacity to equip thousands of soldiers:

Whence the Christians, reflecting on these things, always suppose them to conceal some fraud, and that they may have some wolfish treacheries under a sheep's clothing. For if there had not been treachery and fraud, so many brave western knights might forcibly have penetrated the array of all the orientals, and put them to utter rout. [20]

Unwittingly, he puts his finger on the basic debilitating flaw which underlies the Templar ideology when put into practice.

The taint of treachery never dissipated; if anything it increased towards the end of the Templars' military career. The *Bury St Edmunds Chronicle* offers two interesting contemporary criticisms of presumed Templar treachery. The first example occurs under the *Chronicle* entry for 1270:

On the vigil and on the day of Palm Sunday the Christians and the infidels met in battle between Acre and Safed. First eight emirs and eighteen columns of infidels were killed, then eventually the infidels were victorious, but not without very great loss of men. The Christian army was nearly wiped out because of the sedition of the Templars. [21]

This account refers to the taking of the Templar fortress of Safed by Baybars during his 1266 campaign. Baybars first besieged the castle, but was beaten back three times during the course of July that year. He then offered an amnesty to the native Christians who formed an important part of the garrison; some accepted—although the Templars themselves were suspicious of his offer. It seems that the Templars were in this case betrayed by a Syrian called Leo whom they charged to negotiate with Baybars: he returned with the promise that the besieged garrison would be allowed to retreat safely to Acre, but once they had left the safety of the castle they were captured by Baybars and decapitated to a man. [22] Thus the accusation of the *Chronicle* appears to be unjustified by the facts, but what is more interesting in this case is the perception of events in the Holy Land from the abbey at Bury. Whatever the truth may have been in the distant Holy Land, the Templars were already largely discredited even within the Church.

Another, perhaps equally unfounded, example concerns King Hugh III of Cyprus (1267–84). The *Chronicle* states quites simply that: 'Hugh of Lusignan, King of Cyprus, his son and others of his household were killed by poison by the knights of the Temple.' [23] The modern editor of the *Chronicle* observes that there is in fact no evidence that such a murder actually occurred, and that the case can be explained by the close alliance between the Templars and Charles of Anjou. The then Master, Guillaume de Beaujeu, was following a long-term policy of crushing Hugh with the aim of placing the crown of Jerusalem on Charles. This contrast shows the Templars in a different, less altruistic and more political light. They were closely involved in the long power struggle which allowed what was left of the Kingdom of Jerusalem* to fall apart. Hugh confiscated Templar property in Cyprus in revenge for their manoeuvring against him, and might have been able to recapture Tyre in 1279 if the forces of Acre and the Templars had backed his efforts. He rightly held the Templars responsible for his failure, and the idea that they may have murdered him is at least plausible. [24] Yet again what is most interesting is the fact that from the perspective of Bury St Edmunds the Templars were judged to have been responsible. No value judgement is made, and no particular bias is shown. The

---

* This title was still used even though from 1191 the 'capital' of the Christian possessions in Latin Syria was Acre.

Chronicle simply states as a matter of fact that the Templars murdered Hugh.

Examples adduced in previous chapters corroborate the validity of the Bury perception. There seems to be little doubt that the Templars often acted against the interests of Christendom and the Kingdom of Jerusalem—whether for booty, as at Ascalon, for political advantage, as on Cyprus, or as the result of the rivalry with the Hospitallers that we shall shortly review. Even at the end of their career, the taint remained. Jean Favier comments that at the fall of Acre, 'despite all the knights who died . . . some people spoke of the 'treason' of the Templars'.[25] This suspicion of treason appeared early in the Order's history, and was never fully allayed. On many occasions the Templars were condemned by their arrogance and pride, and these condemnations in turn stimulated their enemies and pushed critics towards attributing failure to them.

Natural Decline of the Crusading Ideal

Yet the Order of the Temple was perhaps necessarily doomed to ultimate failure and suppression, irrespective of the merits of its knights in battle. As the concept of crusade, and the crusading ideal, diminished with the gradual decline of the Latin Kingdom itself, so their *raison d'être* disappeared. It is possible to interpret their decline in the closing years of the thirteenth century as an inevitable consequence of the fading of the crusading ideal. We shall see that the other military orders were ready to adapt to changing circumstances and thereby avoided the fate of the Templars. Favier has commented that the 'Temple perished for having forgotten Jerusalem',[26] but such a judgement presupposes a continuity of crusading purpose which in fact did not exist. Whatever their shortcomings, the Templars were not solely responsible for the loss of Jerusalem and its Kingdom; neither did the Order perish as the result of their having neglected that city. The reason for the inevitability of their decline must be sought in events which were beyond their control.

Maureen Purcell has shown in a fascinating article how the idea of crusade produced a certain frame of mind—exemplified by the 1130s Templar ideology—which outlasted the ideal itself. She finds the roots of change at the battle of Hattin:

As a *vital* idea crusade suffered an immense setback on the fields of Hattin, but no longer vital it survived until the fall of Acre when it rapidly became either merely an ideal stamping ground for political theorists, or a conveniently distractive appellation for the interested policies of cynical politicians.[27]

If she is right, then it was the inability—as a result of the essential mediocrity of Templar leadership—to develop a new role or establish a powerful political base in Western Europe which was the real cause of the downfall of the Templars.

The initial crusades took place within a firmly determined worldview with short-term Christian objectives: the First and Second Crusades were ventures which harmonized a dualism between this immediate objective and longer-term views of the Christian economy of salvation. As the quintessence of the crusading ideal, we might add to Purcell's observations that the Templars exemplified the harmony and accommodation of these views. But after the loss of Jerusalem the crusading ideal, and the accompanying crusading indulgences, were rapidly over-exploited and this harmony was destroyed. Crusade became a tool of political expediency in the hands of successive popes, who fell prey to the attractive idea of what Purcell describes as 'geographical diversions'; these diversions departed radically from the original idea of crusade as an expression of Christian unity against the Syrian Moslems. At first crusade was adopted in *defence of Christian unity* (against Slavs and Tartars); then it was used *against heretics* within Christendom (the Cathars or Albigensians); finally, it was used blatantly against the *enemies of the papacy* or of a single pope (against Frederick II, for example). The *reductio ad absurdum* of this process of degeneration was Boniface VIII's idea of a crusade against the aristocratic Colonna family in Rome, which continually opposed his authority.[28]

The ideal of harmonizing mysticism and militarism, evoked and superbly justified by the knightly monk St Bernard, became impossible to sustain: such a notion of crusade was rendered obsolete by Hattin. Thenceforth the remnants of the once great crusading kingdom were continuously fighting for survival with no sustaining ethos. The practical resolution of the paradox implicit in the concept of the warrior monk was no longer feasible while Jerusalem as the symbolic goal of a pilgrimage to eternity was overshadowed by the desire for financial and military possession of the physical entity named Jerusalem. The Templars' role was also rendered obsolete. In the same period that saw crusade reduced to a matter of political expediency in Western Europe, in the East 'mystical notion reduced it to military impracticality'.[29]

We shall see how the weakness, indecision and lack of future vision of the Templar leadership prevented the Order from changing its structure and role before it was too late. But it already seems clear that their role as conceived by Hugues de Payen and St Bernard was literally out of date by the beginning of the thirteenth century. It was only a kind of historical momentum deriving from the immense power, wealth, and prestige of the Templars, and a desperate clinging to the vestiges of the crusading ideal, which enabled them to survive up to and beyond the fall of Acre in 1291.

THE RECOVERY OF JERUSALEM AND PROPOSED UNION

ONCE their underlying *raison d'être* had lost the vital thrust of its meaning, the objective of the Templars, together with the other crusading orders, the papacy, and European kings, became the *recovery* of the Kingdom of Jerusalem. This idea increased in importance until it became one of the principal obsessions of Western Europe; the idea of the recovery of Jerusalem took root and persisted in the minds of nobles and clergy alike. It was the increasing difficulty of the enterprise, from both a military and a financial point of view, which led to the corollary notion of a union of the military orders: with their combined experience, wealth, and military strength, it was reasoned, the business of recovering the Holy land would be much easier. Thus from about 1248, when St Louis of France suggested the union of the Templars and the Hospitallers, union gradually became perceived as a *necessary precondition* for the recovery of Jerusalem. In a sense, the independent existence of both orders was doomed from that moment, and with hindsight it might be argued that only the order with astute leadership had any chance of survival.

At least in part, the idea of uniting the two main crusading orders derived from the continuous rivalry and bickering between them. Riley-Smith cites eight cases of serious disputes up to 1291. They range from a dispute over the crusader states' policy towards neighbouring Moslem states in 1168, and cases in which the orders took opposite sides in baronial contentions within the Holy Land, to minor arguments over water rights, bread ovens, and land ownership.[1] Internecine feuds which seriously debilitated Christian forces often found the Temple and the Hospital on opposite sides. One such feud concerned Gastin. This territory in the Principality of Antioch was taken from the Templars by Saladin and then passed into the control of Leo of Armenia. The

Templars tried to reclaim their lost lands from Leo and thereby instigated a long and complex disagreement in which Bohemond of Antioch supported them against the combined forces of Leo and the Hospitallers.[2] An even more serious feud was that which resulted in the deaths of 20,000 men at Acre in 1257 and destroyed the commerce of Acre and Tyre: in this case, the forces involved were far larger, with the Templars, Teutonic Knights, Venice, and Pisa marshalled against the Hospitallers, Genoa, and Barcelona.[3]

One of the few successful attempts at reconquest was made by Richard of Cornwall, brother of Henry III, who arrived at Acre in October 1240 and immediately tried to placate the almost open warfare between Temple and Hospital. With great tact and careful negotiation he managed to restore order to the remaining Christian territories and establish good diplomatic relations with the Sultan Ayub. But as soon as he departed, in May 1241, the Templars refused to accept the terms of Richard's treaty with Ayub and attacked the Moslem cities of Hebron and Nablus. A state of virtual civil war ensued, with Templar and Hospitaller knights openly fighting in the streets. In the following year the Templars went so far as to besiege the Hospital compound in Acre. Thus the conciliatory efforts of Richard of Cornwall risked annihilation in what Grousset described as an act of 'criminal folly'.[4]

Union of the Military Orders

These constant feuds, the stalemate in the East, and the criticisms of the Templars listed in the previous chapter must have been present in the minds of delegates to the 1274 Council of Lyons. Pope Gregory X, who was elected to the Holy See in 1271 while in the Holy Land with Henry III's son Edward, maintained his interest in the crusades when he returned to Rome. He appealed for knights to take the cross, and compiled a dossier of reports on the situation in the Holy Land. The lack of enthusiasm for crusades, the corruption of the Church and military orders, and the disappearance of the custom of making penance by going on crusade to the East, were all stressed in these reports. More interesting, from the point of view of a history of the Templars, is the threatening suggestion that there should be a permanent standing army of crusaders.[5] When the dossier was completed, Pope Gregory summoned a General Council of the Church which opened in May 1274 at Lyons. Although the kings of France and England were not present, there were the cardinals and five hundred bishops, the patriarchs of the Eastern Church, and delegates from the military Orders. Guillaume de Beaujeu, who had been elected Grand Master of the Templars a year earlier, represented his order. Two other figures of considerable importance for the immediate future of the Templars were also present: Fidenzio of Padua, the Franciscan Provincial Vicar in the Holy Land, and Girolamo Masci, Gregory's Apostolic Legate in the East. The ideas that these men may have heard for the first time at the Council of Lyons were to have far-reaching consequences.

The man who had such an impact was Raymond Lull (1232–1315). A Spanish knight converted to preacher, a mystic, and the future author of a famous work on chivalry, Lull understood the Moslems and their language. He was also a persuasive thinker and speaker and consistently pursued his idea of converting the Moslems to Christianity by a combination of arms and well-prepared preachers. His ideas were seminal in the later history of the crusades, while in grammar and philosophy his influence endured for centuries.* At the Council of Lyons he made his first mark as principal advocate for union of the military orders. [6] He seems to have convinced Gregory X himself, and Charles II of Anjou, King of Naples and Sicily, in addition to Fidenzio of Padua and Gregory's apostolic legate. At that time there was no practical follow-up, and when Gregory X died in 1276 nothing had been done towards putting Raymond Lull's explicit advocation of union into practice. But the idea had been sown well, and would flourish.

The next twelve years saw a succession of six short-lived popes who never had time to apply themselves seriously to the problems of the Holy Land. But when on 15 February 1288 Girolamo Masci, from Ascoli, was elected to the Holy See as Nicholas IV, his first thoughts concerned the Holy Land, where much of his career had been spent. One of his first actions was to revive the idea of a union of the military orders, and in 1291 the first important text arguing the case was published at his instigation: the *Liber Recuperatione Terrae Sanctae*† of his one-time colleague Fidenzio of Padua. Whatever the initial reception of

---

* As late as the seventeenth century, Leibniz's *Dissertation on the Art of Combination* was written with the same purpose as Lull's *Ars generalis*, which attempted to evolve a method of making the faith intelligible to unbelievers.
† 'On the Recovery of the Holy Land'.

this work had been, the news which came soon afterwards from Acre increased the urgency of Fidenzio's appeal. The next decade saw a proliferation of books advocating union, with titles echoing that of the work of Fidenzio. After the fall of Acre, the combined military strength of the crusading orders under a single leader was considered by many writers—and by Pope Nicholas himself—to be the only means by which the Christians could recover Jerusalem.

Union was no longer an abstract idea, but a desperate need. In 1292 the Council of Salzburg approved the union, although nothing came of this decision. The following year, Nicholas IV wrote letters to the kings and princes of Christendom for consultations concerning union.[7] But in April 1292 Nicholas died. Without his enthusiasm the idea languished: a break of twelve years had preceded the election of a pope who had experience of the East and a personal interest in union. Now, after the brief pontificate of Celestine V, the papacy was controlled for nine years, from 1294 to 1304, by Boniface VIII, a lawyer-pope whose main concern was the completion of Church law and the consolidation of papal power against the great secular lords of Europe—especially Philip the Fair of France. The preoccupation with crusade diminished during his pontificate, and interest in union also faded after Lull's *Petitio pro recuperatione Terrae Sanctae* of 1294 and Galvano de Levanti's *Liber sancti Passagii Christicolarum contra Saracenos pro recuperatione Terra Sanctae* of 1295. This latter volume, prophetically, since it pointed already towards Philip as the potential single leader, was dedicated to the French king.[8] As if unaware of the process behind the scenes, and of the fact that the idea of union was slowly gathering force and only lacked papal support, Jacques de Molay travelled through Europe trying to make up the losses sustained at Acre. The meagre nature of the concessions he obtained, cited in Chapter 7, vividly underlines the Templars' reduced circumstances.* In Europe there was little interest in crusades, despite the enthusiasm of Raymond Lull.

Attention, and diplomatic energy, in Europe were at that time concentrated on the running battle between Philip the Fair of France and the papacy. This had included the celebrated and scandalous attack

---

* Another minor instance of the concessions is the 1295 order of Charles II of Naples, which exempted grain exported to Cyprus by the Knights Templar from the 'jus exiturae' (Yver, *Le Commerce et Les Marchands*, p. 118).

against Boniface VIII at the Pope's summer residence in Anagni, his home town south of Rome. French power was absolute in Europe and in 1305 Philip at last succeeded in electing a Frenchman to the Holy See. Bertrand de Got, from Bordeaux, who took the name Clement V, never went to Rome, but after a vagrant period spent mainly in and near Poitiers established his papacy at Avignon, conveniently in Provence and thus technically outside the territory of France. But there was little doubt that he was a puppet of the French king, and it may be for this reason that he was far more interested in the idea of a crusade than Boniface had been. With his pontificate, the last, and fatal, phase of the idea of union began. The first two years of his rule saw the publication of the two most influential pamphlets on union, Lull's *Liber de Fine* (1305) and Pierre Dubois' *De Recuperatione Terrae Sanctae* (*c*.1305–7).

It was from 1305 that the idea of a new crusade, with Philip or one of his sons as the head of a united crusading order, was propounded with a frequency that Philip himself could not ignore. In Part 2 of the *Liber de Fine*, entitled *De modo bellandi*, Lull argued that the leader of the crusade he is proposing should be a man of royal blood and his successors the sons of kings. All the military orders were to be united under the command of this king, whose title was *dominus bellator rex* or 'warlike king'. Lull spent some years at or near Philip's court, seeking to spread his ideas concerning the recovery of the Holy Land and in fact wrote another book to that purpose, the *Liber de Acquisitione Terrae Sanctae*, in 1309. The attractions to Philip of presenting himself or one of his sons as the *bellator rex* are obvious, as such a status would further his attempt to create a Capetian hegemony over both the Church and Christian Europe. But his most pressing problem was lack of funds for such an enterprise, and it was Pierre Dubois who suggested a potential source of cash for the project.

Dubois was a Norman lawyer and publicist who specialized in writing propaganda in favour of the French monarchy. He seems to have written in order to flatter Philip for personal gain, which may not have been important were it not for his continued polemical stance against the Templars—whom he attacked in three separate pamphlets. It has been said of him that he did much 'to make familiar the idea of abolition of the order and confiscation of its property' from about 1300.[9] His *De Recuperatione* was a long, closely argued pamphlet which from hints and explicit ideas sprinkled throughout the text builds up to a declaration of the value of suppressing the Order of the Temple. The first condition for success in any attempt at recovering the Holy Land was obviously peace in western Christendom, he argues, a position clearly held in support of Philip as the man who should create such peace. He recognizes the need for large cash subsidies, and in paragraph 14 states where they could be obtained: if the properties of the Hospitallers and the Templars—which he describes as 'divided and confused'—were to be united, it would be possible to raise the necessary cash. [10] Paragraph 37 insists on the need for reform of the present situation, while paragraph 60 elaborates a project to create schools for interpreters in Templar and Hospitaller priories in the East. [11] A more clearly anti-Templar measure appears in paragraph 107, where he suggests a common treasury of the Holy Land to be held in the cathedral of each diocese—usurping the Templars' traditional role as bankers to the crusades.

But it is in the *Appendix,* which its modern editor Langlois believes may have been written slightly later, that the nature of his suggestions is made clear. In paragraph 3 of the *Appendix,* he advocates a single military order under the direction of the King of Cyprus; but what is more remarkable is the fact that he specifically excludes the Templars from this order (*exceptus Templariis*). [12] Finally, in paragraph 5, he explicitly mentions the suppression of the Order: 'It was decided with the approval of the council that the Order of the Templars was to be abolished, and that according to justice it be totally annulled, and it was decided to order as mentioned above that their wealth be used towards a general crusade.' [13] *

This statement, made to measure for the consumption of Philip the Fair, climaxes a series of ideas, projects, and pamphlets concerning the recovery of Jerusalem. No one had yet attempted to put the actions recommended into practice, but this 'decision'—and its authoritative backing—was too good to pass over. Once Philip perceived himself in the role of *bellator rex* the next step was logical enough. Hillgarth has commented: 'If one looks at the events of 1305–12 as a whole

* 'Ordinem vero Templariorum cum consilio concilii modis omnibus expedit demoliri, et exigente justicia totaliter adnullari, er sicut predictum est de bonis eorum usque as generale passagium ordinare.'

it is clear that, if one necessary preliminary to a general crusade, in the eyes of Philippe IV, was the capture of Constantinople by a French prince, the second, equally essential, was the destruction of the Temple.'[14]

The Grand Master's Defence

The Grand Masters of the Temple and Hospital were summoned to appear before Pope Clement V at Poitiers on 6 June 1306. They were to give him advice on sending aid to the kings of Armenia and Cyprus, and to discuss the recently propounded idea of union.[15] Jacques de Molay produced two separate memoirs for presentation to the Pope on this occasion: the first concerned the organization of crusades and consisted of an attempt to persuade the Pope to preach a general crusade; the second memoir concerned the mooted union of the two main crusading orders and attacks the idea with all the arguments and authority which de Molay could muster.

This latter memoir, entitled *De Unione Templi et Hospitalis Ordinum ad Clementem Papam Jacobi de Molayo Relatio*, begins with a history of the idea of union since the 1274 Council of Lyons. After this introductory passage he sets out the case for and against the proposed union—with a clear bias against. As Grand Master he refers to the traditions of the Templars, asserting that 'it would not be honourable to unite such ancient orders' (*antiquas religiones*).[16] But he implicitly acknowledges discord between the orders when he argues that it would be unwise to unite them because members of the original orders would be instigated by the devil to quarrel. That would be dangerous since they would be armed.[17] Further discord would result from the suppression of certain preceptories in favour of others, while he also doubted that union would effectively increase their combined power. As far as charitable services are concerned, such as alms and the provision of food for the poor,* he believes they would be considerably diminished.[18]

Yet some of his arguments are very weak—as if he had not thought seriously about the matter or was incapable of understanding the full implications of the situation. For instance, he observes that both the Temple and the Hospital have a marshal, a commander, and a drapier,

---

* It is interesting, and contrary both to popular belief and evidence at the trial, that de Molay states that all Templar houses provided general alms three times weekly to whoever asked, and gave a tenth of their bread to the poor.

and that in the event of union this would create conflicts and rivalry because each of these men would wish to maintain his role.[19] In such comments, as Barber has observed, he 'showed only the faintest sense that the Templars might be vulnerable'.[20] The whole business seems impossible to the Grand Master: he argues that rivalry between the existing orders is a good thing, and had always been to the advantage of the Christians and against that of the Moslems. Apart from the obvious ingenuity of this claim, there is something pathetic in the assertion that while the Hospitallers went on an expedition, the Templars had been able to rest.[21] That would be a matter of military organization, and has little to do with the number of orders. His comparison with the rivalry between Dominicans and Franciscans, and its consequences for the good of the Christian people, is clever but largely irrelevant.[22] Interestingly, however, de Molay also refers to pilgrims in this context, suggesting that the original purpose of the Templars had not been completely forgotten. Pilgrims, he argues, whether greater or common men, always find lodgings and refreshment with one of the two orders; perhaps—and here he is evidently on very weak ground—a single order would not be able to provide such a thorough service.[23]

Once he has set out in separate paragraphs what he takes to be the main disadvantages of union, the Grand Master goes on to make a short and unconvincing statement of what he sees as the main advantages. If the previous section was lacking in conviction, the casuistry of these arguments is blatant. It is clear that Jacques de Molay is arguing against the grain, notwithstanding his attempt to present what appears to be a balanced argument. Yet even he is forced to admit that union would lead to reductions in costs on the grounds of the reduced number of preceptories and houses that would need to be maintained both in Europe and in the East. He concludes his argument as follows: 'Whence, Holy Father, are displayed the advantages and the drawbacks, the honour and the dishonour or the dangers that I perceive and that I recognize in the aforesaid union.'[24] The bias is clear: the document contains 115 lines against union, while 19 lines contain the argument in favour.

The conclusion of the memoir contains a suggestion which demonstrates how distant the Grand Master is from taking the idea of union seriously. Far from expecting such a thing to take place, he seems to anticipate the announcement of a new crusade. He invites Clement V to come to the Templars whenever he requires advice on this matter, arguing that no cheaper way of financing a crusade existed than through the present military orders. His last, honest but hopelessly ingenuous, words were to the effect that if the Pope intended to assign fixed, perpetual, or annual revenues for the military orders it would be better to assign them separately to the Temple and the Hospital, because 'all the world strives to obtain its due even beyond its power'. [25] This final request, which appears pathetic in the light of what was about to happen to Jacques de Molay and his Order, contains the best evidence of his total inability to understand what was happening around him.

The Grand Master rejected the idea of union, and may have accelerated the process of suppression in doing so. The proposal had only been made explicit by Pierre Dubois after decades of preliminary moves by critics of the Templars; once Philip the Fair had espoused the cause there could have been little doubt concerning the outcome. The arrest of the Templars throughout France on 13 October 1307 is often presented as a surprise which no one in Christendom could possibly have foreseen, whereas in fact many signs pointed towards such an inevitable resolution at a single stroke of many of the problems of the French king. Philip had already brought the Church under his control, and could now aim at destroying one of its richest orders in order to relieve a severe shortage of cash. Perhaps a less short-sighted Master than Jacques de Molay would have recognized this and accepted diminished power within a united military order. In the light of Philip the Fair's attacks and confiscations against Church, Jews, and Lombards, it is difficult to argue that this violent attempt at quick suppression was a surprise. 'All the world knew', says Jean Favier. [26] Except, evidently, Jacques de Molay.

But even if financial arguments and these considerations made with the benefit of hindsight are dismissed, there exists contemporary evidence which explains in a new and altogether more satisfactory way the decision to suppress the Order of the Temple. Hillgarth has shown how it may have been Jacques de Molay's *refusal to accept the idea of union* which brought about the downfall of the Order. He supports this hypothesis with a letter written by Christian Spinola of Genoa to James II of Aragon on 2 November 1307:

I understand, however, that the pope and king [of France] are doing this for the money [of the Temple], and because they wish to make of the Hospital, the Temple, and all other military orders one united Order, of which the King wishes and intends to make one of his sons the King. The Temple, however, stood out strongly against these [proposals] and would not consent to them. [27]

Hillgarth's hypothesis is confirmed by two further sources, a cardinal speaking to envoys of James II and by Adam Murimuth's *Continuatio chronicarum*. [28]

The reasons for the arrest of the Templars in France, and later throughout Europe, are manifold and complex. But, as so many times in the past, the trigger may have been their own arrogance. After two centuries of virtually untrammelled privileges and power, the 'ancient order' and its sixty-year-old Grand Master were unable to adapt to the dramatically changed circumstances.

SUPPRESSION

THE real shock concerning the arrest of the Templars in France derived from the fact that a secular ruler had openly charged an Order directly responsible to the Pope with heresy, a crime which fell within the jurisdiction of the Church. The ecclesiastical tribunal known as the Inquisition, at that moment engaged in a battle against Cathars, Spiritual Franciscans, and other heretics in France and northern Italy, was the competent authority. Had there been strong suspicion of heresy within the Order of the Temple before the arrests were made, it should have been denounced to the Inquisition—which would then have carried out investigations and summoned the leaders of the Templars to appear before an inquisitor. In fact, in order to create a semblance of legality, Philip the Fair inserted into the Arrest Order of 14 September 1307 the statement that arrests were being made following the 'just request' of the Inquisitor-General, Guillaume de Paris. [1] * But there is no evidence of such a request having been made, and it was never mentioned again in the trial documents.

Philip had devoted nearly a decade towards bringing the Inquisition in France under his personal control. Furthermore, the inquisitor Guillaume de Paris had been the King's private confessor since the end of 1305. This close personal relationship, and Guillaume's dependence on the goodwill of the King to maintain his position of authority, would clearly encourage him to acquiesce in Philip's policy and allow

---

* The inquisition in France was then divided into eight provinces. Inquisitors in the Province of Paris, which included Rouen, Sens and Reims, were given the title *inquisiteurs in regno Franciae* or *inquisiteurs généraux de France* (J.-M. Vidal, *Bullaire de l'Inquisition Française au XIVe siècle*, Paris: Letouzey et Ané (1913), p. xxi).

his name to be used in the Arrest Order. It was not so much the power or efficiency of the Inquisition that Philip wished to utilize, but the legitimacy which would derive from making the arrests, however ambiguously, in the name of the competent tribunal. The techniques and methods used by the Inquisition were also of importance, and the paradoxical situation which saw one papal institution employed against another without permission or even the knowledge of the Pope—although these too were claimed in the Arrest Order—can be explained as follows: 'Novel forces were arrayed against the papacy when an advanced secular monarchy . . . made uninhibited use of inquisitorial techniques in order to gain the Templars' wealth.'[2] In terms of the history of the Inquisition, the Templar trials can be seen as one of a series of attempts by both secular and religious leaders to employ to their own advantage the notable success which the Inquisition had achieved in the seventy years since its establishment around 1233.

The key to understanding the thinking behind Philip the Fair's move is contained in the Arrest Order sent to royal seneschals three weeks before the arrests were to take place. The carefully calculated, high-flowing rhetoric of the opening passage, obviously designed to convince sceptical officers of the crown when they received this extraordinary order, is justly famous but nevertheless worth repeating:

A bitter thing, a lamentable thing, a thing horrible to think of and terrible to hear, a detestable crime, an execrable evil deed, an abominable work, a detestable disgrace, a thing wholly inhuman, foreign to all humanity, has, thanks to the reports of several persons worthy of faith, reached our ears, not without striking us with great astonishment and causing us to tremble with violent horror, and, as we consider its gravity an immense pain rises in us, all the more cruelly because there is no doubt that the enormity of the crime overflows to the point of being an offence to the divine majesty, a shame for humanity, a pernicious example of evil and a universal scandal.[3]

One may only imagine the effect of this vehement outburst on those who received the Arrest Order, and the astonishment with which they must have read the remaining pages. It goes on to describe the Templars as wolves in sheep's clothing who are guilty of 'astonishing bestiality' (*bestialitate transcendens*), 'supremely abominable crimes' (*scelerum summe nepharia*), and have had recourse to the sensuality of irrational beasts (*refugit ipsarum irrationabilium sensualitas bestiarum*).[4]

In the second paragraph of the order, the assertion that 'persons worthy of faith' were responsible for a report which led directly to the charges is repeated. We know that one of these trustworthy persons was an ambiguous Frenchman called Esquin de Floyran. Esquin had first attempted to convince King James II of Aragon that the Templars had committed certain horrific deeds. This failed because James II was unwilling to accept otherwise unfounded accusations against an Order which had always been loyal to him—unlike the more powerful French Templars in their relations with Philip the Fair. After this rejection in Aragon Esquin returned to France and, Norman Cohn suggests,[5] managed to convince Guillaume de Nogaret, a royal judge and fanatical anti-cleric who had proceeded against Boniface VIII on Philip's behalf a decade earlier. Nogaret, under an unrevoked ban of excommunication from Clement's predecessor Benedict XI (1303–4), was adept at employing such accusations of magical and heretical practices in order to attack the king's enemies. He had already used them against Boniface VIII, and was later to use them against Louis de Nevers, son of the Count of Flanders. Peter Partner has shown how quite suddenly 'around the year 1307, magical charges became one of the standard methods of aggression* among the jealous and competitive servants of King Philip the Fair.'[6]

In the context of manoeuvres towards abolishing the Order of the Temple and founding a new, united military order, the opportunity presented by Esquin's accusations was clearly too good to miss. But Jacques de Molay had also been informed of these charges against his Order and began to insist that there should be a papal inquiry into the accusations in order to clear the Templars' name. It was perhaps for this reason that Philip was forced to show his hand and prepare a pre-emptive strike. While Jacques de Molay and Clement V discussed the possibility of a crusade and also the idea of union at Poitiers, Philip was already planning to thwart any papal inquiry by arresting the Templars before it could take place. Cohn explains as follows: 'There was in Philip at least as much of the fanatic as of the cynic, and he

---

* Not only in France. The trial of Dame Alice Kyteler, at Kilkenny in Ireland in 1324, for diabolism, was a near contemporary example of such charges being used by a secular authority for political motives (cf. Kieckhefer, *European Witch Trials*, pp. 14, 111).

may well have persuaded himself that an organization which was capable of thwarting his aims was capable of any iniquity . . . he realized that a papal investigation, carried out while the Templars were still at liberty and able to conduct their defence, would be unlikely to result in the condemnation and suppression of the order.'[7]

Thus it may be seen that the report sent to Guillaume de Nogaret by the 'trustworthy' Esquin de Floyran acted as the catalyst which triggered the Arrest Order and provided Philip's lawyers with the excuse that they were acting upon reliable information. The appearance of legality was vital, although it clearly rested upon shaky foundations. In fact Esquin appears to have had mercenary motives: he later came into possession of some Templar land, and wrote to James II of Aragon in 1308 claiming 1,000 livres in rents and 3,000 livres in money from Templar property which had been promised to him in the event that his accusations proved to be correct. It is in this letter that he unequivocably asserts that 'I am the man who has shown the deeds of the Templars to the Lord King of France . . .'.[8]

Having thus justified the provenance of the information, the author of the Arrest Order seeks to legitimize its contents even further by referring to the supposed support of Clement V and Guillaume de Paris. On behalf of Philip the Fair, he claims that he had proceeded only 'after having spoken with our most Holy Father in the Lord, Clement' and then mentions an 'earlier inquiry' made by Guillaume de Paris—of which there is neither mention nor trace elsewhere.[9] Removing direct responsibility from the King, he states that it was only in 'acquiescing in the demands of the said inquisitor' that Philip decided upon the arrest of the Templar brothers in France. He reaches the triumphant conclusion that:

we have decreed that all the members of the said order within our realm will be arrested, without any exception, imprisoned and reserved for the judgement of the Church, and that all their moveable and unmoveable property will be seized, placed in our hands and faithfully preserved.[10]

The Arrest Order concludes with a detailed list of procedures to be used during the arrests. It is worth noting that these, unlike the main body of the order, are written in Old French; it seems that this description of the manner in which arrests should be made, together with a brief list of the charges which were to be made against the

Templars, was intended for the consumption of the King's own officers. In this case, the Latin text was for the clergy, higher ranking officers, and potential critics of the King's action. Briefly, royal officers were to use the month between receiving the Arrest Order and its implementation to make secret inquiries into Templar houses. They were to avoid arousing suspicion by making parallel, decoy inquiries into other religious houses at the same time.

In the light of the continuing argument concerning the use of torture to obtain confessions from the Templars, there is a further passage of the Arrest Order of particular interest. As soon as the seizures had been made the royal seneschals and bailiffs—together with auxiliary local forces which had assisted them—were 'to put the persons [i.e. arrested Templars] in isolation under a good and secure guard, make a preliminary inquiry about them, and then call the inquisitor's assistants and examine the truth with care, *using torture if necessary* . . .'[11] On 22 September 1307, a week after the Arrest Order was distributed throughout France, the Inquisitor-General had sent instructions to the inquisitors of Toulouse and Carcassonne to assist in the inquiry.[12] We can therefore see that careful arrangements to obtain confessions of the initial charges had been made even before the arrests were carried out.

It is also important to observe that the arrests occurred at the moment when flagrant and violent use of torture by the Inquisition reached its peak, with regular use of the rack, the pulley torture, the ordeal of water, and the ordeal of fire used to extract confessions at all cost. So much so that Pope John XXII was later forced to issue a decree limiting the use of torture, while the issue was already discussed in the same Church Council that abolished the Order of the Temple in 1312. The most notorious employers of torture were the inquisitors of southern France, where the Cathar threat which had led to the foundation of the Inquisition had been strongest. The famous Dominican inquisitor Bernard Gui in fact complained to John XXII that the proposed limitation of torture would cripple the efficiency of the tribunal.[13] In a sense the Templars were doomed from the moment of their arrest in France: the most powerful European monarch was to combine with the most ruthless and efficient of all tribunals against them, freely using torture to obtain the confessions which Philip the Fair needed to destroy them.

Very few of the Templars arrested were knights or even sergeants, and it is reasonable to assume that many of them did not possess either the will or the courage to endure torture. The 'Templars' interrogated by the Inquisition in Paris numbered 138, ranging in age from sixteen to eighty and including among them stewards, shepherds, agricultural labourers, and carpenters. Barber has provided an analysis of the roles of these 138 men: only fifteen were knights, seventeen were priests, and as many as forty-one were either sergeants or serving-brothers; the remainder were at the most serving brothers but often of even lower status. [14] The number of knights corresponds with our earlier estimates of the proportion of knights within the Order. Given the wide range of age, role, and literacy within this group of men, it is hardly surprising that their confessions constitute a mixture of ignorance, inconsistencies, contradictions, and sheer confusion. Using a well-proven technique, inquisitors guided their prey towards the required answers by means of carefully chosen questions derived from previous testimony and their own imagination.

Yet among the small body of fifteen knights were some of the most important officials of the Order at that time. It may well have been the unusual concentration of high-ranking Templars in Paris which encouraged Philip to move against them in such peremptory fashion. They included Jacques de Molay, Hugues de Pairaud, Visitor of France, Geoffroi de Charney, Preceptor of Normandy, and the Preceptors of Aquitaine, Reims, and Cyprus. Only twelve Templars then in France, including Gérard de Villiers, the Preceptor of France, managed to escape arrest.

The Role of Clement V

It seems likely that Philip the Fair's hope was to deal an irreversible blow to the Templars and bring about the suppression of the Order as soon as possible. But he reckoned without the stalling power of Clement V, whose authority he required to render the operation legal. The pope had been presented with a *fait accompli*, and since the arrests had technically been made with the approval of the Inquisitor-General for France there was no easy way in which he could reverse Philip's pre-emptive strike. His only possible ploy was to assume command of the trial, and thereby maintain some say in the outcome. Thus, after weeks of consultation and consideration of his dilemma near Poitiers, he issued the bull *Pastoralis praeminentiae* on 22 November 1307. Barber has explained the importance of his action as follows:

By this means Clement irrevocably committed himself to a central role and effectively prevented the hasty end to the proceedings which Philip would have preferred. If Clement had been prepared fully to accede to the coup of 13 October, then it is likely that some quiet, although undoubtedly disreputable, settlement would have been arranged to Philip's material advantage, and the Order would have been dissolved. [15]

The bull instructed Christian rulers to arrest all Templars within their jurisdiction and to assume control of Templar property in the name of the Pope. It was addressed to the Kings and Princes of England, Ireland, Castile, Aragon, Portugal, Italy, Germany, and Cyprus. Although Edward II of England had at first defended the Templars against the charges made by Philip the Fair, and had written to other monarchs in support of the Order, this papal bull forced him to act. He ordered that the Templars in his kingdom be arrested on 10 January 1308, in the hope that the matter would be resolved quickly. [16] In comparison to those taken in the French arrests of the previous October the Templars were treated leniently: some brothers were allowed to remain in their preceptories, while others—including the English Master, William de la More—received royal pensions during their arrest. Similarly, James II of Aragon had originally refused to arrest the Templars in his kingdom and wrote to the kings of Castile and Portugal in order to establish a concerted policy concerning the Order in their relations with Philip the Fair. [17]

In both Aragon and England the initial proceedings were severely hampered by the prohibition of torture existing in those kingdoms. Spanish and English interrogators did not obtain such dramatic and condemning confessions as the inquisitors working under the direction of Guillaume de Paris. In fact the only time that the papal Inquisition ever operated on English soil was when two inquisitors, Dieudonné, Abbot of Lagny, and Sicard de Vaur, arrived there to interrogate the Templars on 13 September 1309. The results, without torture being applied, are significant: none of the forty-three brothers examined by the inquisitors admitted as much as a single charge. [18] Elsewhere, especially in Italy and Germany, arrests were sporadic, unplanned, and dependent upon complex local political situations which caused different procedures to be followed and varying degrees of enthusiasm to be applied to the task. Nevertheless, Clement's legitimizing authority compelled all Christian rulers to take *some* action, often where they had previously refused to do so.

But the Pope's conscience troubled him. The Order of the Temple had after all been consistently loyal to the Holy See for nearly two centuries, and it must have been obvious that the unilateral decision to arrest the Templars was part of the gradual process of derogation of papal power. Although the French king had been responsible for the election of Bertrand de Got as Clement V, it was now clear that this was part of a blatant scheme to place the papacy at his service. The frequent indecision, dramatic changes of idea, contradictions, and to a certain extent even the trial of the Templars themselves, were the products of an unequal power struggle between pope and king. In this contest of will, Clement's initial acquiescence was followed by a pressing need to express his protest at Philip's action. In February 1308 he suspended the proceedings against the Templars by the Inquisition, and the imprisoned brothers were involuntarily pushed into a theological and legal limbo which was to last for six years—with all the psychological effects on their consciences and feelings about the guilt of the Order that one may imagine.

The protagonists of this power struggle met at Poitiers in May 1308. The royal case against the Templars was presented in a long speech by the King's minister Guillaume de Plaisians, who sought to convince Clement of the Templars' heresy by reviewing the trials, confessions, and evidence up to the moment at which inquisitorial proceedings had been suspended. He attempted to clinch his argument by suggesting that the Templars had long been suspected of illicit activities in their chapters, which were held at night like those of known heretics. Their pride, avarice, and treachery are all adduced as arguments supporting his case. But Clement was stubborn enough to resist the royal intimidation, manifested at Poitiers by the presence of a military force sufficient to overwhelm the papal retinue.[19] That presence is testimony to the efficacy of Clement's stalling policy. In spite of his long-term plans to limit the power of the Church, Philip the Fair needed the Pope's consent and wished to have it peacefully if that were possible. But, from his more powerful position, he was also prepared to force the issue once again if Clement would not comply.

He arranged for seventy-two Templars—perhaps fourteen knights, three priests, twenty serving brothers, and others unidentified—to appear before the Pope at Poitiers. They were chosen on the basis of their previous confessions, and included brothers who had been tortured before confessing together with some who seem to have borne grudges against the Order. None of the high-ranking Templars appeared. There were many contradictions in the evidence presented, and most of the key points which appear in later trials can be found in the surviving records of depositions made before Clement V. The show was intended as a concession to the papal demand that prisoners should be handed over to him, and now that he had been allowed to save face, arrangements were made for further enquiries into the supposed heresies. A papal commission was set up to investigate the guilt of the Order as a whole, while provincial councils were to investigate that of individual prisoners. The only exceptions were the leaders of the Order, who were to be interrogated by a commission of cardinals appointed by Clement himself. Templar property was to be held until their guilt was established, and in the event of the Order's suppression was to be used to finance activities in the Holy Land.

In this way, with a series of papal bulls issued during the summer of 1308, Clement V formally submitted to the will of Philip the Fair. From that moment the Pope's role diminished in importance, and the papal commissions found great difficulty in carrying out their work as the result of obstacles created by royal officials. The full list of charges against the Templars was established in a bull of 12 August 1308, after which the trials could begin.

The Charges

The original charges made by Philip the Fair can be divided into three main areas: denial of and spitting on the cross, homosexuality, and the worship of idols. As the result of interrogations, confessions under torture, and the fantasy of many of the prisoners and inquisitors, the full final list comprised 127 charges. Many of them were repetitive or parallel, and they can be reduced to eight principal categories:

1. That the members denied Christ, God, the Virgin, or the saints during a secret ceremony.

2. That the members committed a variety of sacrilegious acts on the cross or the image of Christ.
3. That the members practised obscene kisses.
4. That the members encouraged and permitted the practice of sodomy.
5. That the priests of the Order did not consecrate the Host.
6. That the members did not believe in the sacraments.
7. That the members practised various sorts of idolatry.
8. That the Grand Master, or other dignitaries, absolved brethren from their sins.[20]

These generalized charges, rarely admitted in their entirety by a single Templar, remained the basis for the eventual suppression of the Order. But what is most striking is the fact that in the context of contemporary witchcraft trials all these charges are quite familiar. As Norman Cohn observes in his study of the 'inner demons' of European society: 'Clearly the charges against the Templars were simply a variant of those which . . . had previously been brought against certain heretical groups, real or imaginary.'[21] It is also important to note that the charges multiplied and grew more complex throughout the interrogations and trials, with features added as if to convince sceptics of Templar guilt. It is remarkable how efficacious such traditional stereotypes as denial of Christ, devil or image worship, and obscene kisses could be in the context of early fourteenth-century France.

Denial of Christ had been a key charge against heretics in Aquitaine, who were said to have spurned the cross and then held sexual orgies, at the beginning of the eleventh century, and had often been cited in the succeeding centuries. The secondary charge of holding orgies was obviously more difficult to sustain against the Templars, whereas the practice of sodomy would be more feasible amongst a wholly male Order. Finally, with a certain irony considering the explicit Moslem condemnation of image worship, the veneration of an idol or idols was held to be plausible in an Order which derived much of its power and tradition from the East. This latter charge was commonly thought by outsiders to be based upon fact, even though few of the Templars who 'confessed' to worshipping an idol seem to have agreed about its identity. It ranged from the head of Jacques de Molay to ambiguous three-faced images.* Some of the most fantastic charges—that the devil appeared as a black cat to which they gave the obscene kiss, or that they made powders from the bodies of dead brethren—more evidently derive from current witch trials. They show how the Templar trials belong to the group of ten politically motivated trials between 1300 and 1360 which involved charges related to the witchcraft phenomenon.[23] The element underpinning the charges in this case was the general acceptance of conspiracy by the Templars. As Peter Partner has remarked in his brief survey of the trials, 'the peculiar thing about the charges is not the ruthless prosecution methods but the fusion of the idea of political conspiracy with the idea of magical attack'.[24]

Clement V had at first hesitated to believe the accusations made against the Templars, and his struggle with Philip the Fair had brought about a period of respite after the initial hearings, since his suspension of inquisitorial proceedings made it impossible to carry out further interrogations. Thus the formal list of charges issued by the Pope on 12 August 1308 represents a watershed in the story of the trials: from that moment, with papal authority and inquisitorial efficiency sustaining the charges, the Templars were as good as convicted. As the result of shrewd manoeuvres against Clement V, the French king had succeeded in applying against his political enemies the same charges which the Church had used against heretics for at least two centuries. His triumph is only highlighted by the fact that no convincing physical evidence of heresy was ever found.

Defence of the Templars

The carefully manipulated propaganda of Guillaume de Nogaret was not sufficient to convince everyone. After the initial

---

* Salomon Reinach noted how the number of so-called Baphomets belonging to the Templars multiplied dramatically during the nineteenth century from Raynouard's *Monuments Historique* (1813) to Loiseleur's *Le Doctrine Secrète des Templiers* (1872). By 1881, he observes, it was possible to speak of 'baphometic figures' (*La Tête magique des Templiers*, pp. 25–6). The beautiful painted head of Christ in the ex-Templar church at Templecombe, thought by some to be a copy of the Turin Shroud, might suggest a more plausible—and certainly not heretical—form of 'idol-worship'. See illustration 12.

confessions came retractions of previous statements and even stubborn denials. Still more remarkable was the sudden rush which followed the papal commission's announcement that it would hear the evidence of any Templar who would volunteer to defend the Order. Over 500 brothers who had been tortured and imprisoned by the Inquisition in France volunteered to come forward in February 1310; of the 134 Templars who had affirmed the guilt of the Order at Paris in 1307, 81 now wished to defend it.[25] As this movement gathered momentum the number of potential defenders grew from 532 in February to 597 at the end of March.[26] The commissioners visited groups of Templars housed in various parts of Paris and recorded detailed defences and denials of all the charges made against the Order. Two Templar priests, Pierre de Bologna and Renaud de Provins, prepared statements which criticized the procedures used against them. It seems likely that Pierre de Bologna, who was the Templar procurator to the papal court, had studied law at the University of Bologna.[27] His fine legal knowledge and ability to comment on procedural intricacies, together with an eloquent spoken defence, seemed almost to be having their desired effect on the papal commissioners.

The language of a surviving document prepared by these lawyers, dated 7 April 1310, is reminiscent of the noble tone of earlier Templar manuscripts. After observing that no Templar outside France has yet confessed to the charges laid against the Order, they observe that: 'the order of the Temple was created and founded in the charity and love of a true fraternity and that it is . . . close to God the Father, a saintly and immaculate order free of all taints and vices, in which there is and always will be in vigour a regular doctrine, a salutary observance, and that as such it is approved, confirmed and honoured by numerous privileges of the Holy See.'[28] The articles of the accusation are referred to as 'dishonest, horrible, terrifying and detestable as much as they are impossible and supremely shameful'.[29] Another similar and carefully-reasoned defence of the Templars, addressed to the scholars of the University of Paris and perhaps written as early as 1308, has been printed by Cheney.[30]

Several contemporary accounts of the Templar trials also seem to regard the Order on the whole as being innocent of the charges against it. The Dominican friar Pierre de la Palud gave evidence in favour of the Order;[30] the Cistercian theologian Jacques de Thérines was perplexed by contradictions in the evidence and unable to make up his mind;[31] most surprising of all is what Cheney calls the 'bafflement' of Bernard Gui, a Dominican, experienced heretic hunter and inquisitor, and author of one of the most influential manuals for inquisitors.[32] If such an expert lawyer and judge of heresy found himself unable to interpret the evidence, it is legitimate to ask how anyone could, or can today, make confident assertions concerning Templar guilt or innocence. The same doubt was expressed in verse by the chronicler Geoffroy de Paris, whose uncertainty may be taken as representing a widespread sentiment:

> Je ne sai a tort ou a droit
> Furent li Templiers, sanz doutance,
> Touz pris par le royaume de France.[33]

With brethren coming forward to defend their Order, and objective observers and witnesses willing to publicize opinions about their innocence, many Templars must have looked to the immediate future with a certain optimism during the first part of 1310.

But the ruthlessness and determination of Philip the Fair soon brought an end to any such optimism. Once his design was seen to be in real danger, he arranged for fifty-four Templars who had retracted their confessions to be burned in a field outside Paris on 12 May. Again the innocence of the Templars was emphasized, as a contemporary chronicle shows: 'all of them, with no exception, finally acknowledged none of the crimes imputed to them, but constantly persisted in the general denial, saying always that they were being put to death without cause and unjustly . . .'.[34]

Nevertheless, these executions had the desired effect as fresh terror was struck into the hearts of the Templars still in the hands of the Inquisition. Aimery de Villiers-le-Duc, who was interrogated two days later, asserted quite openly that he would rather confess than be burned.[35] Philip's dramatic move had been the decisive blow against the Order of the Temple: by November no one could be found to defend it, and the momentum which had gathered in February and March had completely dissipated. After two year's work, during which members sat for 161 days and heard 231 witnesses, the papal commission officially ended its work. A copy of the depositions was made for the Pope, while another was to be kept at the monastery of Sainte-Marie in Paris.[36]

Suppression and Aftermath

In the summer of 1308, Clement V had announced a General Council of the Church to take place at Vienne in two years. The agenda of this Council was to include the fate of the Templars, reforms within the Church, and the possibility of a crusade to the Holy Land. The Council opened a year after its planned date, on 16 October 1311. Summaries of the trials in all European countries had been sent to Clement before the Council opened, together with views of the clergy—who had been invited to submit their written opinions for consideration.[37] Two surviving reports, one by the future Pope John XXII, were extremely hostile and suggested that the Pope should abolish the Order on his own authority without requesting the assent of the Council. But Clement wished as much as Philip the Fair to act with the legitimizing authority of a General Council.

Once again a surprising resistance nearly thwarted the moves towards suppression. Clement had formally invited the Templars to appear in defence of their Order at the Council of Vienne; just as it appeared that the suppression was imminent—after four long years of interrogations—nine Templars actually appeared with the manifest intention of presenting a defence. Clement immediately ordered their arrest, perhaps because he feared that there may have been others in the area with similar intentions, but more likely because even he now wished to end the affair as soon as possible. Barber suggests that he hoped by concluding the Templar trials to clear the way for a new crusade[38]—returning to the original scope of the propaganda against the Templars by Pierre Dubois. Many of the hundred prelates at the Council were in fact in favour of allowing the Templars to defend their Order, except those from France, who did not dare to oppose the will of Philip the Fair.[39] Clement V was losing his control of the Council as the winter months passed in debates on the right of the Templars to a defence.

Again, it was Philip the Fair who forced the issue. His patience sorely tried by the prevarications of delegates to the Council, he began to issue blunt ultimatums. On 2 March 1312 he argued that since evidence of heresy and other detestable crimes had been found by the papal commissioners the Order of the Temple ought to be suppressed immediately. He continues:

That is why, burning with zeal for the orthodox faith, and that such a great wrong against Christ is not left unpunished, we supplicate Your Holiness affectionately, devotedly and humbly to suppress the above Order and to create a new military order and to assign to it, with their rights, honours and charges, the property of the above Order . . .[40]

This blatant derogation of the powers of the Council intensified Clement's doubts and increased the desire of non-French members of the Council to provide the Templars with a chance to defend themselves.

But further procrastination was impossible. On 20 March Philip the Fair arrived at Vienne with his brothers Charles and Louis, his three sons, and a substantial armed force. The veiled threats of previous months were now transformed into an open military threat. After years of debate, discussion, and prevarication the suppression of the Order of the Temple was voted with a four-fifths majority just two days later at a secret consistory of the Council of Vienne. The decision was rendered public at a ceremony on 3 April 1312, when the bull of suppression, *Vox in Excelso*, was read out in the presence of Clement V—who was flanked by Philip the Fair as if to ensure that there would be no last-minute changes.[41] Philip's purpose was achieved, but the most important fact to observe is that the Temple *was suppressed without being formally condemned*. Notwithstanding the richly-elaborated confessions and fresh testimony provided for the Council of Vienne, the guilt of the Order and of its individual members was never established. It is in this fact that the openly political nature of the Templar trials is most evident.

*　　*　　*

Once the Temple was suppressed there remained two outstanding questions: how to dispose of Templar property and what to do with the leaders still in custody. Philip still hoped to see the formation of a new military order with one of his sons as Master, but even he gradually became convinced that the lukewarm interest of participants at the Council of Vienne militated against such an order. This time Clement V managed to assert his own desire, against that of many members of the Council. In his bull *Ad providam* of 2 May 1312 he ordered that all Templar property should be transferred to the Hospital with the single exception of property on the Iberian peninsular, which was to go to local military orders in Spain and Portugal as the result of diplomatic pressure exerted by the kings of those countries.[42] It was also agreed with Philip the Fair that expenses for the custody of Templar brothers and the administration of their property from the moment of their arrest in 1307 should be deducted from their total property and paid to the French crown.[43]

This property had, however, been gradually eroded since 1307. In England, for example, Edward II had drawn on Templar resources within a month of their arrest and continued to do so until the suppression. He sold their wool, used stores of grain for his war against Scotland, drew on Templar reserves of meat and fish for his coronation feast, and used Templar funds to pay arrears to his clerks and provide alms for religious houses. Similarly, estates had been stripped of horses and stock, kitchen equipment and any other movable property, while Edward even stripped Templar lands of their timber.[44] Furthermore, the process of taking possession of Templar property by the Hospital was by no means straightforward, even with the backing of a papal bull. Perkins describes the rush for land in England:

The removal of the royal keepers seems to have been the signal for a scramble in which the lords of the fees and the king were in a much better position to succeed than the small number of Hospitallers. The Templars had accumulated their extensive properties gradually and held them under various tenures of many different lords. This made it far from easy for the Hospitallers to gain possession of their gift from the pope, especially without the use of the Templars' deeds, charters, and rolls, which they had not secured by August 30, 1324. They early secured some few of the estates, but most were seized by neighbouring lords . . .[45]

This process was repeated throughout Europe. In France, Germany, and Italy the Hospital managed after long and expensive delays to obtain only a part of the papal 'gift'. The immediate consequence of the suppression was therefore a 'wild orgy of plunder which quickly passed beyond papal control'.[46] This orgy was almost exclusively concentrated on land, since inventories of Templar movable property—treasure, cash, gold, and silver—show them to have possessed remarkably little at the time of their downfall. The loss of Acre and the subsequent move to Cyprus must have made huge drains on Templar cash supplies, and perhaps the coffers had not been replenished afterwards. We have seen that Jacques de Molay's visit to Europe had not been particularly successful in this respect.

The second problem, that of the Templar leaders in custody, was resolved by the papal constitution *Considerantes dudum* of 6 May 1312. This established that the leaders were to be reserved for papal judgement, while ordinary brothers would be judged by the provincial councils.[47] The treatment of the latter was generous: those who were found innocent or submitted willingly to the Church were allowed to reside in former Templar houses with pensions paid from the Order's property. Once the initial shock, and accusations, were forgotten, leniency prevailed: in 1317 the Conference of Frankfurt gave German Templars permission to join the Hospital, and a year later Pope John XXII ordered the Franciscans and Dominicans of the Kingdom of Naples to support surviving Templars.[48] In Portugal, many ex-Templars had been allowed to join the new order of Jesus Christ, which received their property in that country, and to maintain their previous rank. Elsewhere ex-Templars were left relatively free as long as they remembered their monastic vows and led quiet lives devoted to prayer; many continued to live and work on their country estates much as they had done before. After the dramatic burnings of 1310 few Templars of any rank who were prepared to confess appear to have suffered. In 1319, Templars were still living in their houses in Aragon in 'fairly large groups', and the last of the Aragonese Templars only died shortly after mid-century;[49] twelve former Templars were still drawing pensions in England as late as 1338;[50] in 1350, the former Templar Berenger dez Coll was still living at the preceptory of Mas Deu in Roussillon.[51]

These isolated and anachronistic vestiges of Templar power post-dated the real end of the Order of the Temple, which may be said to have coincided with the death of Jacques de Molay and other leaders. While they were still alive, there was hope that in some way the Order might be reconstituted or enjoy a continued underground existence. De Molay, Hugues de Pairaud, Geoffroi de Gonneville, and Geoffroi de Charney were taken before a special commission of three cardinals in 18 March 1314 in Paris. Since these men had repeatedly confessed their guilt, the commission was really a formality; they would be sentenced to perpetual imprisonment, the standard punishment for heresy. But, to the surprise of everybody present Jacques de Molay and Geoffroi de Charney denied their previous confessions and sought desperately to defend themselves. Barber comment of Molay: 'He was an old man, probably into his seventies by this time, and he had spent nearly seven years in prison. The pathetic reliance which he had placed in papal judgement, even to the exclusion of some kind of defence of the Order, had failed him.'[52]

At this point the cardinals on the commission had no choice, for retracting a confession was regarded as a relapse into heresy. Perpetual imprisonment was not in fact regarded as a punishment, but rather as a penance after re-entering the Church through confession. Relapse implied the prisoner's being handed over to the secular arm, in this case the royal authorities of Philip the Fair, for burning. With calm and courage which impressed onlookers and fuelled new legends about the Templars, Jacques de Molay and Geoffroi de Charney were burned to death declaring their orthodoxy on a small island in the River Seine on 18 March 1314.

AFTERWORD

IT IS impossible to write nearly seven hundred years later with any degree of certainty about an event which, even at the time, was shrouded in mystery and ambiguity. These qualities, together with the lack of conclusive evidence for or against presumed guilt, have been responsible for the generation of so many hypotheses about the downfall of the Templars. We may note here that there was never more than a strong suspicion (*vehemens suspicio*) [1] concerning the charges made against them. Even the document entitled *Procedure to follow against the Templars* written by Philip the Fair's lawyers in early 1308 admits that 'perhaps not all of them had sinned'. [2] In the last analysis, belief about what the Templars actually did or did not do regarding heretical and magical practices must remain a matter of personal opinion or taste.

Yet they continue to exert fascination. Just as the aura of glory and heroism persisted in spite of continuous military failures, so the taint of magic and heresy remains in spite of scholarly demonstrations of the absurdity of many of the charges. Part at least of this perpetual fascination seems to derive from the association in the mind of many people with the concept of chivalry. The Templars' contribution to the development of chivalry was encapsulated in seminal literary works, and at the same time in the popular historical imagination.

The idea of chivalry began to spread mainly in northern France during the first part of the twelfth century. Although Maurice Keen has recently argued that the Templars were not responsible for this rise of the chivalric ideal, it may be countered that their influence was perhaps greater than he allows. The fundamental aims of chivalry, to attain fame in this world and to achieve salvation in the next, are evidently related to the aims of the Templars—although in their case the former is subjugated to the Order. Furthermore, we have seen how the Templar ideology was fused from a combination of the northern austerity of St Bernard and the more luxurious, secular knightly ideals of southern France. Such a fusion accurately reflects the joining together of the component parts of the idea of chivalry, in which, in Keen's words, crusading or martial pilgrimage 'established itself as the highest mode of expression of the chivalric virtues of courage and endurance'.[3] We have also seen how it was precisely these values which were constantly stressed in the Templar *Rule*, and in comments by observers concerning the Order of the Templar. If crusading pilgrimage was the highest mode of expression of chivalry, then the Templars may be considered as exemplars of the chivalric life in its early phase.

Moreover, the Templars were deeply identified with the literary expression of chivalry. Chrétien de Troyes, who espoused the cause of chivalry in his epic poem *Perceval*, came from the heart of Templar country in Burgundy—as his name implies. He was born just seven years after the Council which gave the Templars their *Rule* was held at Troyes, and seems to have been imbued with their chivalric sense of purpose. Melville has observed that in his poem the figure of Arthur resembles the Master of a military order rather than a real king.[4] An even closer link comes with the reworking of the same story by Wolfram von Eschenbach, who visited the Holy Land around 1218 and was much impressed by the activities of the Templars he saw there. In his *Parzival*, the grail castle of Munsalvaesche was guarded by Templar knights.[5] This literary association of the Templars with the grail legend provided fresh impulse to the mystery of their downfall. It is easy to understand how the eucharistic mysticism implicit in the grail legend could spill over into heresy; equally, the accusation of heresy might be taken as evidence that there was some truth in connections between the grail and the Templars.

In the same way, both the secular and the religious models for chivalry became associated with the Templars. Although they did not derive their ideology from the legends of Arthur, as secular knights did, that king's name became linked with the Temple in the literary context— and thence perhaps in the popular imagination. From the religious point of view, the models were equally fascinating and intertwined again with the grail legend. In the twelfth century, in fact, the Book of Judges was translated into the vernacular for the Templars so that they could study the chivalry of biblical times, in particular stories of the conquest of the Holy Land by Joshua and its later defence by David and Judas Maccabaeus. [6] As the greatest, richest, and most feared of the military orders—already semi-legendary in its own day, as the concealed discrepancies between reputation and achievement imply—the Templars attracted envy, suspicion, and quasi-mythical awe as light attracts moths.

The search for models in the past, representing a pressing need to establish historical roots and legitimize the holding of power or preservation of a secret, was soon applied to the Templars themselves. The archetype of this form of legitimizing of history is Virgil's *Aeneid*, which was written to justify the Emperor Augustus' claim to imperial power. Geoffrey of Monmouth sought to derive English history from Roman legend in a way that echoes Virgil's account of the passage of Aeneas from Troy to Rome. In the same way, when the crusading epoch ended with the fall of Acre other groups sought to provide sustenance for their aspirations by looking back to the Templars. New secular orders of chivalry flourished in the fourteenth century, from the Order of the Band, founded by Alfonso XI of Castile about 1330, to the Order of the Garter, founded by Edward III of England in 1348, and a host of others marked by emphasis on ceremony and elaborate forms of dress rather than the original chivalric ideal. Although there are few precise connections between these orders and the Templars, at least one significant example is provided by the Order of the Golden Fleece, founded by Philip the Good in 1431, which contains echoes of the Templar *Rule* in its statutes. [7] Chivalry took on a more formal aspect and looked back to the adventures of semi-legendary kings like Arthur for inspiration. It was perhaps in this way that the grail, which may indeed have influenced some higher-ranking members of the Temple in its Christian eucharistic form, was associated with the now equally legendary Knights Templars.

In seventeenth-century England this nostalgic vision of the Templars resurfaced in the writings of Elias Ashmole, as Peter Partner has shown. [8] Precursor of a movement towards the revival of noble and knightly orders which took place during the Enlightenment, Ashmole was also one of the first non-craftsmen to become a member of a Masonic Lodge. Once again, although there is no direct link to Ashmole, fuel had been provided for the literary imagination. Partner shows how in the eighteenth century the Templars were drawn into the symbolic system of speculative freemasonry. In Germany the most modern form of 'Templarism' drew on its supposed medieval precursors just as secular chivalric orders in the fourteenth century looked back to biblical and Roman 'knights' for *their* models. Modern literary manifestations of this golden mist of chivalry enclosing the historical past include Spenser's Red Cross Knight in *The Faerie Queene*, who represents the idealized Englishman of the sixteenth century, and Sir Walter Scott's Templar Master in *Ivanhoe*. In this way the Templars may be perceived as a link in a chain of more or less loose associations reaching back to other semi-legendary knights. This perennial need for historical justification, together with the mystery concerning their suppression, makes the Order of the Temple ideal material for those who seek esoteric secrets or simply inspiration. The fact is that these aspects are more a matter of literary and pseudo-scholarly embellishment than reality. We have seen that the real achievement of the Templars was surprisingly limited; but that does nothing to diminish the fascination which surrounds them.

* * *

Many factors contributed to the downfall of the Templars. The mere suspicion of guilt was not sufficient to destroy such a powerful Order and fabricate the fantasies which developed in the course of their trial. It would appear that a combination of the unpopularity of the Templars, the chronic cash shortage of the French treasury, and Jacques de Molay's refusal to contemplate union of the military orders created circumstances in which the consequence of the arrests was a foregone conclusion. A further factor is provided by Malcolm Barber's argument that Philip the Fair's actions were motivated by a genuine belief that the Templars had transgressed the laws upon which medieval society was based. [9] Philip's profound belief in the necessary 'order' of society is demonstrated by his insistence on legality and external form—even at the cost of imposing it by armed force. Yet the greatest charge which can be made against the Templars is one they could do nothing to avoid, and which could not be formulated at the trials: the concept of crusading knight-monks had been rendered obsolete. The Temple was simply anachronistic.

In such a large order it was inevitable that there should be some heretics, some homosexuals, and some members at a higher level who aspired towards mystical experience—perhaps involving the eucharistic grail—and therefore left themselves open to charges of heresy. In the Middle Ages heresy and mysticism were considered equally deviant, and often went hand in hand. But the facts are simple: no convincing evidence of heresy was ever found, and the Order of the Temple was never condemned.

REFERENCES

CHAPTER 1

1. Prawer, *The Latin Kingdom*, p. 253.
2. Runciman, *History of the Crusades*, II, p. 71.
3. Ibid., pp. 91-99, 152-5.
4. Lawrence, *The Castle of Baghras*, pp. 42-6.
5. Smail, *Crusaders' Castles*, p. 137.
6. Richard, *Royaume Latin*, p. 105.
7. Saewulf, *Account of the Pilgrimage*, pp. 8-9.
8. Daniel the Higumene, *Pilgrimage*, p. 9.
9. Ekkehard of Aura, *Hierosolymita*, p. 39.
10. Prawer, *Settlement of the Latins*, p. 493.
11. William of Tyre, *History*, I, p. 507.
12. Prawer, *Settlement*, pp. 495-6.
13. La Monte, *Feudal Monarchy*, p. 173.
14. Prawer, *Settlement*, p. 503.
15. William of Tyre, op. cit., I, pp. 524-5.
16. Jacques de Vitry, *History of Jerusalem*, p. 50.
17. Albert of Aix, *Historia Hierosolymitana*, p. 713.
18. Runciman, op. cit., II, p. 484.
19. e.g. Baigent, Leigh & Lincoln, *The Holy Blood, and the Holy Grail*, London: Jonathan Cape, 1982, pp. 56-7.
20. William of Tyre, op. cit., I, p. 525.
21. Barber, *Origins*, pp. 221-2.
22. Richard, op. cit., p. 105.
23. Bulst-Thiele, *Sacrae Domus Militiae Templi Hierosolymitani Magistri*, pp. 20-21.
24. Albon, *Cartulaire*, p. 1, No. 1.
25. Melville, *La Vie des Templiers*, pp. 18-19.
26. Barber, *Origins*, p. 226.
27. Albon, op. cit., pp. 1-2, No. 2.

28. Barber, *Origins*, p. 226.
29. Leclerq, *Sur les débuts des Templiers*, p. 84.
30. Ibid., pp. 86–9.
31. Daniel-Rops, *Cathedral and Crusade*, p. 18.
32. Hill, *Gesta Francorum*, p. xxi.

CHAPTER 2

1. Prawer, *The Latin Kingdom*, p. 253.
2. Melville, *La Vie des Templiers*, pp. 26–7.
3. William of Tyre, *History*, I., p. 525.
4. Daniel-Rops, *Cathedral and Crusade*, p. 97.
5. Southern, *Western Society*, p. 255.
6. Daniel-Rops, op. cit., pp. 111–13.
7. Prawer, op. cit., p. 254.
8. Curzon (ed.), *La Règle*, §2.
9. Prawer, op. cit., p. 255.
10. *Règle*, §2.
11. Leclerq, *Un document*, p. 81.
12. Richard, *Royaume Latin*, p. 106.
13. Albon, *Cartulaire*, pp. 23–4, No. XXXI.
14. Ibid., p. 5, No. VII.
15. Quoted in Lees, *Records*, p. xxxviii.
16. Ibid., p. xxxix (VCH Essex gives 1136).
17. Ibid., p. lxxiv.
18. Ibid., pp. xlvii–xlviii.
19. Forey, *The Templars in Aragón*, p. 9.
20. Ibid., p. 15.
21. Bini, *Dei Tempieri e del loro processo*, p. 403.
22. Guerrieri, *I Cavalieri Templari*, pp. 15–24.
23. Prawer, *Crusading Institutions*, p. 150.
24. Ibid., p. 152.
25. Riley-Smith, *Templars and Teutonic Knights*, pp. 93–5.
26. Melville, op. cit., p. 33.
27. *De Laude*, p. 1252.
28. Ibid., pp. 1255–6.
29. Prawer, *The Latin Kingdom*, p. 255.
30. *De Laude*, p. 1252.
31. Prawer, op. cit., p. 262.

CHAPTER 3

1. Melville, op. cit., p. 33.

2. Albon, *Cartulaire*, p. 375, No. V.
3. Ibid., pp. 375–9.
4. Riley-Smith, *The Crusades: Idea and Reality*, pp. 92–3.
5. Melville, op. cit., p. 37.
6. Ibid., pp. 42–7.
7. Riley-Smith, *The Knights of St John*, pp. 329–30.
8. Prawer, *Latin Kingdom*, p. 261 and p. 331.
9. Cf. Partner's estimate in *Murdered Magicians*, p. 14.
10. Richard, *Royaume*, p. 107.
11. Ambroise, *The Crusade of Richard Lion-Heart*, ll. 2,500–2 (p. 124); Riley-Smith, *Knights*, suggests 230 dead (p. 325, n. 5).
12. Matthew Paris, *English History*, I, p. 484.
13. Hill, *History of Cyprus*, II, p. 37.
14. Partner, op. cit., p. 59.
15. Lea, *Inquisition in the Middle Ages*, III, p. 251.
16. Ibid., p. 244.
17. Albon, *Cartulaire*, p. 381, No. 8.
18. Daniel-Rops, *Cathedral and Crusade*, p. 95.
19. Ibid.
20. Albon, *Cartulaire*, p. 382, No. 10.
21. Delaville, *Documents concernant les Templiers*, p. 11.
22. Bini, *Dei Tempieri in Lucca*, p. 8; Melville, op. cit., p. 42.

CHAPTER 4

1. Smail, *Crusading Warfare*, p. 19.
2. Ibid., pp. 20–1.
3. Runciman, op. cit., II, p. 211.
4. Ibid., p. 219.
5. Riley-Smith, *Templars and Teutonic Knights*, pp. 93–5.
6. Lawrence, *The Castle of Baghras*, pp. 43–6.
7. Runciman, op. cit., II, p. 215.
8. Ibid., p. 223.
9. Ibid., p. 230.
10. Smail, *Crusaders' Castles*, p. 140.
11. William of Tyre, op. cit., II, p. 203.
12. Runciman, op. cit., II, pp. 237–8.
13. Virginia G. Berry, *The Second Crusade*, in Setton, ed., *History of the Crusades*, I, pp. 469–81; cf. Runciman, op. cit., II, pp. 252–4, and Daniel-Rops, op. cit., pp. 106–7.
14. Runciman, op. cit., II, p. 257.

15. Ibid., p. 268.
16. Delisle, *Mémoire*, p. 17.
17. Odo of Deuil, *De Profectione*, p. 125.
18. Runciman, op. cit., II, p. 288.
19. *Règle*, §138, and notes to p. 110.
20. Smail, *Crusading Warfare*, pp. 112–15.
21. Ibid., pp. 78–80.
22. Ibid., p. 128.
23. Ibid., p. 129.
24. Ibn Wasil, in Gabrieli, *Storici Arabi delle Crociate*, p. 289.
25. Ibn Alatyr, *Extrait de la Chronique intitulée Kamel-Altevarykh*, p. 679.
26. Jacques de Vitry, *History of Jerusalem*, p 52.
27. Ibid.
28. Riley-Smith, *Knights of St John*, p. 136.
29. Riley-Smith, *Templars and Teutonic Knights*, p. 280.
30. William of Tyre, op. cit., II, p. 312.
31. Hamilton, *Latin Church*, p. 109.
32. Smail, *Crusading Warfare*, p. 204.
33. Fedden, *Crusader Castles*, p. 20.
34. Hamilton, op. cit., p. 149.
35. Smail, *Crusading Warfare*, p. 207.
36. Smail, *Crusaders' Castles*, p. 147.
37. Prawer, *Settlement*, p. 135.
38. Prawer, *Crusader Institutions*, p. 214.
39. Ibid., p. 322.
40. Riley-Smith, *Knights of St John*, p. 79.
41. Ibid., p. 74.
42. Smail, *Crusaders' Castles*, p. 148.
43. Theoderich, *Description of the Holy Places*, pp. 30–2.
44. Smail, *Crusading Warfare*, p. 33.
45. Runciman, op. cit., II, pp. 280–1.
46. Berry, op. cit., p. 507.
47. Smail, op. cit., p. 31 & p. 33.
48. Runciman, op. cit., II, pp. 282–3.
49. Berry, op. cit., p. 510.
50. William of Tyre, op. cit., II, p. 203.
51. Ibid., p. 227.
52. Cf. the account by Marshall Baldwin, in Setton, op. cit., I, pp. 536–8.
53. Smail, op. cit., pp. 102–3.
54. Baldwin, in Setton, op. cit., p. 539.
55. William of Tyre, op. cit., II, p. 312.

56. Runciman, op. cit., II, pp. 390–1.
57. Smail, op. cit., p. 96.
58. Fedden, op. cit., p. 61.
59. Richard, *Royaume*, p. 107.
60. Smail, op. cit., p. 96.
61. La Monte, *Feudal Monarchy*, p. 219.
62. Smail, op. cit., p. 96; Runciman, op. cit., II, pp. 452–4.
63. Riley-Smith, *Knights of St John*, p. 74.
64. Lizerand, *Clément V et Philippe le Bel*, p. 77.
65. Melville, *Vie des Templiers*, p. 30.
66. *Cartulaire*, p. 28, No. XXXVIII.
67. Melville, op. cit., p. 29.
68. Forey, *Templars in Aragón*, p. 15.
69. Cf. Forey, op. cit., pp. 24-62, & Burns, *Medieval Colonialism*, pp. 14–16.
70. Forey, op. cit., pp. 285–9.
71. Hillgarth, *The Spanish Kingdoms*, I, p. 22.
72. Lees, *Records of the Templars*, pp. xl–xli.
73. Ibid., p. xlv.
74. Poole, *Domesday to Magna Carta*, p. 155.
75. Lees, op. cit., p. 1.
76. Gransden (ed.), *Chronicle of Bury St Edmunds*, p. 150.

CHAPTER 5

1. Postan, *Medieval Trade and Finance*, p. 134.
2. Postan, *Essays on Medieval Agriculture*, p. 98.
3. Little, *Religious Poverty and the Profit Economy*, pp. 15–16.
4. Bini, *Dei Tempieri e del loro Processo*, pp. 460–501.
5. Prawer, *Latin Kingdom*, pp. 65–6.
6. Runciman, op. cit., pp. 318–19.
7. In Gabrieli, *Storici Arabi*, p. 80.
8. Postan, *Essays*, p. 33.
9. Richard, *Royaume Latin*, p. 108.
10. Hamilton, *Latin Church*, p. 284.
11. Byrne, *Genoese Trade*, pp. 213–14.
12. Heyd, *Histoire du Commerce du Levant*, II, p. 29.
13. Yver, *Commerce et Marchands dans L'Italie Meridionale*, pp. 167–8.
14. Little, op. cit., p. 13.
15. Thompson, *Economic and Social History*, I, p. 431.
16. Albon, *Cartulaire*, p. 79, No CXI.
17. Forey, op. cit., p. 46.
18. Ibid.

19. Atiya, *Crusade and Commerce*, pp. 46–7.
20. Heyd, op. cit., I, p. 186; Prawer, *Latin Kingdom*, p. 197.
21. Prawer, op. cit., p. 198.
22. Baldwin, *Business in the Middle Ages*, p. 96.
23. Lees, *Records*, p. lv.
24. Hamilton, op. cit., pp. 246–7.
25. Forey, op. cit., p. 346.
26. Delisle, *Mémoire sur les Opérations Financières des Templiers*, pp. 4–5.
27. Bini, *Dei Tempieri e del loro Processo*, pp. 441–3.
28. Hill, *History of Cyprus*, I, pp. 312–13.
29. Delisle, op. cit., p. 10.
30. Ibid., pp. 11–13.
31. Ibid., p. 12.
32. Little, op. cit., p. 36.
33. Ibid.
34. Ibid., p. 39.
35. Ibid., p. 56.
36. Postan, *Medieval Trade*, pp. 11–12.
37. Forey, op. cit., p. 351.
38. Ibid., p. 352.
39. Hillgarth, *Spanish Kingdoms*, I, p. 272.
40. Delisle, op. cit., p. 17.
41. Lopez & Raymond, *Medieval Trade*, pp. 101–2.
42. Postan, *Medieval Trade*, p. 54.
43. Delisle, op. cit., p. 20.
44. Ibid., p. 21.
45. Ibid., p. 12.
46. Ibid., p. 21 & pp. 32–7.
47. Brundage, *Medieval Canon Law and the Crusader*, p. 185.
48. Lees, op. cit., p. lviii.
49. Delisle, op. cit., p. 27.
50. Ibid., p. 28.
51. Ibid., p. 25.
52. Burns, *Medieval Colonialism*, p. 19.
53. Ibid., p. 19 & p. 217.
54. Delisle, op. cit., p. 31.
55. Melville, *La Vie des Templiers*, p. 151.
56. Ibid., p. 154.
57. Mundy, *Europe in the High Middle Ages*, p. 171.
58. Riley-Smith, *Knights of St John*, p. 390.
59. Delisle, op. cit., pp. 32–7.

60. Perkins, *Templars in the British Isles*, p. 213.
61. Ibid., pp. 216-17.
62. Perkins, *Wealth of the Knights Templar*, pp. 255-6.
63. Ibid., p. 254.
64. Ferris, *Financial Relations*, p.4.
65. Ibid., p. 5.
66. Ibid., p. 6.
67. Powicke, *The Thirteenth Century*, pp. 1-3.
68. Ibid., p. 17.
69. Ibid., pp. 146-7.
70. Lees, op. cit., p. xxxvii.
71. *Victoria County History, London*, Vol. I, p. 486 (henceforth cited as VCH).
72. Yver, op. cit., p. 118.
73. Matthew Paris, *English History*, I, p. 484.
74. Lea, *Inquisition of the Middle Ages*, III, p. 251.
75. Perkins, *Wealth*, p. 254.
76. Forey, op. cit., p. 60.
77. Postan, *Medieval Economy and Society*, p. 92; cf. VCH, *Lincolnshire*, II, pp. 210-13, and VCH, *Yorkshire*, III, pp. 256-60.
78. Perkins, *Wealth*, p. 253.
79. Lees, op. cit., pp. xxix-xxx.
80. Ibid., p. xxxiii.
81. Ibid., p. lxxi.
82. Ibid., p. 141.
83. Ibid., p. lxxiv.
84. Ibid., p. xciv.
85. Ibid., p. lxxxv; cf. VCH, *London*, I, pp. 485-91.
86. VCH, *London*, I, p. 485.
87. VCH, *Cambridgeshire*, II, pp. 259-60.
88. VCH, *Lincolnshire*, II, pp. 210-13.
89. VCH, *Somerset*, II, pp. 146-7.
90. VCH, *Kent*, II, p. 175.
91. VCH, *London*, I, p. 486.
92. Lees, op. cit., pp. xcv-c.
93. VCH, *Sussex*, p. 92.
94. VCH, *Yorkshire*, III, pp. 256-60.
95. VCH, *Oxfordshire*, II, pp. 106-7.
96. VCH, *Shropshire*, II, p. 86.
97. Lees, op. cit., p. lxxi.

CHAPTER 6

1. Based on Hitti, *Salah-al-Din*, pp. 117–23, and Gibb, *The Rise of Saladin* pp. 563–89.
2. Gibb, op. cit., p. 564.
3. Runciman, *History of the Crusades*, II, pp. 417–18.
4. Gibb, op. cit., p. 573.
5. Cf. Lyons and Jackson, *Saladin*, p. 287.
6. Cf. Baldwin, in Setton, *History of Crusades*, I, pp. 599–606, and Runciman, op. cit., II, pp. 436–45.
7. Baldwin, *Raymond III of Tripolis*, pp. 86–95.
8. Ibid., pp. 90–1; Runciman, op. cit., pp. 452–4; Ernoul, *Chronique*, pp. 148–52.
9. Ernoul, op. cit., p. 152.
10. Ambroise, *Crusade of Richard Lion-Heart*, ll. 2,500–2, p. 124.
11. In Gabrieli, *Storici Arabi*, p. 118.
12. Baldwin, in Setton, op. cit., p. 610; cf. Prawer, *Crusader Institutions*, pp. 488–91 for detailed description of the topography.
13. Ibn al-Athir, in Gabrieli, op. cit., p. 118.
14. Prawer, *Crusader Institutions*, p. 487; Runciman, op. cit., pp. 455–6.
15. Ibn al-Athir, op. cit., p. 120.
16. Cf. Baldwin, in Setton op. cit., I, pp. 610–11.
17. Smail, *Crusading Warfare*, p. 195.
18. Cf. Ernoul, op. cit., pp. 161–2.
19. Lyons and Jackson, op. cit., pp. 259–60.
20. Ibid., pp. 260–1.
21. Prawer, *Crusader Institutions*, p. 496.
22. Lyons and Jackson, op. cit., p. 261.
23. Richard, *An Account of the Battle of Hattin*, p. 169.
24. Baldwin, *Raymond III of Tripolis*, p. 123.
25. Imad ad-Din, in Gabrieli, op. cit., p. 134.
26. Cf. Baldwin, in Setton, op. cit., pp. 612–15; Lyons and Jackson, op. cit., pp. 262–4.; Prawer, *Crusader Institutions*, pp. 496–500; Runciman, op. cit., II, pp. 458–9; Ibn al-Athir, op. cit., pp. 121–4; Imad ad-Din, op. cit., pp. 125–36.
27. Ambroise, op. cit., ll, 3,021–34, p. 143.
28. Ibn al-Athir, op. cit., p. 124.
29. Quoted by Riley-Smith in *The Knights of St John*, p. 76.
30. Imad ad-Din, op. cit., p. 76.
31. Prawer, *Crusader Institutions*, p. 487.
32. Lyons and Jackson, op. cit., p. 266.
33. Gibb, op. cit., p. 57.

34. Ibn al-Athir, op. cit., pp. 140–1.
35. Ibid., p. 143.
36. Lyons and Jackson, op. cit., pp. 283–90.
37. Quoted in Lyons and Jackson, op. cit., p. 289.
38. Ibid., p. 290.
39. Riley-Smith, *The Knights of St John*, p. 327n.

CHAPTER 7

1. Poole, *Domesday Book to Magna Carta*, p. 344.
2. Munz, *Frederick Barbarossa*, p. 371n.
3. Sidney Painter, *The Third Crusade: Richard the Lionhearted and Philip Augustus*, in Setton, *History of Crusades*, II, p. 47.
4. Munz, op. cit., pp. 391–6;
5. Runciman, op. cit., III, p. 17.
6. Cf. Ibn al-Athir, in Gabrieli, op. cit., p. 205.
7. Cf. Painter, op. cit., p. 50.
8. Cf. Bahà ad-Din, in Gabrieli, op. cit., p. 191.
9. In Gabrieli, op. cit., pp. 184–5.
10. Bahà ad-Din, in Gabrieli, op. cit., p. 192.
11. Painter, op. cit., pp. 61–9; Runciman, op. cit., III, pp. 43–50; Poole, op. cit., pp. 347–78.
12. Morgan, *La Continuation de Guillaume de Tyr*, p. 135.
13. Hill, *History of Cyprus*, II, pp. 34–5.
14. Morgan, op. cit., p. 135.
15. Hill, op. cit., p. 36.
16. Ibid., p. 37.
17. Ibid., III, p. 1042.
18. Morgan, op. cit., p. 136.
19. Poole, op. cit., p. 361.
20. Painter, op. cit., p. 74; Runciman, op. cit., III, pp. 55–6.
21. Bahà ad-Din, in Gabrieli, op. cit., pp. 221–2.
22. Runciman, op. cit., p. 59.
23. Painter, op. cit., p. 85.
24. Ibid., pp. 74–85; Runciman, op. cit., III, pp. 55–74.
25. Poole, op. cit., p. 362.
26. Morghen, *Medioevo cristiano*, p. 157.
27. Epist. XVI, 30, quoted in Fliche, *Histoire de l'Église*, p. 39.
28. Cf. Delisle, op. cit., p. 31.
29. Epist. XIII, 1210, quoted in Fliche, op. cit., p. 106.
30. Melville, op. cit., p. 129.

31. Cf. Jacques de Vitry, *History*, pp. 56–91.
32. Benvenisti, *Crusaders in the Holy Land*, pp. 284–8.
33. Lawrence, *The Castle of Baghras*, p. 46.
34. Riley-Smith, *Templars and Teutonic Knights*, p. 110.
35. Van Cleve, Thomas Curtis, *The Fifth Crusade*, in Setton, *History of Crusades*, pp. 394–5.
36. In Benvenisti, op. cit., p. 176.
37. Johns, *Excavations at Pilgrim's Castle*, p. 159; see also the description in Benvenisti, op. cit., pp. 175–85.
38. Johns, op. cit., p. 153.
39. Ibid., p. 162.
40. Van Cleve, op. cit., p. 395.
41. Johns, op. cit., p. 152.
42. Fedden, *Crusader Castles*, p. 92; Benvenisti, op. cit., p. 177.
43. Fedden, op. cit., p. 92.
44. Burchand of Mount Sion, *Description*, p. 93.
45. Gabrieli, op. cit., p. 251.
46. Van Cleve, op. cit., p. 396.
47. Ibid., p. 405.
48. Ibid., p. 408.
49. Ibid., p. 414.
50. Ibid., p. 413.
51. Cf. Ibn al-Athir, in Gabrieli, op. cit., pp. 252–5; Runciman, op. cit., III, pp. 151–70.
52. Van Cleve, *The Emperor Frederick II*, p. 184.
53. Ibid., p. 193.
54. Ibid., pp. 196–7.
55. Ibid., p. 215.
56. Van Cleve, *The Crusade of Frederick II*, in Setton, *History of the Crusades*, II, p. 444.
57. Van Cleve, *The Emperor Frederick II*, p. 218.
58. In Gabrieli, op. cit., p. 264.
59. Van Cleve, *The Emperor Frederick II*, p. 220.
60. Van Cleve, *The Crusade of Frederick II*, in Setton, op. cit., II, p. 457.
61. In Gabrieli, op. cit., p. 271.
62. Van Cleve, *The Emperor Frederick II*, p. 226.
63. Ibid., p. 227.
64. Van Cleve, *The Crusade of Frederick II*, in Setton, op. cit., II, p. 460.
65. Van Cleve, *The Emperor Frederick II*, pp. 428–9.
66. Heyd, *Histoire du Commerce*, I, p. 186.
67. Riley-Smith, *Knights of St John*, p. 178.

68. Ibid., p. 179.
69. Delaville Le Roulx, *Documents*, p. 27.
70. La Monte, *Feudal Monarchy*, p. 220.
71. Joseph R. Strayer, *The Crusades of Louis IX*, in Setton, *History of the Crusades*, II, pp. 487–518.
72. Riley-Smith, *Knights of St John*, pp. 180–3; Strayer, op. cit., pp. 488–9.
73. Strayer, op. cit., p. 499; Ibn Wasil, in Gabrieli, op. cit., p. 285.
74. Strayer, op. cit., p. 505.
75. Delisle, op. cit., p. 6.
76. Mustafa M. Ziada, *The Mamluk Sultans to 1293*, in Setton, *History of the Crusades*, II, p. 735.
77. Ibid., pp. 738–42.
78. Nicholson, *Literary History of the Arabs*, pp. 447–8.
79. Ziada, op. cit., p. 746.
80. Grousset, *Histoire des Croisades*, III, pp. 626–7.
81. Quoted in Riley-Smith, *Knights of St John*, p. 126.
82. Lawrence, op. cit., p. 46.
83. Ziada, op. cit., p. 749.
84. Ibn 'Abd Az-Zahir, in Gabrieli, op. cit., pp. 316–18.
85. Schlumberger, *Prise de Saint-Jean-d'Acre*, p. 23.
86. Ibid., pp. 6-7.
87. Abu L-Mahasin, in Gabrieli, op. cit., p. 339.
88. Abu L-Fidà', in Gabrieli, op. cit., p. 337.
89. Runciman, op. cit., II, p. 416.
90. Schlumberger, op. cit., p. 47.
91. Quoted from Benvenisti, op. cit., p. 92.
92. Abu L-Mahasin, in Gabrieli, op. cit., p. 340.
93. Ludolph von Sachem, *Description*, p. 57.
94. In Gabrieli, op. cit., pp. 338–9.
95. Hill, *History of Cyprus*, II, p. 187.
96. Barber, *James of Molay*, p. 92.
97. Ibid., p. 94.
98. Ibid., pp. 94–5; Hill, op. cit., pp. 202–3.
99. Favier, *Philippe le Bel*, p. 431.
100. La Monte, op. cit., p. 220.

CHAPTER 8

1. William of Tyre, *History*, I, pp. 526–7.
2. Prawer, *Latin Kingdom of Jerusalem*, p. 259.
3. Barber, *Trial of the Templars*, p. 12.
4. Grousset, *Histoire des Croisades*, II, pp. 598–602.

5. Quoted in Seward, *Monks of War*, p. 28.
6. Martin, *Trial of the Templars*, p. 18.
7. Cf. Barber, op. cit., p. 261, n.34.
8. Matthew Paris, *History*, e.g. I. p. 387.
9. Riley-Smith, *Knights of St John*, p. 177.
10. E.g. 17 November 1206, in Fliche, op. cit., p. 183.
11. Riley-Smith, op. cit., p. 387.
12. Melville, op. cit., p. 129.
13. Barber, *Trial*, pp. 12-13; Lea, op. cit., III, p. 243.
14. Partner, *Murdered Magicians*, p. 30.
15. Lizerand, *Clément V et Philippe le Bel*, p. 78.
16. Bini, *Dei Tempieri e del loro Processo in Toscana*, pp. 401-13.
17. Forey, op. cit., p. 197.
18. Ibid., pp. 281-2.
19. Ibid., p. 267.
20. Matthew Paris, *History*, I, p. 484.
21. Gransden (ed.), *Chronicle*, p. 47.
22. Runciman, op. cit., III, pp. 320-1.
23. Gransden, op. cit., p. 82.
24. Cf. Hill, *History of Cyprus*, II, pp. 172-4.
25. Favier, *Philippe le Bel*, p. 431.
26. Ibid., p. 9.
27. Purcell, *Changing Views of Crusade*, p. 3.
28. Ibid., pp. 11-17.
29. Ibid., p. 19.

CHAPTER 9

1. Riley-Smith, *Knights of St John*, p. 151 & pp. 444-50.
2. La Monte, *Feudal Monarchy*, p. 223n.
3. Ibid.
4. Grousset, *Histoire*, II, p. 397; cf. Runciman, op. cit., III, pp. 218-20.
5. Cf. Runciman, op. cit., III, pp. 338-42.
6. Atiya, *Crusade in the Later Middle Ages*, p. 36.
7. Lizerand, *Clément V et Philippe le Bel*, pp. 80-1.
8. Atiya, op. cit., p. 71.
9. Macdonell, *Historical Trials*, p. 27.
10. Dubois, *De Recuperatione*, p. 13.
11. Ibid., pp. 30-2 & pp. 49-50.
12. Ibid., p. 133.
13. Ibid., p. 134.
14. Hillgarth, *Ramon Lull and Lullism*, p. 86.

15. Barber, *James of Molay*, p. 103.
16. Lizerand, *Dossier*, p. 4.
17. Ibid., p. 6.
18. Ibid.
19. Ibid., p. 8.
20. Barber, *Trial*, p. 15.
21. Lizerand, *Dossier*, p. 8.
22. Ibid., p. 10.
23. Ibid.
24. Ibid., p. 12.
25. Ibid., p. 15.
26. Favier, op. cit., p. 427.
27. Hillgarth, op. cit., p. 93.
28. Ibid., p. 94.

CHAPTER 10

1. Lizerand, *Dossier*, p. 23.
2. Lambert, *Medieval Heresy*, p. 173.
3. Lizerand, *Dossier*, p. 16.
4. Ibid., p. 18.
5. Cohn, *Europe's Inner Demons*, p. 83.
6. Cf. Partner, *Murdered Magicians*, pp. 51–5.
7. Cohn, op. cit., p. 84.
8. Quoted from Barber, *Trial*, p. 51.
9. Lizerand, *Dossier*, p. 20.
10. Ibid., p. 22.
11. Ibid., p. 26.
12. Barber, *Trial*, p. 52.
13. Gui, *Gravamina*, quoted in Lea, *Inquisition of the Middle Ages*, I, p. 424.
14. Barber, *Trial*, pp. 58–9.
15. Ibid., p. 73.
16. Ibid., p. 195.
17. Ibid., pp. 204–5.
18. Ibid., pp. 195–6; cf. Perkins, *Trial in England*, pp. 434–5.
19. Barber, *Trial*, pp. 89–97.
20. Gilmour-Bryson, *Trial of the Templars*, p. 17; Barber, *Trial*, gives a full list of charges in translation, *Appendix A*, pp. 248–52.
21. Cohn, *Europe's Inner Demons*, p. 88.
22. Cf. Russell, *Witchcraft in the Middle Ages*, p. 86.
23. Ibid., pp. 194–8.
24. Partner, *Murdered Magicians*, p. 58.

25. Cohn, op. cit., p. 95.
26. Barber, *Trial*, p. 132.
27. Ibid., p. 142.
28. In Lizerand, *Dossier*, p. 182.
29. Ibid., p. 184.
30. Ibid., pp. 192–5.
31. Cheney, *A Letter in Defence of the Templars*, p. 315.
32. Ibid.
33. Quoted by Cheney, op. cit., p. 316 & Raynouard, *Monuments Historique*, p. 30.
34. Quoted from Barber, *Trial*, p. 157.
35. Lizerand, *Dossier*, p. 190.
36. Barber, *Trial*, p. 177.
37. Ibid., p. 233.
38. Ibid., p. 224.
39. Ibid., p. 226.
40. Lizerand, *Dossier*, pp. 196–9.
41. Barber, *Trial*, p. 229.
42. Ibid., p. 231.
43. Cf. Philip's letter to Clement on 24 August 1312, in Lizerand, *Dossier*, pp. 198–203.
44. Perkins, *Wealth of the Knights Templars*, pp. 256–7.
45. Ibid., p. 259.
46. Ibid., p. 263.
47. Barber, *Trial*, p. 238.
48. Lea, *Inquisition of the Middle Ages*, III, p. 324.
49. Forey, *Templars in the Corona of Aragón*, p. 364.
50. Barber, *Trial*, p. 239.
51. Lea, op. cit., III, p. 316.
52. Barber, *Trial*, p. 241.

AFTERWORD

1. Cf. the legal review of the case in Macdonell, *Historical Trials*, especially, p. 42.
2. Lizerand, *Dossier*, p. 80.
3. Keen, *Chivalry*, p. 76.
4. Melville, *La Vie des Templiers*, p. 181.
5. Cf. Keen, op. cit., p. 59 & p. 118.
6. Ibid., pp. 120–1.
7. Ibid., pp. 179–80.
8. E.g. Partner, *The Murdered Magicians*, pp. 96–8.
9. Cf. Barber, *The World Picture of Philip the Fair*.

SELECT BIBLIOGRAPHY

THE bibliography of the Templars, mainly contained in the works of Dessubré and Neu cited below, is of vast and ever-increasing dimensions. Much of it is irrelevant to a book such as this: of about 1,200 items in Dessubré, for instance, as many as 318 concern local history; a further 100 volumes deal with the trial, and nearly 100 with the so-called secret doctrines and possible occult practices. No attempt has been made to incorporate such works, except occasionally when they contain otherwise unavailable information. The same is true of over 3,000 published pages of trial documents in Dupuy, *Traittez concernant l'histoire de France* (1685), Raynouard, *Monumens Historiques Relatifs a la Condamnation des Chevaliers du Temple* (1813), Michelet, *Le Procès des Templiers* (1841-51), Schottmüller, *Der Untergang des Templer-Ordens* (1887), Prutz, *Entwicklung und Untergang des Tempelherrenordens* (1888), and Finke, *Papsttum und Untergang des Templeordens* (1907). Some of these works have been cited to illustrate particular points, but no attempt has been made to analyse them since only a small part of this volume deals with the trial. The series has now been completed with the publication of the transcripts of the only remaining unpublished trials by Anne Gilmour-Bryson, in *The Trial of the Templars in the Papal State and the Abruzzi* (1982). The Select Bibliography given here contains only those works cited in the text.

Albert of Aix, *Alberti Aquensis: Historia Hierosolymitana*, Paris: Recueil des Historiens des Croisades, Historiens Occidentaux, 5 vols. (1844-95), Vol. IV, pp. 265-713.

Albon, Marquis d', *Cartulaire de l'Ordre du Temple*, Paris: Champion (1913).

Ambroise, *The Crusades of Richard Lion-Heart*, (tr, Merton Jerome Hubert), New York: Columbia University Press (1941).

Atiya, Aziz Suryal, *The Crusade in the Later Middle Ages*, London: Methuen (1938).

_____, *Crusade, Commerce and Culture*, Bloomington & London: Indiana University Press & OUP (1962).

Baldwin, Marshall Whithed, *Raymond III of Tripolis and the Fall of Jerusalem (1140-1187)*, Princeton: Princeton University Press (1936).

Baldwin, Summerfield, *Business in the Middle Ages*, New York: Henry Holt (1937).

Barber, Malcolm, 'The Origins of the Order of the Temple', *Studia Monastica*, XII, (1970), pp. 219–40.

——, 'James of Molay, the Last Grand Master of the Temple', *Studia Monastica*, XIV (1972), pp. 91–124.

——, *The Trial of the Templars*, Cambridge: CUP (1978).

——, 'The World Picture of Philip the Fair', *Journal of Medieval History*, Vol. 8, No. 1 (March 1982), pp. 13–43.

Benvenisti, Meron, *The Crusaders in the Holy Land*, Jerusalem: Israel Universities Press (1970).

Bernard of Clairvaux, *Liber Ad Milites Templi De Laude Novae Militiae*, in *Sancti Bernardi Opera Omnia*, ed. J. Mabillon, Paris: Apud Gaume Fratres, Bibliopolas, 1839, vol. 1, pp. 1252–78.

Bini, Telesforo, *Dei Tempieri in Lucca*, Lucca: Tipografia Bertini (1839).

——, *Dei Tempieri e del loro Processo in Toscana*, Lucca: La Reale Accademia Lucchese (1845).

Blancard, L., 'Documents relatifs au procès des Templiers en Angleterre', *Revue des Sociétés Savantes*, 4ᵉ Ser. VI (Octobre 1867), pp. 414–23.

Brundage, James A., *Medieval Canon Law and the Crusader*, Madison, Milwaukee, and London: University of Wisconsin Press (1969).

Bulst-Thiele, Marie Luise, *Sacrae Domus Militiae Templi Hierosolymitani Magistri: Untersuchungen zur Geschichte des Templerordens 118/9–1314*, Göttingen: Vandenhoeck & Ruprecht (Abhandlungen der Akademie Der Wissenschaften in Göttingen) (1974).

Burchand of Mount Sion, *Burchand of Mount Sion, AD 1280: A Description of the Holy Land* (tr. Aubrey Stewart), London: Palestine Pilgrims' Text Society, XII (1896).

Burns, Robert Ignatius, *Medieval Colonialism: Postcrusade Exploitation of Islamic Valencia*, Princeton: Princeton University Press (1975).

——, *The Crusader Kingdom of Valencia: Reconstruction on a Thirteenth-Century Frontier*, Cambridge, Mass: Harvard University Press, 2 vols. (1967).

Byrne, E. H., 'Genoese Trade with Syria in the Twelfth Century', *American Historical Review*, XXV (1919–20), pp. 191–219.

Cheney, C. R., 'The Downfall of the Templars and a Letter in their Defence', in *Medieval Texts and Studies*, Oxford: Clarendon Press (1973), pp. 314–27.

Cohn, Norman, *Europe's Inner Demons*, London: Paladin (1976).

Curzon, Henri de (ed.), *La Règle du Temple*, Paris: Librairie Renouard (1886).

Daniel-Rops, H., *Cathedral and Crusade: Studies of the Medieval Church 1050-1350*, London: Dent (1957).

Daniel the Higumene, *The Pilgrimage of the Russian Abbot Daniel in the Holy Land 1106-7* (tr. C. W. Wilson), London: Palestine Pilgrims' Text Society, IV, 1895.

Delaville le Roulx, J., *Documents concernant les Templiers, extraits des Archives de Malte*, Paris: Plon (1882).

Delisle, Léopold, *Mémoire sur les Opérations Financières des Templiers*, (Mémoires de l'Institut National de France, Académie des Inscriptions et Belles-Lettres, Vol. 33, Part 2), Paris: Imprimerie Nationale (1888).

Dessubré, M., *Bibliographie de l'Ordre des Templiers*, Paris: Librairie Critique Emile Nourry (1928).

Dubois, Pierre, *De Recuperatione Terre Sancte: Traite de Politique Générale* (ed. Ch.-V. Langlois), Paris: Alphonse Picard (1891).

Edwards, John, 'The Templars in Scotland in the Thirteenth Century', *The Scottish Historical Review*, Vol. 5 (1908), pp. 13–25.

Ekkehard of Aura, *Ekkehardi, Abbatis Uraugiensis: Hierosolymita, de Oppressione, Liberatione, ac Restauratione Jerosolymitanae Ecclesiae*, Paris: Recueil des Historiens des Croisades, Historiens Occidentaux, 5 vols., 1844-95, Vol. V, pp. 1–40.

Ernoul, *Chronique d'Ernoul et de Bernard le Trésorier* (ed. M. L. De Mas Latrie), Paris: Jules Renouard (1871).

Favier, Jean, *Philippe le Bel*, Paris: Fayard (1978).

Fedden, Robin, & Thomson, John, *Crusader Castles*, London: John Murray (1957).

Ferris, Eleanor, 'The Financial Relations of the Knights Templar to the English Crown', *American Historical Review*, VIII (October 1902), pp. 1–17.

Fidenzio of Padua, *Liber Recuperationis Terrae Sanctae*, in Biblioteca Bio-Bibliografica della Terra Sancta (ed. G. Golubovich), Vol. 2, Florence: Quaracchi (1913).

Fliche, A., Thouzellier, C., Azais, Y., *Histoire de l'Église, Vol. X: La Chrétienté romaine (1198-1274)*, Paris: Bloud & Gay (1950).

Forey, A. J., *The Templars in the Corona of Aragón*, London: OUP (1973).

Gabrieli, Francesco (ed.) *Storici Arabi delle Crociate*, Turin: Einaudi (1963).

Gibb, Sir Hamilton, *The Life of Saladin, from the works of 'Imād ad-Dīn and Bahā' ad-Dīn*, Oxford: Clarendon Press (1973.)

Gilmour-Bryson, Anne, *The Trial of the Templars in the Papal State and the Abruzzi*, Città del Vaticano: Biblioteca Apostolica Vaticana (1982).

Gransden, Antonia (ed.), *The Chronicle of Bury St Edmunds 1212-1301*, London: Nelson (1964).

Grousset, René, *Histoires des Croisades de du Royaume Franc de Jérusalem*, Paris: Plon, 3 vols. (1934-6).

Guerrieri, Giovanni, *I Cavalieri Templari nel Regno di Sicilia,* Trani: Vecchi (1909).

Hamilton, Bernard, *The Latin Church in the Crusader States: The Secular Church,* London: Variorum (1980).

——, *The Medieval Inquisition,* London: Edward Arnold (1981).

Heyd, W., *Histoire du Commerce de Levant au Moyen Age,* Leipzig: Otto Harrassowitz, 2 vols. (1923).

Hill, Sir George, *A History of Cyprus,* Cambridge: CUP, 4 vols. (1948–52).

Hill, Rosalind (ed.), *Gesta Francorum: The Deeds of the Franks and other Pilgrims to Jerusalem,* Oxford: Clarendon Press (1972).

Hillgarth, J. N., *Ramon Lull and Lullism in Fourteenth Century France,* Oxford: Clarendon Press (1971).

——, *The Spanish Kingdoms 1250-1516,* Oxford: Clarendon Press, 2 vols. (1976).

Hitti, Philip K., 'Salah-al-Din: Hero of the Anti-Crusades', in *Makers of Arab History,* London: Macmillan (1969), pp. 116–42.

Johns, C. N., 'Excavations at Pilgrim's Castle, 'Atlit (1932)', *Quarterly of the Department of Antiquities in Palestine,* Vol. III, No. 4 (1933), pp. 145–64.

Keen, Maurice, *Chivalry,* New Haven and London: Yale University Press (1984).

Kieckhefer, Richard, *European Witch Trials: Their Foundation in Popular and Learned Culture, 1300-1500*, London: Routledge & Kegan Paul (1976).

Knowles, David, & Hadcock, R. Neville, *Medieval Religious Houses: England and Wales*, London: Longman, Green (1953).

Lambert, Malcolm, *Medieval Heresy, Popular Movements from Bogomil to Hus,* London: Edward Arnold (1977).

La Monte, John L., *Feudal Monarchy in the Latin Kingdom of Jerusalem,* Cambridge, Mass: The Mediaeval Academy of America (1932).

Lawrence, A. W., 'The Castle of Baghras', in Boase (ed.), *The Cilician Kingdom of Armenia*, Edinburgh & London: Scottish Academic Press (1978), pp. 34–83.

Lea, Henry Charles, *The History of the Inquisition of the Middle Ages,* New York: Macmillan, 3 vols. (1908).

Leclerq, Jean, 'Un document sur les débuts des Templiers', *Revue d' Histoire Ecclésiastique,* LII (1957), pp. 81–91.

Lees, Beatrice, *Records of the Templars in England in the Twelfth Century: The Inquest of 1185 with illustrative charters and documents,* London: OUP (1935).

Leonard, E. G., *Introduction au Cartulaire Manuscrit du Temple (1150-1317), Constitué par le Marquis D'Albon*, Paris: Edouard Champion (1930).

Little, Lester K., *Religious Poverty and the Profit Economy in Medieval Europe,* London: Elek (1978).

Lizerand, Georges, *Clément V et Philippe le Bel,* Paris: Hachette (1910).

——, *Le Dossier de L'Affaire des Templiers,* Paris: Honoré Champion (1923).

Lopez, Robert S., Raymond, Irving W., *Medieval Trade in the Mediterranean World,* New York: Norton (n.d.).

Ludolph Von Sachem, *Ludolph von Sachem's Description of the Holy Land and of the way thither, Written in the year AD 1350* (tr. A. Stewart), London: Palestine Pilgrims' Text Society, XII (1895).

Lyons, Malcolm Cameron, & Jackson, D. E. P., *Saladin: The Politics of the Holy War,* Cambridge: CUP (1982).

Macdonell, Sir John, *Historical Trials,* Oxford: Clarendon Press (1927).

Maillard de Chambure, Charles Hippolyte, *Règles et Statuts secrets des Templiers,* Paris: Brockhaus & Avenarius (1840).

Martin, Edward J., *The Trial of the Templars,* London: George Allen and Unwin (1928).

Melville, Marion, *La Vie des Templiers,* Paris: Gallimard (1951).

Michael the Syrian, *Chronique de Michel le Syrien,* Vol. III (ed. J. B. Chabot), Paris: Ernest Leroux (1905).

Michelet, Jules, *Le Procès des Templiers,* Paris: Imprimerie Royale (Collection de Documents Inédits sur L'Histoire de France), Vol. I (1841), Vol. II (1851).

Mollat, G., *Les Papes D'Avignon (1305-1378),* Paris: Letouzey & Ané (1949, 9th Edition).

Morgan, Margaret Ruth (ed.), *La Continuation de Guillaume de Tyr (1184-1197),* Paris: Paul Geuthner (1982).

Morghen, Raffaello, *Medioevo cristiano,* Bari: Laterza (1978).

Mundy, John H., *Europe in the High Middle Ages, 1150-1309,* London: Longm n (1973).

Munz, Peter, *Frederick Barbarossa, A Study in Medieval Politics,* London: Eyre and Spottiswoode (1969).

Neu, H., *Bibliografie des Templer-Ordens 1927-1965,* Bonn: Wissenschaftliches Archiv GMBH (1965).

Nicholson, Reynold A., *A Literary History of the Arabs,* London: T. Fisher Unwin (1907).

Odo of Deuil, *De Profectione Ludovici VII in Orientem: The Journey of Louis VII to the East* (ed. & tr. Virginia Gingerick Berry), New York: Norton (1948).

Otto of Freising, and his continuator Rahewin, *The Deeds of Frederick Barbarossa* (tr. Charles Christopher Mierow), New York: Columbia University Press (1953).

Paris, Matthew, *English History from the year 1215 to 1273* (tr. Revd J. A. Giles), London: Henry G. Bohn, 3 vols. (1852).

Partner, Peter, *The Murdered Magicians: The Templars and their Myth,* Oxford: OUP (1982).

Perkins, Clarence, 'The Trial of the Knights Templars in England', *English Historical Review,* XCV (July 1909), pp. 432–47.

_____, 'The Wealth of the Knights Templar in England', *American Historical Review,* XV (1910), pp. 252–63.

——, 'The Knights Templars in the British Isles', *English Historical Review,* XCVIII (April 1910), pp. 209–30.

Poole, Austin Lane, *From Domesday Book to Magna Carta 1087-1216,* Oxford: Clarendon Press (1955).

Postan, M. M., *The Medieval Economy and Society: An Economic History of Britain 1100-1500,* Berkeley & Los Angeles: University of California Press (1972).

——, *Essays on Medieval Agriculture and General Problems of the Medieval Economy,* Cambridge: CUP (1973).

——, *Medieval Trade and Finance,* Cambridge: CUP (1973).

Powicke, Sir Maurice, *The Thirteenth Century: 1216-1307,* Oxford: Clarendon Press (1953).

Prawer, Joshua, 'The Settlement of the Latins in Jerusalem', *Speculum,* XXVII (1952), pp. 490–503.

——, *The Latin Kingdom of Jerusalem: European Colonisation in the Middle Ages,* London: Weidenfeld & Nicholson (1972).

——, *Crusader Institutions,* Oxford: Clarendon Press (1980).

Purcell, Maureen, 'Changing Views of Crusade in the Thirteenth Century', *The Journal of Religious History,* Vol. 7, No. 1 (June 1972), pp. 3–19.

Raynouard, M., *Monumens Historiques Relatifs à la Condamnation des Chevaliers du Temple, et à l'Abolition de leur Ordre,* Paris: Adrien Égron (1813).

Reinach, Salomon, 'La Tête magique des Templiers', *Revue de l'Histoire des Religions,* LXIII (1911), pp. 25–39.

Rey, E. G. (ed.), *Les Familles d'Outremer de Du Cange,* Paris: Imprimerie Impériale (Collections de Documents Inédits sur l'Histoire de France) (1869).

Richard, Jean, 'An Account of the Battle of Hattin Referring to the Frankish Mercenaries in Oriental Moslem States', *Speculum,* XXVII (1952), pp. 168–77.

——, *Le Royaume Latin de Jérusalem,* Paris: Presses Universitaires de France (1953).

Riley-Smith, Jonathan, *The Knights of St John in Jerusalem and Cyprus c. 1050–1310,* London: Macmillan (1967).

——, 'The Templars and the castle of Tortosa in Syria: an unknown document concerning the acquisition of the fortress', *English Historical Review,* CCCXXXI (April 1969), pp. 278–88.

——, 'The Templars and the Teutonic Knights in Cilician Armenia', in Boase (ed.), *The Cilician Kingdom of Armenia,* Edinburgh & London: Scottish Academic Press (1978), pp. 92–117.

——, 'Crusading as an Act of Love', *History,* Vol. 65 (1980), pp. 177–92.

Riley-Smith, Jonathan & Louise, *The Crusades: Idea and Reality 1095-1274,* London: Edward Arnold (1981).

Runciman, Steven, *A History of the Crusades,* Harmondsworth: Peregrine, 3 vols. (1978).

Russell, Jeffrey Burton, *Witchcraft in the Middle Ages*, Ithaca and London: Cornell University Press (1972).

Saewulf, *An Account of the Pilgrimage of Saewulf to Jerusalem and the Holy Land in the Years 1102 and 1103* (tr. W. R. Brownlow), London: Palestine Pilgrims' Text Society, IV (1896).

Schlumberger, Gustave, *Prise de Saint-Jean-d'Acre en l'an 1291 par l'armée du Soudan d'Egypte*, Paris: Plon (1914).

Setton, Kenneth M., (General Editor), *A History of the Crusades*, Madison, Milwaukee & London: University of Wisconsin Press (1969), Vol. I: *The First Hundred Years*, and Vol. II: *The Later Crusades 1189-1311*.

Seward, Desmond, *The Monks of War: The Military Religious Orders*, London: Eyre Methuen (1972).

Smail, R. C., 'Crusaders' Castles of the Twelfth Century', *The Cambridge Historical Journal*, Vol. X, No. 2 (1951), pp. 133–49.

_____, *Crusading Warfare (1097-1193)*, Cambridge: CUP (1956).

Southern, R. W., *Western Society and the Church in the Middle Ages*, Harmondsworth: Penguin (1970).

Strayer, Joseph R., *The Reign of Philip the Fair*, Princeton: University of Princeton Press (1980).

Theoderich, *Theoderich's Description of the Holy Place (circa 1172 AD)*, (tr. & ed. Aubrey Stewart), London: Palestine Pilgrims' Text Society, V (1896).

Thompson, James Westfall, *Economic and Social History of the Middle Ages*, New York: Frederick Ungar, 2 vols. (1959).

Van Cleve, Thomas Curtis, *The Emperor Frederick II of Hohenstaufen*, Oxford: Clarendon Press (1972).

Vitry, Jacques de, *History of Jerusalem* (tr. Aubrey Stewart), London: Palestine Pilgrims' Text Society, XI (1896).

Wendover, Roger of, *Flowers of History, comprising the history of England from the descent of the Saxons to AD 1235* (tr. J. A. Giles), London: Henry G. Bohn, 2 vols. (1849).

William of Tyre, *A History of Deeds done beyond the Sea* (tr. and annotated by Emily Atwater Babcock & A. C. Krey), New York: Octagon Books, 2 vols. (1976).

Wolff, Philippe, *Cartulaires des Templiers de Douzens*, Paris: Bibliothèque Nationale (Collections des Documents Inédits sur l'Histoire de France, Série in 8°-Vol. 3), (1965).

Yver, Georges, *Le Commerce et Les Marchands dans L'Italie Meridionale au XIII° et au XIV° Siècle*, Paris: Albert Fontemoing (1903).

INDEX

The INQUISITION

THE HAMMER OF HERESY

EDWARD BURMAN

The often loosely-used term 'Inquisition' covers a complex and amorphous phenomenon of fundamental importance in the history of Western Europe. As an institution, it came into being early in the thirteenth century. Its effects are still felt today.

This panoramic study offers the general reader a description and interpretation of the Inquisition and its methods based on two essential moments in its history: the gradual establishment of the Holy Office and its dramatic reflowering three hundred years later. Such an approach shows how the Inquisition functioned as an elastic response to heretical and political pressure, and how its power was in direct proportion to specific geographical and temporal needs.

In the course of his survey Edward Burman describes the crucial role of the Dominican Order in the work of the Inquisition and demonstrates that the Franciscans—in spite of the gentle piety of their founder—were also involved in stamping out heresy. In addition he provides a wealth of fascinating detail concerning the Inquisitors' methods (including torture, confiscation of property, and the terrible trials for the dead), their manuals, the Inquisition in Italy, the Inquisition in France from the Albigensian Crusade to the burning of Joan of Arc, the persecution of witches, the Spanish Inquisition, the economic and cultural effects of the Inquisition in Europe, and the legacy of the Inquisition.

Drawing on an array of sources, many of them little known to English readers, the author paints a terrifying but complete picture of one of the most efficient systems of repression ever devised.